"I Sweat the Flavor of Tin"

PITT LATIN AMERICAN SERIES

John Charles Chasteen and Catherine M. Conaghan, Editors

"I Sweat the Flavor of Tin"

LABOR ACTIVISM IN EARLY

TWENTIETH-CENTURY BOLIVIA

Robert L. Smale

UNIVERSITY OF PITTSBURGH PRESS

Published by the University of Pittsburgh Press, Pittsburgh, Pa., 15260

Manufactured in the United States of America

Printed on acid-free paper

10 9 8 7 6 5 4 3 2 1

Frontispiece: Cancha de barrillas. Empresa Minera "La Salvadora." Uncía, Bolivia, 1913. *The Nettie Lee Benson Latin American Collection. Photographic Collection. Rare Books and Manuscripts. The University of Texas at Austin. Gift of Dr. Peter J. Bakewell and Judith Reynolds.*

Library of Congress Cataloging-in-Publication Data

Smale, Robert L.

"I sweat the flavor of tin" : labor activism in early twentieth-century Bolivia / Robert L. Smale.

p. cm. — (Pitt Latin American series)

Includes bibliographical references and index.

ISBN 978-0-8229-4399-0 (hardcover : alk. paper) — ISBN 978-0-8229-6117-8 (pbk. : alk. paper)

1. Tin miners—Bolivia—History—20th century. 2. Tin mines and mining—Bolivia—History—20th century. 3. Tin miners—Labor unions—Bolivia—History—20th century. I. Title.

HD8039.M72B668 2010

331.88'123453098409041—dc22   2010020947

Sudo sabor a estaño
En los negros socavones.
Sudo sabor a estaño,
Orgullo de mi Bolivia.

I sweat the flavor of tin
In the dark mineshafts.
I sweat the flavor of tin,
The pride of my Bolivia.

Rubén Porco Herrera, "Minero de corazón"

CONTENTS

Acknowledgments ix

Prologue 1

CHAPTER 1: Laboring in the Boss's Shadow 7

CHAPTER 2: Artisan Initiative 38

CHAPTER 3: Crisis and Organization 61

CHAPTER 4: Strikes and Contracts 82

CHAPTER 5: The Uncía Massacre, 1923 110

CHAPTER 6: The Vicissitudes of Republican Rule 144

CHAPTER 7: An Ideology of Their Own 166

Epilogue: The Chaco War and Its Aftermath 193

Notes 201

Bibliography 229

Index 235

ACKNOWLEDGMENTS

I would like to acknowledge the following for their financial support: the University of Missouri-Columbia Research Council; the Department of History, the Tereza Lozano Long Institute of Latin American Studies, and the Graduate College, all at the University of Texas at Austin; the Tinker Foundation; and the U.S. Department of Education for a Foreign Language Area Studies Fellowship and a Fulbright-Hays Doctoral Dissertation Research Abroad Fellowship.

I express my thanks to the administration and staff of the following archives and institutions in Bolivia: the Prefecture of Oruro, the Supreme Court of Oruro, the Subprefecture of the Cercado Province of Oruro, the Municipal Library of Oruro, the Casa de la Cultura of Oruro, the Casa Simón Patiño of the Technical University of Oruro, the Historical Archive of La Paz, the Archive and Library of the Casa de la Moneda in Potosí, and the National Archive and Library of Bolivia in Sucre. I would also like to thank Gilberto Pauwels and his staff at the Centro de Ecología y Pueblos Andinos in Oruro for their support. In the United States, I would like to thank the administration and staff at the Nettie Lee Benson Latin American Collection of the University of Texas at Austin and the librarians at the University of Missouri's library.

I thank a number of professors and historians in the United States for their teaching, mentorship, and assistance: Jonathan Brown, Susan Deans-Smith, Virginia Burnett, Margot Beyersdorff, Erick Langer, Thomas Wright, and Brooke Larson. In Bolivia, I would like to acknowledge María Luísa Soux, Magdalena Cajías, Ximena Medinaceli, Pilar Mendieta, and Eugenia Bridikhina. I would also like to thank my colleagues in the Department of History at the University of Missouri, especially Jonathan Sperber who read and commented on the complete manuscript. Tristan Platt deserves thanks for providing me with an unpublished article on Northern Potosí.

I express gratitude to my fellow history graduate students at the University of Texas at Austin, many of them now professors. I especially thank

Matt Childs and Russell Lohse for their theoretical insights. Gabrielle Kuenzli deserves special mention for her friendship during two years in the archives of Oruro.

At the University of Pittsburgh Press, I would like to thank Joshua Shanholtzer, Deborah Meade, David Baumann, Ann Walston, and Devin Fromm. I must also acknowledge the copy editor Bruce Bethell and the cartographer Bill Nelson. Two anonymous readers for the University of Pittsburgh Press provided me with observations leading to substantial alterations of the book, and I thank them for their comments.

Finally, I thank my family for years of support: Linda Smale, Scott Smale, and Eloise Koenig. I could not have completed this project without the love and support of my beautiful wife, Daveiva Murillo, and the joyful diversion of our three children, Skip, Scott, and Marilinda.

"I Sweat the Flavor of Tin"

Prologue

JUNE NIGHTS in the Bolivian Andes are clear and cold. In the mining town of Uncía, in the department of Potosí, the night of June 4, 1923, was bloody too, for on it Bolivian soldiers turned their rifles and a machine gun on a crowd of striking miners, killing workers and artisans assembled in the Plaza Alonso de Ibañez—an incident popularly considered Bolivia's first labor-related massacre. The laborers had gathered to protest the arrest of their federation's leaders, men eventually exiled from Uncía to break the momentum of organization. After the bloodshed, the government ensured the return of company control over the region's mines and mills, but the conflict presaged future confrontations between the working class, on the one side, and government and business, on the other.

The Uncía Massacre highlights a formative period for Bolivia's militant tradition of organized labor. The Andean republic's working class began the twentieth century with little ideological autonomy and only rudimentary organizational schemes—a late start by European and North American standards and tardy even when compared to some South American neighbors. Just five decades later, however, in 1952, Bolivia's unions crafted one of Latin America's most surprising social revolutions and one of the world's few workers' revolutions.[1] What sparked the sudden evolution of thought and organization that allowed the popular classes to defeat a government representing the country's dominant classes?

The fundamental supports of Bolivian labor's organizational strength and militancy developed between 1899 and 1931 as the country's tin mines industrialized and expanded their production exponentially. These three decades marked the apogee of economic liberalism and oligarchic governance in Bolivia, during which the popular classes labored in the dominant classes' shadow. Those on top included business leaders, urban professionals, state bureaucrats, prosperous merchants, and large landowners. The pejorative for this group as a whole was *la rosca* (the ring). This privileged element, a small fraction of the national population, used division and intellectual obfuscation to rule the majority.

The popular classes sustained the economy with their labor. Bolivia began the twentieth century as an overwhelmingly rural nation. The 1900 census classed only 26.8 percent of the country's residents as urban. To get even this number, statisticians employed a definition of *urban* so broad as to be absurd: "cities, towns, cantons, missions, and vice-cantons with more than 200 inhabitants."[2] The country retained its rural character during the following decades. In 1950, 72 percent of the population still labored in agriculture and related economic activities.[3] Still, although it constituted only a minority of the popular classes, the urban element was important and diverse: artisans, petty merchants, domestics, and wage laborers. Urban residents had better access to the trappings of modernity than did the rural population, including schools, newspapers, transportation, and electoral politics. In 1900 Bolivia had only six cities with more than 10,000 residents: La Paz, Cochabamba, Potosí, Sucre, Santa Cruz, and Oruro. The largest city was La Paz, with 60,031 inhabitants. Oruro, the administrative capital of Bolivia's wealthiest tin mining region, was the sixth largest, with 13,575 residents and an additional 2,323 in nearby mining camps.[4] The urban popular classes would experience significant growth during the early decades of the twentieth century, however. Ultimately, this collection of artisans, petty merchants, and workers crafted a tradition of organization and radical ideology to rival the oligarchy's historical dominance.

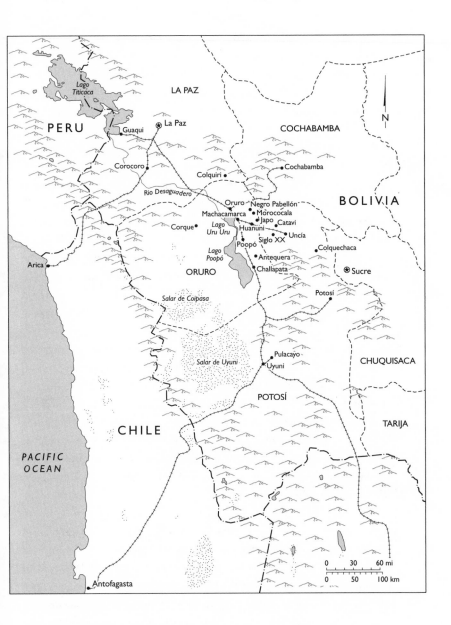

Map 1. Early Twentieth-Century Highland Bolivia. *Map by Bill Nelson.*

Tin mining expanded enormously between 1899 and 1931, eclipsing the supremacy of silver. The department of Oruro and a neighboring, northern segment of the department of Potosí lay at the center of this industrial boom (see map 1). The new century continued the trends of previous decades, but specific aspects—industrialization, state building, and the growth of the working class—developed with greater intensity and vigor. Foreign capital poured in during the first three decades of the twentieth century, creating epic mining companies. The region produced the country's greatest "tin baron" in the person of Simón I. Patiño, who by the end of 1924 controlled mines and mills in Uncía, Llallagua, Catavi, Siglo XX, and Huanuni. He owned the railroad that ran between Machacamarca and northern Potosí, and his company had offices and a bank in Oruro.

Relative political stability accompanied the growth of tin mining. The Liberal Party dominated politics between 1899 and 1920. In 1920 the Republican Party—an offshoot of the Liberal Party—seized control and held onto the government until the mid-1930s. While presidents changed, economic and political policies remained consistent throughout the period. The government defended and promoted the mining industry's interests. Wage labor, public education, a professional police force, and the promise of electoral democracy became the norm in Oruro and northern Potosí's cities and towns, but always in the shadow of the mines and the bosses.

Despite oligarchic governance and the dominance of liberal economic policies, between 1899 and 1931 the urban popular classes made significant progress in developing vigorous labor associations and alternative political ideologies: socialism, Marxism, and anarcho-syndicalism. The impositions of industry and the disappointments of oligarchic rule spurred these developments. The urban popular classes—especially the miners—came to understand capitalism and the liberal state in their most unadulterated forms. Although the popular classes suffered occasional repression and the dominant classes' deadening political tutelage, workers and artisans laid the foundation for movements that would bear revolutionary fruit once the liberal oligarchic order collapsed under the weight of its own incompetence in the 1930s. The Chaco War with Paraguay (1932–1935) and the economic dislocation of the Great Depression discredited the old socioeconomic order. The post–Chaco War era presented surprising opportunities for the working class. Elements of the Bolivian military and new political parties experimented with a variety of reforms. The working class and its intellectual allies achieved heady levels of national power. It was a new epoch, but one built on the innovations of the century's first three decades.

Analyzing organizational and ideological developments among the working class is key to understanding the course of Bolivian politics. Organization provided the strength to confront seemingly more powerful segments of society. Ideology gave that strength direction. In fact, Bolivia's labor movement embraced a radical and idiosyncratic brand of socialist thought, drawing heavily from Leon Trotsky, that took root in the 1920s. The anthropologist June Nash, who lived and worked in Bolivia during the late 1960s and early 1970s, recalled, "My encounter with Marxism came in the field where Bolivian miners took upon themselves the project of educating me in their basic principles as well as the daily praxis of mine union activism." She added, "I came to know more about Trotskyism than I would have received in most graduate schools, especially in the United States where it was treated as a failed branch of Marxist-Leninist philosophy."[5] The Bolivian labor movement first emerged in the years just before Russia's Bolshevik Revolution. As Bolivians built their own labor unions, the working class's intellectual allies ensured that Oruro and northern Potosí's laborers understood the example of the great European revolution.

Workers also experienced a conjuncture between socialist, Marxist, and anarcho-syndicalist explanations of Bolivian society and their own lived experience in the 1920s: the Uncía Massacre. In some ways, this incident was perhaps aberrant. During the twentieth century's first three decades some officials lent working-class and artisan organizations a sympathetic ear, especially since educated artisans and workers formed a significant body of political clients. Beyond that, the government adopted a variety of social reforms, especially in the 1920s. Even though enforcement of this legislation was often lax, such official sympathy contradicted leftist descriptions of a capitalist state hostile to workers. The Uncía Massacre, however, seemed to confirm the image of a cold and violent government

—a tangible affirmation of radical arguments. But old habits died hard. While organized labor partially reconciled with state officials in the massacre's wake, the more radical assertions of government's innate hostility never completely faded away. With the disasters of the 1930s, workers understood the prescience of radical political thinkers.

This book is a regional study of the urban popular classes of Oruro and northern Potosí. It is not a comprehensive history of the mining industry and only occasionally addresses working-class formation in other parts of Bolivia.[6] Today, Oruro and northern Potosí bear the marks of poverty and economic decay; during the twentieth century's first three decades, the region presented a different panorama. Between 1899 and 1931 the area saw the infusion of foreign capital and the creation of massive mining enterprises. For decades Oruro and northern Potosí (more specifically that portion of the department known as the Bustillos Province) functioned as the nation's industrial heartland. The mining industry was the government's central preoccupation in the region. Chronologically, the book begins with Bolivia's transition from silver mining to tin around the year 1899. It briefly addresses the country's colonial and nineteenth-century past to set the stage for the twentieth century. The study ends with the Great Depression. Industry and the working class experienced a formative period between 1899 and 1931. The twin crises of the Great Depression and the Chaco War led to the temporary suppression of open labor activism, yet the government and the dominant classes could never completely extirpate the organizational and ideological models first developed in the 1910s and 1920s. Once the crises passed, the working class and its allies emerged as more powerful arbiters of national power than their rivals ever imagined they could be.

CHAPTER 1

Laboring in the Boss's Shadow

MINING IN twentieth-century Bolivia produced no greater magnate than Simón I. Patiño. From modest provincial beginnings Patiño became the country's richest man and one of the wealthiest individuals in the world. His initial success depended on the willingness of his earliest workers to fight and perhaps die to defend his property. In 1895, while working as a clerk for the small Germán Fricke mining company in the city of Oruro, the future impresario purchased a partial stake in "La Salvadora," a claim located in the northern reaches of the neighboring department of Potosí. He bought out his partner in 1897, yet legal disputes hampered the mine's development. Pedro Armando Artigue, a Frenchman, insisted that his own claim overlapped Patiño's. Artigue had never occupied his claim but nevertheless pursued a lawsuit. In 1901 Patiño's workers discovered a rich seam of tin in La Salvadora's main mineshaft. Artigue intensified his attempts to dispossess Patiño, setting about to seize the claim by force. The Frenchman recruited a band of around seventy men for the assault. Patiño turned to his own outnumbered workers, who scraped together an irregular assortment of firearms and prepared to defend La Salvadora. Patiño's men used the mountainous terrain against the attackers, rolling boulders down the hill as Artigue's men sought to make their ascent. Patiño's workers held their position through a whole day. The future "tin king" received a minor bullet wound, yet surprisingly only one person was killed in the fight. As night fell, Artigue's followers abandoned the struggle, convinced that Patiño's men planned to counterattack the following day. While wrangling in the courts continued to occupy Patiño and his lawyers for years, his workers' tenacious defense of his claim guaranteed the man from Cochabamba the foundation of his empire.[1]

Personal bonds formed in an isolated mining camp allowed Simón I. Patiño to mobilize his workers in defense of his claim. Such situations were typical, for mine owners sought to foment the dependence of their workers and develop an accompanying sense of benevolent paternalism. These practices and antiquated workplace arrangements inherited from the colonial period retarded the development of a union movement in Oruro and northern Potosí during the early years of the twentieth century. Nonetheless, hostilities existed, and incipient industrialization sparked by silver mining in the nineteenth century exacerbated the tensions and resentments. The transition to tin mining at the dawn of the twentieth century accelerated the flow of ore through the region's mills and led to the adoption of more expensive machinery. Labor arrangements inherited from earlier periods gave way to modern wage labor. Workers felt a growing economic chasm developing between themselves and the bosses, yet alienation advanced only slowly. Dependence proved a durable phenomenon. A politically powerful sense of class did not immediately emerge, but the momentum of Bolivia's industrial and political development continued to propel history in that direction.

THE LEGACY OF SILVER

An Indian named Diego Huallpa discovered Potosí's silver in 1543. Chroniclers disagree as to the details of his story; two slightly different versions exist. In both, nightfall caught Diego Huallpa and a herd of livestock on the slopes of Potosí's Cerro Rico, or Rich Mountain, so he made camp there. Some chroniclers relate that he stumbled on a rich vein of silver the following day. A misstep caused him to lose his footing while chasing a deer, and to save himself from tumbling down the mountain, he grabbed a bush, which tore out by the roots. As he lay supine on the hillside, he noticed a rich coat of silver on the clump of earth in his hand. The second version records that the night Diego Huallpa spent on the mountain was exceptionally cold; to warm himself he built a fire of grass and twigs. The next morning he found rivulets of molten silver had poured from the fire during the night. No matter how he made the discovery, Diego Huallpa sought to conceal the news from the Spaniards, for he hoped to grow wealthy working the silver in secret. One of his companions eventually revealed the strike after a fight over the division of profits. In 1545 the rush to Cerro Rico began; Potosí soon became the largest city in the Americas.[2]

Diego Huallpa's secret exploitation of Cerro Rico's silver highlights the emergence of a segment of Andean society that gravitated toward mining and away from the agricultural vocations of the countryside. Here was the sixteenth-century appearance of what would become the twentieth-century working class of the mines. Right after the Spanish Conquest, an important nucleus of Indian miners quickly developed. As the colonial period advanced, a special stratum of the popular classes devoted to mining consolidated itself even further. Significant numbers of unskilled rural migrants, both voluntary and involuntary, came to populate the silver mines of colonial Potosí and Oruro, but professional miners formed the core of the colonial labor force. Many of these miners identified themselves as Indians, but they were not Indians of the same type as those devoted to agricultural occupations in the countryside. Over time, members of this mining stratum moved in the direction of a mestizo identity—a mixture of European and Andean culture.

While the infamous involuntary labor draft known as the *mita* dominates popular thinking about silver mining in the colonial period, the industry employed significant numbers of free laborers. During the initial rush to Potosí in the mid-sixteenth century, Andean people enjoyed surprising autonomy in their exploitation of Cerro Rico's more accessible

silver deposits—although declining ore quality in the 1570s and the introduction of new technology such as mercury amalgamation milling led the
Spaniards to assert greater control in the workplace. Even then, however,
while the *mita* forced Spain's rural, Andean subjects to labor in Potosí and
other mining camps, not all cities enjoyed the same level of royal patronage. In particular, the city of Oruro, founded in 1606, had to function with
an assortment of free labor arrangements. Potosí itself attracted numerous
voluntary laborers despite the influx of draft workers. These willing mine
workers built a flourishing urban culture uniquely Andean and uniquely
colonial with its own, often illicit, economic underpinnings.

During Potosí's early decades, Andeans dominated silver production
employing their own pre-Columbian methods.[3] Diego Huallpa had ties to
the nearby Inca mining settlement of Porco, which provided Potosí with
its first settlers and laborers. Andean prospectors preferred high-grade
surface deposits and developed techniques to exploit them efficiently. The
most striking invention of this type was a wind-powered furnace called a
wayra.[4] Pedro de Cieza de León, a Spanish chronicler, described it thus:
"To extract the metal they make pottery forms in the size and manner of
earthen pots in Spain; they have in a number of places holes or ventilation.
In these contraptions they place charcoal with the metal on top. Sited on
hills and heights where the wind blows with more force, they extract the
silver, which is then purified and refined with small bellows or cane tubes
through which they blow."[5] Another chronicler, Luis Capoche, counted
6,497 *wayras* in Potosí in the late sixteenth century.[6] De Cieza de León said
of the thousands of small furnaces, "At night there are so many of them
on all of the hills and heights that they resemble decorative lights."[7]

Using the *wayra* and other inventions, Andean people extracted and
refined much of the mountain's silver with little Spanish supervision. The
first Indian laborers produced two marks of silver (or a bit over sixteen
ounces) per week for their European masters; anything beyond that they
kept.[8] Noting workers' independence during this period, Pedro de Cieza
de León wrote, "As the Indians have not had supervisors, and nor is it possible to control their extraction of silver, as they go and take it from the
hills, it is believed that many of them have grown rich and carried off to

their lands a great quantity of this silver."[9] In fact, during the 1550s and 1560s a class of Indian contractors emerged to organize mining operations. European owners held the claims, but they leased those claims to Andean bosses who employed other Indians as laborers. The contractors shared a portion of the ore with Spanish owners.[10] Luis Capoche, a mine owner himself, described these arrangements: "Many entrepreneurial Indians have of their own volition entered into agreement with the mine owners so that they might work a few meters of the mine. And the mine owner gives them metal bars, which they then set and sharpen at their own cost—they [the Indians] also supply the candles. And the recompense and interest that they receive is that the mine owner sells them the rich ore that they have extracted." Capoche summed up the arrangement by declaring, "The Indians possess all the riches of the kingdom."[11]

Declining ore quality and the introduction of mercury amalgamation milling changed the balance of power between the Andean population and Spanish mine owners. The amalgamation technique first appeared in the Americas in Mexico in the 1550s, but Potosí's mine owners did not start employing the new technology until the 1570s. Amalgamation allowed for the extraction of silver from low-grade ore resistant to traditional Andean methods.[12] During the years of *wayra* milling workers discarded mounds of rock judged to be worthless, and these accessible piles of waste became the initial source of ore for the new amalgamation mills.[13] Viceroy Francisco de Toledo, the great organizer of sixteenth-century Perú, firmly believed in the technology's promise. "The new process of amalgamation is what shall determine the restoration of this kingdom," he wrote in 1574.[14] The infrastructure to support amalgamation required an enormous investment of capital and labor, so the viceroy hoped to promote the continued growth of mining by having government play an active role in marshaling the necessary labor. The colonial administration ultimately threw its bureaucratic weight behind reforms promoting the profitability of amalgamation. This is when the infamous labor draft known as the *mita* emerged as a central element of colonial rule in the Andes. Precursors to the *mita* existed in Potosí prior to Francisco de Toledo's arrival, but the new viceroy gave the system royal sanction and placed the authority of the colonial government behind its administration. In its ideal form, the *mita* would marshal one-seventh of the adult male population of fifteen provinces in Perú and Alto Perú each year for labor in Potosí or other nearby mines. *Mitayos* (as the draft laborers were known) had to work for one year before returning to their rural homes. Spanish law established the wage, hours, and conditions of labor. Viceroy Toledo organized his first *mita* for Potosí in 1572; by the end of the year some 9,500 Indian men found themselves ordered to the mines.[15]

Potosí's silver production peaked in 1592; Cerro Rico would never again yield that much silver. The boom did not immediately end, but production began a long, slow decline over the course of the seventeenth century. By the early eighteenth century production had fallen back to the level of the 1570s.[16] But Potosí's is not the only story of silver mining in Alto Perú. Over the course of the seventeenth century other districts sought to challenge the Imperial City's dominant position.

The city of Oruro, with its own rich hills, stands out as an important rival. The Spanish founded Oruro on November 1, 1606.[17] Some hoped to develop the city's mines along the same lines as Potosí's—with coercive *mita* labor. Despite petitions from Oruro's mine owners, however, the region never received the royal patronage of a *mita*, for Potosí's mining lobby consistently swayed royal officials against the idea. Throughout the colonial period Oruro relied on wage labor and its colonial variants. Spaniards sometimes transferred *mita* Indians to Oruro (often illegally), but compulsory labor never became the norm.[18] Mine workers in Oruro enjoyed relatively high wages, opportunities for illicit enrichment, and a strong bargaining position vis-à-vis their employers. Over the course of the colonial period, the city's labor force developed a strong, acculturated, urban nucleus—a trend that eventually marked mining settlements throughout Alto Perú.[19]

Potosí's labor force developed in a similar manner despite the presence of thousands of *mita* Indians. By 1600 more than half the workers employed in the region's mines and mills had no connection to the *mita*. During the seventeenth and eighteenth centuries a growing number of laborers came to depend on wages and related income to support their families. The skilled workers who drove the advance of the shafts, men known as *barreteros*, provide an example of Potosí's wage labor arrangements. Using metal rods and heavy hammers, the *barreteros* followed the mountain's hidden veins of ore. Because of their importance, these laborers could demand cash advances on their wages even though employers complained of the fraud that plagued the system, for workers sometimes sought money from several mine owners but then labored for only one or none. Skilled workers also demanded a cut of the ore as a supplement to their regular wages.[20]

The practice of *kajcheo* (illicit mining carried out at night or on holidays) also strengthened the position of the urban popular classes in mining zones. Potosí's silver attracted determined and creative plebeians seeking to cheat the powerful of their riches. Royal officials and mine owners deplored these men, the *kajchas*. Such bandit miners sometimes occupied abandoned shafts, but they also raided active mines, bribing or overpowering any guards. Some *kajchas* lived exclusively from their illegal activities; others engaged in occasional raids to supplement their wages. Small, quasi-legal mills powered by human labor alone complemented clandestine mining. These mills processed silver provided by *kajchas* or by workers seeking to dispose of ore pilfered from the workplace.

Wage laborers and the socially related *kajchas* formed an important stratum of colonial urban society. One of Potosí's more flamboyant *kajchas*, Agustín Quespi, appeared in the work of Bartolomé Arzáns de Orsúa y Vela, an eighteenth-century chronicler. The chronicler identified the indomitable Quespi as an Indian but used the term as a racial marker and not a cultural indicator. The bandit miner was a native of Potosí—"his home was this city"—raised in the household of an influential Basque colonist. Quespi understood perfectly the society, culture, and economy of the colonial urban environment. Potosí's mine owners despised and feared this *kajcha*. "He became so feared on the Hill that the bravest Spaniards fled from his presence," wrote Arzáns de Orsúa y Vela. Despite Quespi's ferocious reputation, the chronicler found much to admire in his character and noted that the working class of Cerro Rico respected the *kajcha* as a popular leader: "Many *kajchas* (those who violently go in search of metal during holidays with the strength of their arms and danger to their lives) called him their captain." Yet the mine owners wanted to destroy Quespi. "So great was his fame, that the owners wanted to drink his blood," Arzáns de Orsúa y Vela recorded; "they planned ambushes, surrounding him with thirty or fifty men, and he, sometimes alone and sometimes with his companions, attacked and beat them with sheathed blades, sabers, clubs, slings, and stones. Because of his valor and strength, all fell before him." The chronicler mentioned that all this created the dark suspicion that Quespi "had a pact with the devil": "'Certainly,' they said, 'a small Indian of such ruinous appearance could not naturally raise such resistance.'" But Arzáns de Orsúa y Vela noted that the *kajcha* leader executed his raids with a certain care and consideration. "This Indian Agustín did no damage in active mines," the chronicler wrote; "true, he went to work with a pair of pistols, because he did not own his own mine and entered abandoned ones or, through passages and tunnels, those owned by others, but he took metal without knocking down supports or causing considerable damage."[21]

Arzáns de Orsúa y Vela, a Creole, enjoyed a cordial acquaintance with Agustín Quespi. He recorded that one September day—a day of religious celebration—he visited a chapel popular with the *kajchas*. There he encountered Quespi, who greeted him with "much courtesy." Acting as host of the celebration, the bandit miner invited the chronicler to a drink: "Agustín with his natural courtesy placed in my hands a large glass of that alcoholic beverage which is called *chicha* [a fermented beverage made from corn] and asked me with sweet words to drink, for surely the sun was fatiguing me." Yet even in this moment of friendly celebration, the *kajcha* was not a man to provoke. While the chronicler drank, a group of four Frenchmen stopped to converse, "having come to see the Indian celebration." Quespi invited the four to a drink as well, offering them, in addition to *chicha*, "rich wine and *aguardiente*." The four lacked Arzáns de Orsúa y Vela's tact. "The Frenchmen spurned the invitation, and Agustín, seeing their condescension, hurled at them a couple of insults." The foreign visitors responded with declarations of bravado, at which point Quespi "grabbed the staff of a banner that was there as a decoration and threw himself at the foreigners, breaking the head of one and administering such blows to the other three, who came at him with swords, that they and their mules were forced to flee." After this incident, Arzáns de Orsúa y Vela enjoyed the hospitality of the celebration a bit longer but acknowledged a sense of relief at departing: "I found myself quite happy in getting far from those Indians."[22]

Despite the occasional outburst, Agustín Quespi possessed a keen political instinct. He assiduously cultivated the patronage of influential Creoles and Spaniards in the Imperial City. Arzáns de Orsúa y Vela wrote that the bandit miner was "magnanimous and liberal" and that whoever came to him "presenting their needs, he would succor them generously." Quespi especially courted the priesthood, providing "the priests with parties and the divine cult with donations." When royal officials succeeded in capturing and incarcerating Quespi sometime around 1725, José Callejas Flores, who was a priest at the San Pablo church and a member of the Holy Office of the Inquisition, mobilized a campaign to liberate him. After appeals and wrangling involving the archbishop of Chuquisaca, officials in Potosí released the bandit miner.[23] *Kajchas* such as Agustín Quespi played an important role in the mining economy of the late colonial period—an economy struggling to recapture the dynamism of earlier centuries.

In the eighteenth century the new Bourbon monarchs of Spain sought to shake Andean mining from its seventeenth-century lethargy. Administrative reforms and other factors succeeded in stimulating silver production. Between 1730 and 1790 silver exports rose continuously, but Alto Perú's recovery faltered in the 1780s with the Tupak Amaru and Tupak Katari rebellions, the largest Indian revolts of the colonial period.[24] The nineteenth century's wars of independence further debilitated the silver economy. Chronic European warfare interrupted the shipment of Spanish mercury to the American colonies. Fighting throughout South America shrank commerce across the continent. Civil war and invasion took a heavy toll on the economic order of Alto Perú. The *mita* broke down completely; mines flooded or collapsed; and on three occasions—1811, 1813, and 1815— the patriot army of Argentina invaded and occupied the city of Potosí only to be evicted by royalists each time.[25] Despite the disorder, neither mining nor its accompanying plebian culture ever completely disappeared. In the nineteenth century republican Bolivia eventually succeeded in restoring the country's silver mines to vibrancy.

After the establishment of an independent republic in 1825, Bolivia's leaders sought to revitalize the mining economy, with uneven results. Simón Bolívar and Antonio José de Sucre both promulgated laws seeking to spark investment in mining and agriculture, but to little effect.[26] The country struggled to attract foreign capital, and mine owners complained of a dearth of laborers. Despite these difficulties, however, Bolivia experienced a miniboom in silver production during the 1830s and 1840s. This early blossoming presaged the more prolonged expansion of the late nineteenth century, an upswing driven by foreign investment and liberal economic policies. The miniboom introduced a number of innovations. To enhance their operations' profitability, several entrepreneurs began to experiment with technological improvements. Potosí's mine owners also had to abandon the *mita* as a dependable source of cheap labor; government officials judged the system anathema to their modern, liberal goals.[27]

Despite the modernizing changes, some colonial currents flowed into the nineteenth century. A plebian mining culture continued to flourish in the shadow of better-funded entrepreneurs. Small mills and the rambunctious *kajchas* played a critical role in Potosí's economy in the 1830s and 1840s. During the early republican period illicit mining provided an important safety net for national silver production. The labor force of the early nineteenth century also maintained a strong bargaining position with employers. Mine owners still viewed workers as undisciplined and undependable. Some laborers continued to scam potential employers out of cash advances, while others continually smuggled the richest rock from the mines.[28] *Kajchas* even sought to expand their access to ore and official sanction for their endeavors. The government and mine owners resisted their pretensions.

In 1837 Potosí's *kajchas* penned a letter to government officials outlining a proposed modification of property rights in the mining industry. The *kajchas* began by acknowledging that both government officials and mine owners viewed their vocation with "aversion and repugnance." They admitted past transgressions. "Certainly the men dedicated to this vocation have only sought to enrich themselves, extracting the best ore with little planning and without considering the accompanying damages to the owner," they wrote. But, they argued, much of the damage resulted from the illicit nature of their entry into the mines, and they concluded that "ending the cause" would "end the effect." The bandit miners proposed a "regulated *kajcheo*"—that is, an understanding with the mine owners including specific provisions:

> That they permit us to enter their works from Saturday until Monday night—that the respective watchmen turn the shafts over to us with a precise examination of their condition—we will then bear the responsibility of guaranteeing to them, in whatever manner they wish, that we will return the shafts to the same watchmen without risk and with no damage done. In this period, with all of the formality of the Regulations, we will exploit the metal with our tools and whatever else may be necessary. The extracted metal will then be divided between the individual mine owner and ourselves; he may even buy our part at a just price established by a third party, as long as we agree.

The *kajchas* claimed their proposal would benefit the mine owners, who would "not have to make up-front payments" and would "be spared the cost of tools." In fact, they argued, this would leave the owners in a better position than that of the *kajchas*, who labored with no certainty of recompense. Finally, the *kajchas* claimed a service to the republic in cushioning the blow of a mining slowdown: "There is the need that exploitation continue in order to conserve the working class and amass metal."[29]

All Potosí's major mine owners rejected the proposal, complaining, "Experience has proven how prejudicial the *Kajchas* are." Nonetheless, mine owners sometimes employed *kajchas* as contract workers, but on their own terms. They concluded, "Voluntary arrangements are not prohibited by the Law; in this way the petitioning workers might enter into agreement with those mine owners who wish to employ them in their works."[30] The bosses sought to keep government out of the contracting process. The *kajchas* sought to obtain a greater range of legal options and to force open mines previously closed to them. The government declined to act on the *kajchas'* petition. As the nineteenth century advanced and modernization continued, the mine owners never succeeded in completely disciplining strong-willed laborers.

In the 1850s and 1860s new Chilean, North American, and European investors began to express interest in Bolivia's mining industry, and a handful of the nation's businessmen emerged as the representatives and managers of this investment. The historian Antonio Mitre has termed these privileged individuals the "silver patriarchs," and they all came from prestigious, land-owning clans: the Aramayos, the Pachecos, and the Arces. To make Bolivia productive in the late nineteenth century, mine owners contracted European engineers and industrialized with steam-powered machinery. Doing this required a greater capital investment than even the wealthiest Bolivian families might afford alone.[31] Foreign capital became a necessity.

Mine owners wedded to foreign backers required new laws congenial to their liberal, free-trade ideology. Vocal elements among the popular classes, however, resisted the loss of protective regulations developed during the colonial period. The government eventually sided with the silver patriarchs. The mining oligarchy achieved its greatest legal triumph on October 8, 1872, when the government legalized the export of silver bullion. The new law reversed the colonial practice of exporting only silver coin and paved the way for an even greater influx of foreign capital and the progressive consolidation of mining in the hands of a few powerful companies.[32]

Support for colonial protectionism did not immediately disappear; elements among the popular classes fought the ascendancy of the silver patriarchs. In 1876 Sucre's artisans directed a protest to President Hilarión Daza (1876–1879) calling for the suspension of the new silver export law. The artisans complained that liberal economic policy damaged the public good: "The free export of bullion . . . has done nothing more than move the monopoly of purchase, once exercised by the State for the public good, into the hands of bankers, mine owners, and merchants for their own particular benefit." The artisans insisted on the principle, established during the colonial period, that mineral deposits belonged to the state and not individual mine owners. The state conferred only a "usufruct contract" to mineral deposits, and the mine owners had to accept this "with the implicit condition to sell the bullion at a fair market price" to the government. Sucre's artisans argued that the principles of liberal "economic science" did not apply to mining and that the "industrial liberty" of the mine owners needed limits. "Liberty, this precious gift that God has given to man, has as its soul justice and is guided by reason: lacking these conditions it is nothing more than an antisocial element," they contended. Finally, the artisans ridiculed the oligarchic assembly of 1872 that first approved the law, calling its members "men of much knowledge, who so often lose themselves in the realms of their vast illusions."[33] The government sided with the influential men of "vast illusions" and upheld the laissez-faire export law of 1872. The legal enthronement of economic liberalism helped open a new era in Bolivian mining in the 1870s.

Bolivia's silver production rose throughout the final decades of the nineteenth century, and foreign capital flooded in despite a steady decline in silver's international value during the same period. In the 1860s the country exported an average of 344,000 marks of silver annually; by the 1890s Bolivia was exporting an average of 1.6 million marks annually. Between 1875 and 1890 Bolivia stood as the world's third-largest silver exporter, contributing around 10 percent of global production. Production peaked in 1895, when the country's mines produced around 2.6 million marks.[34]

The silver boom and the mining oligarchs' accompanying political dominance had important repercussions for Bolivia's popular classes. In the countryside the government imposed laws to privatize land belonging to Quechua and Aymara communities, though the plan sometimes met effective resistance.[35] In addition, the working class resisted the discipline that the oligarchs sought to bring to the mines. The bosses employed every legal device available, including fines, criminal charges leveled against "ore thieves," and educational programs. In 1852 José Avelino Aramayo published a series of internal regulations for his firm, the Anacona Society, the first such guide published by a Bolivian mining company. Internal regulations of this type made an uneven advance in many mines during the final decades of the nineteenth century. Mining companies also began to encourage the creation of municipal mining police or their own private security squads. These forces sought to eliminate absenteeism and limit the consumption of alcohol. The mine owners further set them to guard against the theft of ore and to suffocate sedition among the workers. Mine owners also launched a sustained campaign against religious celebrations that might keep workers away from the mines.[36] At best, however, the campaign for greater discipline achieved only moderate success.

The mine workers, who numbered a little more than 6,500 in the mid-nineteenth century, sometimes fought the impositions openly but principally employed more subtle tactics of everyday resistance.[37] Workers had their own ideas about proper treatment and reacted vigorously to perceived infringements. When the Colquechaca-Aullagas Company fell behind on its payroll in the early 1890s, for example, threatening flyers began to appear around the northern Potosí mining town. The postings depicted a bundle of dynamite about to be lit and bore a caption reading "The dynamite asks the administrator to pay the working people who are poor and frustrated."[38] Laborers bristled at greater regulation and supervision, especially when mine owners failed to reciprocate with prompt and adequate compensation.

The mining labor force of the nineteenth century was a mix of skilled urban workers and seasonal rural migrants, but industrialization magnified the importance of experienced laborers settled permanently in the mining camps. Steam power and the slow but steady mechanization of mining eliminated many job categories previously filled by temporary rural laborers; the labor-intensive work of mercury amalgamation and the manual transport of ore grew rare in better-financed mines. Mechanization required new technical skills—the introduction of more machinery led to specialized positions such as engine operator—and the mechanics' workshop became an essential division of any large operation. At the same time, to meet the shrinking but still unavoidable demand for unskilled labor, the bosses began replacing some migratory male laborers with women and children permanently settled in mining communities.[39]

The nineteenth century also saw the advance of wage labor and an accompanying loss of workplace liberty. For example, between 1850 and

1872 highly varied and flexible contract arrangements dominated in the Huanchaca Mining Company's tunnels and shafts.[40] After 1872, however, wage labor began undercutting the autonomy embodied in earlier practices, with workers feeling increasingly distant from and exploited by the company. A nineteenth-century carnival song from Pulacayo, Potosí—a tune sung by children—illustrates the perceived chasm: "I am the little miner, sir, and I earn my bread with my labor. I have blisters on my hands and chest. The boss is harsh, and the silver that we take from the mine is never for us."[41] This antagonism between owners and miners exploded into open conflict in the twentieth century.

Silver mining's growth continued uninterrupted until 1895, when the price of silver reached a nadir following a five-year downward spiral that had begun in 1890.[42] At the end of the nineteenth century silver faltered as the engine of Bolivia's export-oriented economy; in the twentieth century tin rose to take its place. But silver had left its mark, and subsequent labor activism among Bolivian tin miners grew from this legacy.

THE FEDERALIST WAR AND WORKING-CLASS SOLDIERS

In 1896 Fernández Alonso, the favored candidate of the incumbent Conservative Party, won election as president of the republic. He inherited a legacy of corrupt one-party rule. Fernández Alonso supported reconciliation between the nation's quarreling Conservative and Liberal parties, and because of this, both his allies and his enemies derided him as "timid" and "effeminate." The proposed reconciliation inflamed the combative tendencies of hard-liners in both parties. By 1898 a debate about federalism and a squabble over fixing the seat of government in La Paz versus Sucre began to mix explosively with preexisting party antagonisms. On December 12, 1898, the wealthy and powerful of La Paz, primarily affiliated with the Liberal Party, declared themselves in rebellion. The Federalist War of 1898–1899 began as a dispute among the dominant classes, but in the countryside the conflict developed into a vicious rural revolt beyond the control of urban leaders.[43]

The rural, indigenous population of the Altiplano revolted in conjunction with the Liberal Party and the oligarchy of La Paz. José Manuel Pando, a professional military officer, led the Liberals' army, yet the insurrection in the countryside developed with chaotic autonomy. The rural rebels even followed their own chief, Pablo Zárate Willka, an Aymara from Imilla-Imilla on the border between the departments of La Paz and Oruro. Zárate Willka claimed the title of "general and commander in chief of the Indian Army." In theory he answered to Pando; in practice, he enjoyed significant liberty. Yet even Zárate Willka could not completely control the widespread rural rebellion. On a number of occasions mobilized peasants vented their ire on Conservatives and Liberals alike. The oligarchy's civil war allowed for the eruption of rural rage over the recent loss of community land to neighboring haciendas and a festering resentment over the cultural, social, and economic subjugation of Bolivia's Andean population. Zárate Willka and his followers believed that Pando would address their grievances after a Liberal victory; as things turned out, they had misplaced their faith.[44]

Following the war's resolution, the Liberal oligarchs and Pando turned on their rural allies. The new government circulated a series of orders seeking to demobilize the countryside. "The indigenous race, always removed from the political events of the country due to their special condition of ignorance, has been forced in the present fight to participate in the horrors of civil war," the government declared. "With the recent triumph, the martial services of the indigenous race are no longer necessary. Because of that, please order all of the priests and cantonal *corregidores* . . . to encourage them to return to their labors and the peaceful lives they have always enjoyed."[45] When rebellion did not abate, Pando ordered a general repression, and in late April 1899 the Liberals arrested Zárate Willka. Two years later the guards charged with escorting him from an Oruro prison to a similar cell in La Paz shot the rebel chief during a supposed escape attempt.[46]

The Quechua and Aymara followers of Zárate Willka lent enormous support to the insurgent Liberal Party in the hope of winning concessions from the oligarchy; the working class of the mines played a more ambiguous role. In the copper town of Corocoro, within the department of La Paz, the urban popular classes cooperated with the rural population to drive the Sucre Squadron, a division of the Conservatives' army, from the town.[47] Elsewhere, in the mines of Colquechaca, Potosí, there were labor difficulties associated with the Federalist War.[48] But the mining city of Oruro, where many workers sided with the Conservative cause, provides a contrasting example of miner participation in the conflict; laborers there fought for the incumbent political party and against the rural rebellion. President Fernández Alonso owned a controlling stake in the city's San José mine, and bonds of paternalism influenced many workers to side with his party.

Fernández Alonso acquired a stake in the San José mine in March 1893; when elected president in 1896, he would have occasion to call upon the mine's laborers.[49] The unit they formed, the Alonso Battalion, proved the most reliable and disciplined detachment in the Conservatives' army. It enjoyed the leadership of skilled officers and was well equipped with arms and ammunition. The unit also contained a rather homogeneous soldiery of—according to its commander, Emilio Benavides—"young miners . . . endowed with loyalty, subordination, and valor."[50] First organized in 1898 in response to a rumored invasion by Argentina or Chile, the battalion originally consisted of "500 soldiers selected from among 1,500 workers of the San José mine of Oruro."[51] During the Federalist War the squadron marshaled 300 soldiers. The battalion's commander had been the San José mine's administrator before the war. Benavides acknowledged this previous relationship between himself (among others) and the battalion's soldiers when he wrote that "its officers, inspired by the rough camaraderie of labor in the mine, knew how to capture the troop's affection."[52] In early 1899 the Alonso Battalion participated in the Conservatives' aborted advance on the city of La Paz but saw no action. In March the battalion undertook a new mission that brought it into direct conflict with Zárate Willka's irregular rural fighters.[53]

The Conservative Party tasked the San José mine's soldiers with escorting a shipment of ammunition and rifles from Oruro to the besieged prefect of Cochabamba.[54] The Andean farmers populating the mountains between the two departments sought to ambush the detachment in the Huayllas Valley. The Alonso Battalion's men understood the price of defeat. Two months earlier insurgents in the department of La Paz had captured, tortured, and killed some two-dozen Conservative Party soldiers and three priests in the church of Ayo Ayo. The Alonso Battalion arrived on the scene soon after and buried the mutilated bodies. At Huayllas no quarter was given and none was expected. The battalion's commander later reported that "disguised mestizos" led the irregular force of some three thousand men; other sources record that the Aymara chief Zárate Willka commanded the ambushing force.[55] Although outnumbered, the Alonso Battalion was better trained and better armed; each soldier carried a rifle and one hundred rounds of ammunition. The Andean insurgents carried "rifles, clubs, spears, and slings." In the first encounter the insurgents sought to overwhelm the soldiers with the force of numbers. "Making an infernal noise with gunshots, horns, dynamite, and rockets they assaulted us with terrible fury, intending to disarm us by force," reported Benavides. San José's miners prepared to receive the onslaught by forming a hollow square three ranks deep on each side. When Willka's men closed to within one hundred yards, the Alonso Battalion's soldiers opened fire, repulsing the attackers. After regrouping, the insurgents, "carrying the three banners of the Willkas," launched a second assault with the same results. That night the Conservative Party detachment occupied and fortified the small settlement of Huayllas. The following morning, hoping to take advantage of the predawn darkness, Zárate Willka ordered a third and final attack. This time the Alonso Battalion followed up its repulsion of the insurgent assault with a counterattack to rout Willka's men from the slopes of the valley. The fighting degenerated into a massacre and continued until three that afternoon. The Alonso detachment's commander, Benavides, wrote with a hint of guilt two decades later: "Poor Indians! Their situation must be improved, and the hate they profess for the whites must be dispelled with good, civilizing acts." Willka saw his force dispersed. He withdrew to the Altiplano to rebuild his following. Despite the Conservative victory, the Alonso Battalion's mission ultimately failed; Cochabamba fell to the Liberal Party before the shipment of arms could arrive.[56]

In early April the Alonso Battalion returned to Oruro to rejoin the bulk of the Conservatives' army as it prepared for its final encounter with José Manuel Pando's Liberal army and irregular Andean allies. During the last significant battle of the civil war, the Alonso's soldiers again acquitted themselves with determination. At the Battle of the Second Crossroads (April 10, 1899)—a resounding Liberal victory—the battalion stood as the last Conservative unit to withdraw from the field. The San José mine's working-class soldiers covered the retreat of other defeated Conservative units. In this battle the Alonso Battalion occupied a small hill overlooking the Liberal army and unleashed a torrent of rifle fire. Benavides remembered, "For a moment I thought the victory was ours, when my assistant informed me that the '25th of May' and the 'Olañeta' [two Conservative battalions] were firing in retreat." The defeated units were "terribly pursued by the victorious army and by the Indians who in numerous groups covered the hills, waiting like hungry wolves for the final, bloody result." The Alonso Battalion covered the retreat as well as it could, losing some 40 percent of its men. After the defeat, the battalion's surviving members abandoned their uniforms and returned to Oruro's mining camps to blend in with the bulk of the urban population.[57]

Following their victory in the Federalist War, the Liberal Party did little to modify the nation's political and economic structure. In fact, the spectacular growth of tin mining in the twentieth century amplified the industrial developments of the previous century, and despite an expanding pool of industrial laborers, the political tutelage of the dominant classes continued to burden the urban popular classes.

THE NEW CENTURY IN ORURO
AND NORTHERN POTOSÍ

In October 1899 the victorious José Manuel Pando assumed the republic's presidency, inaugurating two decades of Liberal Party dominance.[58] The new ruling party quickly came to resemble the defeated Conservative Party in its persecution of political opponents. Oruro's newspaper *Ideales* editorialized on the political climate in 1900:

Once master of the political situation, the Liberal Party promised that it would implement a complete reform[;] . . . that all guarantees would be respected; that meritorious men of honor and talent would participate in all branches of public administration; that hostility toward political adversaries would cease; that both the majority and the minority would participate in the Legislature as a manifestation of genuine public opinion; that the soul of Bolivia would be fortified by union and fraternity. But what has happened? It is sad to say: an unprecedented persecution of the adherents of the fallen party began in various forms; criminal prosecution for invented crimes, imprisonment for supposed misdemeanors; whippings in the barracks for the crime of having been a Constitutionalist; bold-faced fraud in the last election, in which those who spent the most money have triumphed, in the greater part of the electoral districts, according to accusations in the press; the total exclusion of members of the Constitutional Party from Congress, from the municipalities, and all other branches of administration.[59]

The ascendant Liberal Party decided against modifying the country's constitution. Federalism, an important ideal during the war, was soon abandoned.[60] Liberal presidents sought to rule with the same centralized authority once enjoyed by their Conservative predecessors.

The Liberal Party's early years in power were relatively free of political strife. José Manuel Pando served as chief executive from 1899 to 1904. Another general succeeded Pando in office: Ismael Montes. Montes cast a long shadow over early twentieth-century Bolivia, serving two terms as president: 1904–1909 and 1913–1917. He did much to shape the intolerant character of Liberal rule and employed an iron hand in pursuing economic development. Montes inaugurated the construction of railroads connecting the cities of La Paz, Cochabamba, Potosí, and Sucre to the existing rail network that linked Oruro with Antofagasta, Chile.[61] The country's political situation began to heat up again only in 1914 with the establishment of a new opposition, the Republican Party. This development coincided with the acceleration of autonomous organizing among the country's urban popular classes, that is, artisans and the working class. The growth of tin mining and the increased pace of industrialization pushed along by the Montes presidencies significantly enlarged the number of urban laborers and their political importance.

Bolivia's mines had always produced a mix of silver and tin, but a primitive transportation network and limited European demand kept the market for tin local. The construction of railroads, growing industrial demand, and a production collapse in Europe's mines all created favorable conditions for the expansion of tin exports at the end of the nineteenth century. Silver's declining value in the 1890s solidified tin's dominance, and this transition moved the geographic locus of mining in Bolivia northward. Activity shifted from Potosí's southern reaches to that department's northern fringes. Mines in the neighboring department of Oruro also expanded. Few silver oligarchs made the transition from one metal to the other. Tin thus created opportunities for a number of foreign companies and for a new group of Bolivian entrepreneurs. Despite the shake-up, Bolivia remained a monoexport country.[62] Tin dictated the nation's industrial evolution for most of the twentieth century.

A handful of massive companies quickly came to dominate tin production. By 1909 just eight concerns accounted for nearly three-fourths of Bolivia's annual output. The department of Oruro and the northern fringe of the department of Potosí contained five of these eight. The Llallagua-Uncía region in northern Potosí alone produced 37 percent of the country's tin. There, the Llallagua Tin Company (a Chilean enterprise) and La Salvadora mine of Simón I. Patiño controlled production.[63] Some government officials expressed unease about this increasing consolidation. In 1909 Oruro's prefect, Moisés Ascarrunz, called on the president and Congress "to draft laws and decrees that tend to succor the small producers." He hoped "to make it so that small industrialists might struggle successfully with large owners."[64] In 1911 a different prefect, Constantino Morales, complained, "The large mining companies appear to have monopolized industrial activity to such an extent that no one can begin a new operation."[65] The boom benefited a small group of owners, and—despite isolated misgivings—the government never took vigorous action to slow the advance of monopoly.

Even during the early boom, however, economic growth occasionally stumbled. The mining industry of Oruro and northern Potosí suffered one significant depression during the twentieth century's first decade. Tin production experienced a sharp contraction beginning in 1908. Writing in 1909 Oruro's prefect, Moisés Ascarrunz, reported, "The extractive mining industry, which for several years has given the department of Oruro a superior level of prosperity when compared to other population centers in the republic, today finds itself restrained." The depression caused widespread unemployment. "Thousands of laborers who were employed in the mining industry have, in the course of just a few months, abandoned the mines to return to their distant homes or to stay here and dedicate themselves to some other activity," reported the prefect. The recession contributed to the consolidation of industry. "The current picture of this district is painful for every truly patriotic heart. Only a few foreign companies continue working, thanks to their significant capital investment and valuable facilities." Ascarrunz continued, "The smaller producers, those who constitute a direct improvement of the fatherland by maintaining their capital inside its territory, are no longer working. The lack of resources, increased costs, and the low price of tin . . . have determined their inactivity."[66] This and other periodic recessions affected working-class Bolivians most acutely.

At the beginning of the twentieth century mine workers constituted less than 1 percent of Bolivia's population. The 1900 census recorded 12,625 individuals who reported their occupation as "miner." Census officials applied the designation to anyone associated with the mining industry; their generic definition erased class differences. The category included "mine owners, businessmen, managers, overseers, and laborers in mines and mills." The census also failed to consider individuals laboring part-time in mining and miners' families—a group acutely dependent on the industry. Even allowing for the census's imperfections, mine workers and their families formed only a minuscule part of the population. Yet the concentration of workers in just a few settlements critical to the country's export-oriented economy magnified their importance. Just three departments contained the bulk of the country's mine workers: Oruro, La Paz, and Potosí. Within these departments, a few important cities contained substantial concentrations of mine laborers: Potosí and Pulacayo in the department of Potosí and Oruro in the department of Oruro. The miners of Potosí numbered 2,230; Oruro, 1,913; and Pulacayo, 1,720. Outside these three cities miners spread across highland Bolivia in small camps and towns huddled around rich or promising seams of ore (see table 1.1).[67]

Table 1.1 Notable Mining Towns, 1900

Town	Department	Miners
Potosí	Potosí	2,230
Oruro	Oruro	1,913
Pulacayo	Potosí	1,720
Provincia de Pacajes*	La Paz	848
Colquechaca	Potosí	695
Poopó	Oruro	661
Huanuni	Oruro	496
Aullagas	Potosí	256
Tolapampa	Potosí	218
Río Blanco	Potosí	169
Provincia del Cercado*	La Paz	156
Ocurí	Potosí	150
Machacamarca	Oruro	149
Provincia de Inquisivi*	La Paz	129
Llallagua	Potosí	120
Maragua	Potosí	114
San Cristóbal	Potosí	112
Machacamarca	Potosí	103
Salinas de Garci Mendoza	Oruro	104
Antequera	Oruro	99
Sorasora	Oruro	97
Dalence	Oruro	95
Provincia de Larecaja*	La Paz	93
Huanchaca	Potosí	92
San Vicente	Potosí	91
Porco	Potosí	85
Santa Isabel	Potosí	85
Amaya Pampa	Potosí	69
Ventaimedia	Oruro	52
Uncía	Potosí	47

*The 1900 census reported population figures only for whole provinces in the department of La Paz, not for individual towns.

Source: Oficina Nacional de Inmigración, Estadística y Propaganda Geográfica, *Censo general . . . 1900*, 2:36, 116–19, 137–38.

Mine laborers and their families formed a flexible, migratory socioeconomic group continually seeking better employment opportunities in new settlements. They occupied a cultural position somewhere between rural Andean agriculturalists and urban artisans, shading more toward the mestizo pole of the artisans. While the mining camps received a constant influx of new workers from the countryside, the core of this socioeconomic group had roots stretching deep into the colonial period. An examination of Pulacayo and Oruro's populations in 1900 provides a picture of this group at the start of the twentieth century.

In 1900 Pulacayo possessed all the superficial characteristics of an isolated industrial enclave and company town. The town sits in an arid and still sparsely populated quarter of the Altiplano. Without silver mining Pulacayo never would have existed. One industry and one company—the Huanchaca Mining Company—dominated the town's economic life. Of the settlement's 6,512 residents at the dawn of the twentieth century, over a quarter claimed "miner" as their occupation. But the town was no rambunctious collection of single male workers. The settlement's ratio of men to women came close to the national average. Men in Pulacayo constituted 50.3 percent of the population, and women, 49.7 percent. Of the town's 4,703 residents over the age of thirteen, 48.7 percent were married or widowed, which neared the national average. Ethnically, Pulacayo was distinct from the rest of Potosí, where Indians made up 57.3 percent of the departmental population. In the mining town 13.5 percent of the population claimed to be white, and 69.3 percent called themselves mestizo, but only 16.2 percent were listed as Indians.[68] Pulacayo's population enjoyed a higher level of education than did the population of the rest of the department. Among individuals over the age of seven, 23 percent claimed some classroom experience. In the department as a whole, only 8.2 percent of the population over the age of seven could make a similar claim.[69] Pulacayo was thus a solid collection of working-class families, disproportionately mestizo and better educated than those of more rural places.

Oruro's working class presented a similar demographic picture, but overall the city possessed a population more diverse than that of isolated Pulacayo. Oruro depended on mining, but other economic and adminis-

Table 1.2 Oruro's Population in 1900: Origin

	Dept. of Oruro	Other Bolivian Dept.	Foreign Born
Socavón mine	40.90%	55%	4.10%
Itos mine	48.80%	48.90%	2.20%
San José mine	39.60%	58.20%	2.20%
City of Oruro	59.90%	35.70%	4.80%

Source: Oficina Nacional de Inmigración, Estadística y Propaganda Geográfica, *Censo general . . . 1900*, 1:16–17.

trative activities contributed significantly to the city's character. A departmental capital, it attracted numerous commercial enterprises and a large concentration of urban professionals. Luckily, a small quirk in the execution of the 1900 census simplifies an exploration of the city's working class. The census divided Oruro's inhabitants into urban and rural categories, yet the rural segment was industrial, not agricultural. Thus the census counted the population of the Itos and San José mines as rural despite their proximity to the city. In all, those two mining camps and one in the heart of the city, the Socavón mine, held 2,927 inhabitants; the city proper contained 12,971 residents (many of whom might also have worked in mining). The population of the city's three major mining camps exemplified the migratory character of Bolivia's mine laborers (see table 1.2). Other Bolivian departments constituted the points of origin for 55 percent of the 704 individuals living at the Socavón mine, 48.9 percent of the 756 living at the Itos mine, and 58.2 percent of the 1,567 individuals living at the San José mine. Contrast this with the residents of Oruro proper: 59.5 percent claimed the department of Oruro as their place of birth, only 35.7 percent came from other parts of Bolivia, and 4.8 percent were foreign born.[70] These numbers reflect the miners' long history of migration in search of greater employment opportunities.

As production accelerated, the tin mines attracted former silver miners and migrants from the countryside. The historian Antonio Mitre estimates that 3,000 individuals labored in the country's tin mines in 1900; for 1910 his estimate climbs to 13,147. The explosive growth of previously unimportant mining camps such as Llallagua and Uncía in northern Potosí and a transition from silver to tin in older settlements such as Oruro and Huanuni drove the expansion. Despite this increase, mine workers and their families never exceeded 3.5 percent of the national population during the early decades of the twentieth century, yet simple demographics do not really capture their importance.[71] In twentieth-century Latin America workers employed in critical export industries generally wielded enormous influence on the national stage—but only when they organized.[72]

THE WEIGHT OF PATERNALISM

Despite all the changes, the modern only slowly replaced the archaic in some mines, in terms of both technology and politics. The bosses used antiquated labor practices intentionally to slow the development of working-class organization. At the dawn of the twentieth century wage labor shared the mines of Oruro and northern Potosí with other contracts that closely resembled colonial and nineteenth-century arrangements as management probed the boundaries of legality with various coercive employment schemes. Contracts that fell short of wage labor encouraged workers to defend the bosses' property as their own. An ore-sharing arrangement called *kajcheo* (distinct from the banditry of the same name) created the illusion of worker coproprietorship. These and other employment habits in the mining camps subverted the development of working-class ideology. In particular, the subtle yet controlling paternalism of some bosses slowed working-class organization as many labor contracts sought to obscure workers' dependence on the mining magnates.

Some companies had yet to reconcile themselves to all the implications of "free" labor—a legal fiction generally supported by the government. In November 1899 Oruro's prefect, Óscar de Santa Cruz, denied a San José mine administrator's request for assistance in controlling the movement of the company's laborers. Santa Cruz reminded the administrator that the government had no "jurisdiction to impede citizens from employing their labor where they wished," since the constitution recognized "absolute liberty on this point." The prefect recommended that the company instead "adopt prudent and sagacious methods" that would "tend to prevent workers from looking for employment in other parts."[73] Other companies also schemed to limit their workers' liberty but used methods with greater constitutional standing.

Bosses frequently sought to pay a part of their workers' wages in company scrip. Local officials often objected, but the central government sometimes sanctioned the practice. Just days before rebuffing the San José mine's request for legal limits to worker migration, Prefect Óscar de Santa Cruz had complained to his superiors that the Mining Company of Oruro used "tokens to pay the greater part of their workers' services, obliging them to buy from company stores, which," he claimed, had "excessively priced merchandise." The prefect remarked that some merchants in Oruro accepted the tokens but only at a "notable discount." The whole system, he lamented, led to a "costly speculation" in a variety of currencies. When Santa Cruz wrote the company to demand that it "convert into coin all the tokens" it had issued and admonished it that the law demanded that wages be rendered "in national currency," he received a reply noting a special dispensation from the government issued in September 1897. The dispensation authorized the enterprise to employ company tokens as pay. The prefect wrote government ministers in La Paz and expressed his opinion that the dispensation should be rescinded to "guarantee the efforts of the laborers."[74] The government eventually resolved to oppose the widespread use of company scrip. In November 1901 an Oruro newspaper praised a new ordinance prohibiting payment in scrip: "This law satisfies one of the greatest aspirations of the mining class, who were anxious to see themselves liberated from a tie that bound them to the companies."[75] Although statutes would consistently prohibit the use of scrip, the Mining Company of Oruro and other employers often circumvented the injunction. As late as 1920 workers in Oruro continued to demand that wages not be paid in "tokens or vouchers."[76] As this shows, modernizing laws could not always restrain powerful mining companies.

Oruro and northern Potosí's mines inherited a number of nineteenth-century and colonial contracting practices that circumvented standard wage labor, among them *kajcheo*. By the twentieth century *kajcheo* had come to mean a kind of contract labor rather than a clandestine theft of ore—its definition in earlier centuries. Under a *kajcheo* agreement, gangs of workers divided the ore that they extracted with the company; the *kajchas* worked for a cut of raw mineral rather than wages. These arrangements enjoyed special prominence in companies lacking substantial capital. Juan Prout, the administrator of the Colquechaca-Aullagas Company of Bolivia (a silver mine), described that enterprise's ruinous financial position in 1900: "There is nothing promising or satisfactory: without its own capital to advance its works, with enormous debts owed to numerous creditors, caught up in lawsuits motivated by contracts that will never make sense." The company's weakened state led the firm to rely on the "ruinous system of *kajcheo* labor." Such ore-sharing agreements engendered a false sense of ownership among workers that made some employers uncomfortable. Thus Prout, who had inherited his company's system of *kajcheo* from his predecessor, took steps to modify it "with special contracts, with strict terms, and for a limited time." He feared that workers might "claim acquired rights that could jeopardize future negotiations."[77]

Ore-sharing agreements varied considerably from company to company. Even within individual enterprises different *kajcha* gangs might have different contracts. *Kajcheo* arrangements in Colquechaca's mines varied according to the labor required to extract ore from the company's numerous shafts. Prior to October 1899 the Colquechaca-Aullagas *kajcha* gangs had hauled ore from the company's Amigos mineshaft "on their backs." Because of the manual labor involved, the workers and the company split the ore fifty-fifty. In late October workers began extracting ore by the Desmond shaft; the change improved efficiency. Prout noted, "The extraction of their ore cost them much less, and they had more equipment for it; we assisted them with the free use of carts and an engine." Because of the change, the company began keeping 60 percent of the mineral.[78]

The results of *kajcheo* did not always please mine administrators. Since *kajchas* profited from the extraction of ore alone, they skimped on maintenance. The Colquechaca-Aullagas administrator Prout complained, "All the principal tunnels and paths in both sections appear completely abandoned, with rubble that has built up because of the work done by the *kajchas.*" The company also suffered periodic invasion by individuals seeking to steal ore; some of the trespassers had worked as *kajchas* in the recent past. Simple economics also limited the *kajchas'* utility. While ore-sharing agreements worked in shafts producing high-grade mineral, other tasks required even undercapitalized mines to employ wage labor. The struggling Colquechaca-Aullagas company employed a number of poorly paid wage workers. A report from 1900 noted 100 laborers hired at 1.20 bolivianos (Bs) a day. The administration employed these men in the operation of the pumps and the perforation of new tunnels—tasks the *kajchas* refused.[79]

Companies sometimes employed contract labor for advancing new tunnels or maintaining preexisting shafts. These contracts differed from *kajcheo* in that there was no ore to share. In 1907 the Andacaba Company of Cuchu Ingenio, Potosí, employed several contractors. The company had yet to locate a rich seam of mineral, making *kajcheo* impossible, and its contractors worked primarily to rehabilitate the mine.[80] These men frequently employed their own workers. In three of its shafts, the company employed four different contractors, each having between three and eight laborers. Only in two of the company's five shafts did the administration employ its own workers "who labored for wages." All the contractors in the Cuchu Ingenio mine received a set sum for every meter they advanced the company's tunnels.[81]

A 1907 contract from Colquechaca illustrates the workings of these piecework agreements. In October of that year the Consolidated Company's administrator, Zacarías Ponce, complained that one Matías Paredes, a contractor employed to rehabilitate the mine, charged too much for his services. Paredes demanded Bs 70 for each meter his crew advanced a shaft. Ponce hoped to find another contractor to replace him but could not find anyone willing to take the job for less than Bs 70–80 per meter. He returned to negotiations with Paredes, reasoning that "he should be preferred as a long-standing worker of the Company and dependable."[82] The two men eventually reached an accord. The company agreed to loan Paredes "a cart and the necessary tools," which he was to return when his contract ended. Paredes promised to "cover the cost of materials, the repair of the tools, etc., . . . at no expense to the company." The contractor undertook to extend the Daza shaft by thirty meters at the pace of two meters per week. The company agreed to pay Bs 60 per meter, to be allocated at the rate of Bs 50 for each meter advanced in a given week with a bonus of Bs 300 on completion. The company stipulated the dimensions of the shaft: one meter and eighty centimeters high by one meter and fifty centimeters wide. Paredes promised to transport the waste rock from the shaft to the San Miguel section of the mine. He also enjoyed complete liberty to hire workers to assist him. If Paredes broke any part of the contract, he faced a fine of Bs 50.[83]

Despite strict terms such as those in Paredes's agreement, contractors and other workers often found ways to manipulate employment practices to their advantage. Some workers continued to raid mines at night and on the weekends, harkening back to what *kajcheo* meant in the colonial period. Ore-sharing agreements also allowed for an assortment of deceptive practices. Workers frequently withheld the richest ore, turning over only low-grade rock. Contract workers and wage laborers sometimes took advantage of cash advances offered by the companies. In June 1909 the mill owner Carlos Ayala complained to Oruro's departmental authorities of "being many times the victim of fraud and tricks on the part of persons . . . asking for work and then not completing it—people asking for cash advances and then not working."[84] Yet during the twentieth century's first fifteen years, resistance to the bosses generally stopped at fraud and swindles —more organized and calculated opposition came later.

The bosses' paternal schemes and the nuances of some labor contracts induced many workers to defend the mine owners' property as their own. Workers employed by one enterprise sometimes came to blows with those of another. In 1911, for example, a series of confrontations broke out between the workers of two competing companies in Huanuni. The problems began on March 27, when a tunnel belonging to the Mining Company of Huanuni intersected with one belonging to the Penny and Duncan Company. Oruro's prefect, Constantino Morales, hoped to head off any violence by dispatching the Cercado Province subprefect to place an "iron grate where the intersection between the workings of the two companies occurred."[85] The measure only postponed the conflict, however, and the potential for an armed confrontation persisted. On July 21 Morales informed the police chief that smoke from the Mining Company of Huanuni's shafts had filled those of the Penny and Duncan Company and was "asphyxiating the workers."[86] On the night of July 23 the Mining Company of Huanuni again began burning "sulfur and chili peppers" in its shafts, resulting in severe consequences for Penny and Duncan personnel. The police chief wrote the prefect that "all their people had to abandon the mine" and all work had ceased.[87] The following morning fighting broke out as the Penny and Duncan Company's workers sought revenge. "Workers employed by the Penny and Duncan Company blew up two bridges with dynamite," reported the police chief.[88] A worker for the Mining Company of Huanuni received a bullet wound in the leg and was reported to be in "a very grave state."[89] Eventually, the prefect and other officials succeeded in calming the situation, but similar conflicts occurred with alarming frequency. Because of the earlier clash, when the Penny and Duncan Company reported another intersection of tunnels on October 16, 1911— this time with the Balcón Company—the prefect ordered immediate action. He contacted the management of both companies and ordered the police chief to ensure that they would "suspend all their work in the place where the intersection occurred, and . . . prevent conflicts between their workers."[90] Archaic employment practices, especially *kajcheo*, thus propelled gangs of workers to attack rivals who might infringe on their small piece of the boss's mine, and any broad sense of class solidarity suffered as a result. As the century progressed, however, this would change.

CHAPTER 2

Artisan Initiative

BOLIVIA'S ARTISAN and working classes exhibited growing political confidence during the twentieth century's early decades, as the blossoming of May Day celebrations clearly illustrates. In 1915 Oruro's Mutual Aid Society of Artisans organized the city's annual May Day celebration. The artisans were inspired by "the most noble sentiments of unity, fraternity, and the love of work." They exalted May Day as "the democratic holiday of labor" and developed a program including artisans, workers, and students from the city's artisan-run schools. The society planned a general ringing of church bells on May 1 and a procession of the city's "distinct laboring associations together with the students of the night schools 'Mutual Aid Society of Artisans' and 'The Inca.'" Santiago Franichevich and Francisco Armaza, two artisan leaders, promised Oruro's prefect, Eduardo Diez de Medina, that "the civic procession" would be "conducted with proper seriousness" and would "observe all the city's municipal ordinances and laws."[1] The prefect approved the plans; "Let me inform you that I applaud the enthusiasm of the Laboring Societies in celebrating this agreeable holiday," he wrote.[2] Not all government officials responded so positively to organizing among the popular classes.

Here as elsewhere, artisans and their local mutual aid societies provided the working class its first organizational models. Early activists rarely distinguished between artisans and industrial laborers, considering both working class. This blurring of economic distinctions facilitated cooperation. The participation of two artisan-run schools in Oruro's 1915 May Day celebration is especially noteworthy. Artisan schools provided an alternative to government and municipal institutions—bodies dominated by the oligarchy's political and social thought. Artisans and educated workers —especially those in influential mutual aid societies—formed an important pool of potential electoral clients. As a result, reforms favored by artisans and workers began to make progress in the halls of government, but politicians typically had a double agenda. Officials hoped to prevent conflict and activism with legislation. At the same time, the government strengthened the police and military, steps favored by the mining companies. By 1910 Bolivia was the world's second-largest exporter of tin, producing around one-fifth of the world's stock of the mineral.[3] With that output and the profit to be made, class antagonism continued despite reform.

THE ARTISAN PRECURSORS

In 1876 Oruro's artisans founded the Industrious Society of Artisans, an organization destined to have significant influence in the region during the early twentieth century. The society's regulations illustrate the principal objectives of nineteenth-century mutual aid associations. The Industrious Society of Artisans gave as its primary goal to "unite all artisans for mutual protection and aid"—an expansive objective. The society sought the "intellectual, moral, and industrious" improvement of its members, employing "a paternal Supremacy so as to educate them as to their duty, order, work, and morality."[4] While the language suggests moralizing impositions by the dominant classes, such traditions of discipline could have positive results for the labor movement, for they laid the groundwork for disciplined unions. What matters is who is doing the disciplining.[5]

The Industrious Society of Artisans built on older, established guilds. Despite its federated character, the society claimed extensive regulatory powers. While individual guilds might still name "their respective masters, officials, and other employees according the methods of their own special regulations or according to established custom," the society claimed the right to schedule and supervise elections. The society even asserted a power to intervene in the personal lives of its members: "to impose small corrective penalties and to seriously rebuke any artisan who has fallen into frequent drunkenness and the vice of gambling." Membership in the organization was nearly irreversible: "No collective guild or any individual master might separate themselves from the interests of the artisans without the consent of all artisans."[6] Bodies such as the Industrious Society of Artisans played a pivotal role in creating a disciplined and educated element among the urban popular classes.

On March 11, 1900, Oruro's artisans met to reforge the Industrious Society of Artisans as the Mutual Aid Society of Artisans—an organization that still exists.[7] The reinvigorated society's leadership had met five days earlier to plan the ceremony. Men who would play prominent roles in creating more aggressive labor associations during the century's second and third decades attended the meeting. León M. Loza, a lawyer who would cooperate with the Oruro Workers' Labor Federation after its creation in 1916, was the Mutual Aid Society of Artisans' first vice president. Nícanor Leclere, a founding member, would serve as the society's president six times between 1905 and 1929. In 1916 Leclere would become the first secretary of the Workers' Labor Federation. The society's leaders convened "a general reunion of all the artisan class of Oruro," including "the masters of workshops and the whole public in general without discrimination because of political colors." They expected a large crowd and requested the use of the city's high school "to give the reunion greater space and solemnity."[8] The Mutual Aid Society of Artisans became a fixture in Oruro, and similar associations appeared throughout Bolivia at the end of the nineteenth century and during the early decades of the twentieth. These organizations eventually carried their message of association and solidarity to the working class of the mines. Their active promotion of educational initiatives played an important role in spreading their influence.

Artisans and workers understood the importance of education, and many government officials agreed, but effectively implementing educational programs proved a separate and thorny issue. During the early twentieth century the government made moderate progress in expanding primary education in urban areas, although plans for the countryside saw less success. Artisan associations actively promoted these projects, and some mutual aid societies even moved to establish their own schools. Artisan schools sought to serve children and young people marginalized by government schools, in particular, those who worked during the day and had time for class only at night. Providing a supplement to government and artisan schools, the law eventually demanded that mining companies maintain schools for their workers' children. With the concentration of educational institutions in urban areas and the active role of artisan associations, the working class and its allies became the most politically savvy segment of the popular classes.

The children of miners and artisans had greater access to the limited but growing system of primary education than did rural youth. Efforts to construct rural schools in the department of Oruro began as early as 1897. In July of that year the teachers at the Quillacas Canton's municipal school complained that Indian community members were "refusing to comply with the constitutional requirement that they enroll their children in elementary school." The teachers blamed a variety of local authorities, citing "the negative influence of the *corregidor*, the indigenous chiefs and mayors" who exercised "absolute authority" in the community.[9] Indian communities had cultural reasons for resisting the Hispanizing impositions of most teachers. The government had greater initial success in the department's mining towns. In May 1897 Prefect González Portal visited Poopó, home to an important silver mill, "to secure locations for the immediate installation of public schools." He noted that the town already had a school for boys and needed only a few things to start a new primary school for girls: "a chalk board, a table and a chair for the teacher, and the publication of a decree or order in a peremptory tone reminding parents to enroll their daughters."[10] Provincial capitals continued to receive the bulk of government attention. In a 1905 dispatch Oruro's prefect, Andrés Muñoz, described the placement of primary schools in three of the department's four provinces: Poopó, Abaroa, and Carangas. All three contained a significant, dispersed rural population. In Poopó Province the subprefect maintained a school in the capital. The Abaroa Province's subprefect maintained a school in his provincial seat, Salinas de Garci Mendoza. And in the expansive Carangas Province the subprefect maintained one school in the capital, Corque.[11] The existence of only one school in each of these three large provinces made education inaccessible to the majority of rural families. In 1907 Prefect Víctor E. Sanjinés identified the reason public education had failed to spread beyond a few towns: "the lack of competent personnel willing to live in the isolated regions of the department."[12]

Nonetheless, rural education occasionally scored minor successes. During Prefect Constantino Morales's 1911 inspection tour of an elementary school in Carangas Province, he became convinced of the feasibility of Indian boarding schools. Corque's elementary school enrolled fifty students, of whom Morales said "a little less than half" came from "the cantons or *ayllus*." He noted, "Their parents leave them with those who live in town, so that they might employ their services under the condition that they go to school." The prefect felt that this indicated a receptiveness among the Indian population to a system of boarding schools: "This is eloquent proof that the Indian of Corque is not opposed to the education of his children, and the easiest and most effective manner to attract them would be to found a boarding school."[13] By the end of the 1920s many rural communities—both Quechua and Aymara—would begin to demand their own schools, but only if they had a strong say in their operation and curriculum. Generally, though, rural areas lagged far behind urban areas in educational access.

Oruro's government schools started slowly but saw moderate growth during the twentieth century's first fifteen years. In 1906 Prefect Víctor E. Sanjinés informed the minister of state that the city of Oruro had eleven government or municipal schools and four private ones. Altogether the fifteen schools enrolled 946 students. Most of these students were concentrated in primary education. The sole secondary school, Bolívar High School, had 9 teachers and 120 students. Sanjinés had a low opinion of the local high school, writing, "The teachers leave much to be desired." Oruro also enjoyed the theoretical presence of a university. The University of San

Agustín was established in 1892 to teach law and engineering, but as the prefect noted, it had no students.[14] Sanjinés reported a moderate growth in enrollment throughout the system one year later and provided data as to the sex of the students. In the city of Oruro he counted five boys' primary schools with 576 students and 13 teachers and six girls' schools with 410 students and 14 teachers. In Cercado Province he reported eight schools with a mixed-sex enrollment of 213 students and 8 teachers. As for the all-male Bolívar High School, it had 134 students and 8 teachers. The city also had a new secondary school for young women with 70 students and 7 teachers.[15]

Determining which level of government should have primary charge of education prompted some debate in Oruro. In July 1910 the prefect Constantino Morales complained, "In Oruro that which has happened in the rest of the Republic has also occurred—Primary Education has been abandoned to the Municipal councils and bodies; it has fallen into the most lamentable empiricism; it has become necessary that the Executive Power again take charge of the schools' administration."[16] Morales continued his exposition on the importance of government-run schools in a speech to the University of San Agustín in 1911, where he noted grave conflicts in modern society and proclaimed, "These grave social problems can be resolved or alleviated with great currents of love; with the strong intervention of a charitable spirit; and with the constant application of an unselfish, self-sacrificing, and tolerant conduct." He also celebrated public education as one remedy for class conflict: "An environment of peace, of good manners in school, a democratic school in the best meaning of the word, I mean to say, a school in which the children of all are educated together," could prevent strife between capital and labor.[17] Despite this prefect's passion for government schools, a variety of institutions dabbled in education.

During the early twentieth century the national government, local municipalities, and artisan societies all ran schools in Oruro. Moisés Ascarrunz, prefect in 1908, noted one unusual absence: "Not one parochial school exists in this whole Department."[18] Enrollment in Oruro's schools continued to grow, and by 1915 Prefect Eduardo Diez de Medina reported 2,726 students in primary and secondary institutions. He noted two schools supported by artisan mutual aid societies—the Inca School, run by the Workers' Union of Artisans, with 45 students, and a school run by the Mutual Aid Society of Artisans, with 160 students.[19] Artisan associations were the only autonomous bodies in Oruro supporting their own educational institutions; the national or municipal governments ran all other schools. Artisan organizations provided education to 7.5 percent of the department's students.

The Mutual Aid Society of Artisans established its night school in 1902. The project had a rocky start but eventually won the support of Oruro's prefects—the start of a rapport with government authorities that lasted fifteen years. In July 1902 the society's leadership wrote Prefect Guillermo Sanjinés requesting previously pledged funds to support the school. Initially Sanjinés balked at the request. He noted the "difficult and precarious situation" of the treasury. He criticized the night school, saying that it had "produced negligible results" and downplaying its importance: "No artisans receive instruction . . . , just some twenty children who also attend the Municipal Schools."[20] The prefect changed his opinion when rebuked by the ministry of education and development. The chastened Sanjinés quickly wrote, "The Prefecture in my charge has made the decision to support the Artisans' Night School," adding that the "monthly budget for the salaries of the teaching body" would be given "with the required punctuality." In addition, he promised a continued relationship: "This Prefecture will provide even greater cooperation in the development of said institution in deference to the instructions of this respectable Ministry."[21] Later prefects provided more spontaneous support.

By the end of 1906 the night school was well established, and the Mutual Aid Society of Artisans continued to cultivate departmental prefects assiduously. On December 5 Prefect Víctor E. Sanjinés presided as a guest of honor at that year's final exams.[22] The courting of the prefect paid off, and the night school won an established line of Bs 1,000 in the national budget.[23] In July 1907 Víctor Sanjinés wrote that the government was "persuaded as to the importance of mass education" and understood its "special duty" to ensure that such educational centers provided "the highest degree of culture" to the artisan class.[24] In December of that year the Mutual Aid Society of Artisans made Sanjinés an honorary member.[25]

The government sought to spread similar institutions to other mining settlements in the department, and mining companies sometimes cooperated. In 1908 the government carved out a budgetary line for a night school in Huanuni. The town's companies supported the idea—after all, they did not have to pay for it. The prefect Moisés Ascarrunz hoped for the initiative's success because, he said, Huanuni was an "important and populous mining town" with a "growing population."[26] The government hired Demóstenes Peláez to run Huanuni's public schools and its night school.[27] They paid him sixty bolivianos a month and provided an additional fourteen bolivianos to pay for electricity, since a night school needed electric light.[28]

Artisan night schools addressed more than just basic academic topics; high culture and Bolivian nationalism figured prominently in the curriculum. Mutual aid societies sought to provide a broad education to their members' children, and the government supported their commitment to cultural education. In December 1910 the Mutual Aid Society of Artisans solicited permission to use a collection of musical instruments that the government had donated to the city of Oruro. The society planned to use the instruments in its night school. Prefect Constantino Morales acceded to the request "without any vacillation," so that the "children of this country's artisans" could "acquire the knowledge of music so indispensable in popular education."[29] In March 1911 the society celebrated the tenth anniversary of its reorganization with the opening of a library and a few literary presentations. The magnate Simón I. Patiño was the invited sponsor of the proceedings, demonstrating that the artisans' passion for cultural improvement crossed class lines.[30]

Authorities proved even more enthusiastic about the artisan school's inculcation of Bolivian patriotism. Militarism and nationalism intertwined in early twentieth-century Bolivia. In July 1911 Prefect Constantino Morales gave the Mutual Aid Society of Artisans' night school Bs 200 to purchase uniforms so that the schoolchildren might present themselves "uniformed in the great scholastic procession" that would pass before "the patriotic altar on the glorious anniversary of August 6, 1825 [Bolivian independence day]."[31] Morales also supported the students' military education. That same July he loaned the society the "necessary rifles" for their "military exercise."[32] The next year the society again requested assistance in defraying the cost of new uniforms for its students. On this occasion a disappointed Morales had to decline: "The patriotic committee that I preside over, at this moment, has no money to pay for what you have solicited." He assured the artisans that he would bring the request to the attention of the whole committee.[33]

Constantino Morales's patronage of the artisan night school continued into 1913. In May of that year the Mutual Aid Society of Artisans inaugurated a new space for the school in an event that also commemorated the one-hundredth anniversary of Bolivia's first printing press. The prefect was a guest of honor at the ceremony.[34] The society's leaders took advantage of the moment to mention their need for one hundred benches, and the prefect forwarded the request to the minister of public education with his endorsement. He praised the school for its "marked benefits for the proletarian class" and noted that the students attended it "with a praiseworthy assiduity." His message conveyed some of the difficulties the children of workers and artisans faced: "The many children that attend the school, at the present moment, have to do their work standing."[35]

With the Mutual Aid Society of Artisans' success, other laboring associations sought to establish their own schools. In late 1911 a new society appeared in Oruro, the Workers' Union of Artisans. Constantino Morales praised the new organization for its "altruistic and patriotic goals."[36] Just two years after its founding, the organization started its own educational institution, the Inca School, where the artisans taught "reading and writing to the children of the town and particularly to the indigenous class."[37] On May 1, 1913, the Workers' Union of Artisans hosted a gala to raise funds for the new school. Prefect Morales arranged for seven musicians from a detachment of the Bolivian army to play at the event.[38] In July 1913 it requested an annual budgetary line of Bs 500 from the government, and Morales endorsed the request, pointing to "the progress made by this institution in the short time since its foundation." He also noted that the patriotic date of August 6 was approaching: "The students of the Inca School are preparing to present themselves . . . in a great scholastic procession before the patriotic altar—which all of the students of the department's public schools should do—for which they need a special uniform, which they are making."[39] By 1915 the Inca School had 45 students, while the Mutual Aid Society of Artisans' night school had 160. The prefect Eduardo Diez de Medina praised both schools and noted that the second had been providing "evident services to the working class" for fourteen years. Diez de Medina noted that many of the students at the mutual aid society's school were "workers of the mining companies."[40] This was the high point of artisan-run schools, for government cooperation soon evaporated.

In 1916 officials in La Paz backed away from their traditional support of the Mutual Aid Society of Artisans' night school. Economic difficulties stemming from World War I explain the stinginess somewhat, but the change also suggests a growing distance between government and the popular classes. A more aggressive laboring association emerged in Oruro in 1916, and other departments experienced similar developments. Many of these new organizations sympathized with the nascent Republican Party, an oppositional offshoot of the ruling Liberal Party. In November 1916 Oruro's prefect, Melitón Lemaitre, forwarded a request for "furnishings and scholastic material" from the Mutual Aid Society of Artisans to his superiors in La Paz. The minister of education, L. Salinas Vega, dispatched the material with a grumbling admonition, complaining that the government lacked "scholastic material in the warehouses" and that it was able to meet requests from the republic's public schools "only with difficulty." Despite some fifteen years of support, the minister now wrote: "I must inform you that because of the economic crisis and . . . the European war, the Ministry cannot in the New Year provide material to any private schools; they must be developed with their own resources"[41] By 1917 the Mutual Aid Society of Artisans' night school dropped from Oruro's departmental reports. Other artisan schools continued to appear but never captured similar levels of government support. In February 1918 the San José Workers' Society invited Oruro's prefect to a religious ceremony accompanying the inauguration of their Sebastián Pagador School, but this was a minor addition at odds with the general trend.[42]

Working-class children did not lose educational access, however, for the number of schools maintained by mining companies and other industrial enterprises, such as railroads, increased sharply during this period. This was a response to government orders issued in July 1913. In a series of regulations to be applied to the mining industry and its workers, the government ordered, "If the number of workers reaches fifty, the Company or mine owner should secure the installation of a mixed-sex primary school in cooperation with the respective authorities."[43] Government and company schools continued to provide greater urban educational opportunities than those available in the countryside; what was perhaps lost, though, was the autonomy of teaching in artisan-run schools. The legacy of artisan schools becomes apparent when viewed alongside other innovations introduced by mutual aid societies during the early twentieth century.

If 1916 marked the beginning of a decline in Oruro's artisan-run schools, it also marked the emergence of more politically active laboring associations in the region. During the twentieth century's first fifteen years, the country's mutual aid societies—in addition to promoting education—worked to create a national federation of artisans. They also sought to expand their membership to include the working class of the mines. Indicative of their expanding political outlook, the artisans introduced the international holiday of May Day to the urban popular classes. All these developments laid the foundation for an autonomous labor movement that would eventually emerge as an arbiter of national power.

During the 1910s a few mutual aid societies began to express an interest in forming a federation transcending local issues, something national in scope. The May 25 Mutual Aid Society of Potosí provides an example.[44] In August 1912 the association circulated a letter of invitation to other labor societies throughout Bolivia. "Taking into consideration the great universal and altruistic principle of fraternity, the society that I have the honor to preside over has decided by unanimous vote to form a federation of all analogous societies that might exist in the republic's territory," its president wrote. "When realized, there will come into being in Bolivia one of the most powerful of organizations. The federation will organize our force and power, amplify our members' work, facilitate the interchange of ideas, and finally, form a true confraternity among those who end up joining our ranks." Despite the rhetoric, the proposal did not modify the traditional local role of an artisan association. Instead, the suggested national federation would mainly seek to make it easier for artisans to move around the country and transfer their membership from one local to another. An artisan moving to a new city would carry "a president's certificate" testifying to "his good conduct," as well as "a recent receipt" verifying "his most recent membership payment." The artisan would then "enjoy all the usual benefits in either the society to which he used to belong or the society to which he . . . moved."[45] The proposed federation thus would not expand the mutual aid societies' traditional activities, membership, or political clout, but the addition of a national vision was still an important step.

Economic distress spurred some societies to greater advocacy. The country's limited social safety net aggravated working-class insecurity, and mutual aid societies sought to improve the situation. In February 1915—with Oruro reeling from an economic slump sparked by the outbreak of World War I—the Mutual Aid Society of Artisans wrote Prefect Eduardo Diez de Medina requesting expanded social welfare programs. It also sought preferential treatment for society members in those programs and proposed some uses for public funds: "In view of the critical period through which the country is passing, the sum which is destined for a public reception in the Government Palace on the Sunday of Carnival might instead be used to increase the funds of the 'Soup Kitchen.'" Various society members also requested that their leaders urge the prefect to send work their way: "When there is work sponsored by the government, they would like you to give them preference because they find themselves among those most without a means to earn their daily bread."[46] Prefect Diez de Medina responded positively. As for the reception during Carnival, he wrote, "The Departmental Budget does not recognize a single expenditure for this reception, but if there were special funds, the Prefecture would with great pleasure implement the recommendation." On the subject of government projects and a preference for society members, the prefect responded, "I am pleased to inform you that this Office will keep the subject in mind at the opportune moment."[47]

The May Day holiday allowed mutual aid societies to raise their public profile even higher. Some used it to reach out to Bolivia's mine workers. In 1915, for example, the Defense of Labor, a Potosí artisan society, sought to expand the social base of its May Day celebration. The organization noted that it would be only the third time that Potosí had commemorated the holiday. With an itinerary of events typical of early twentieth-century May Day celebrations in Bolivia, the group used the holiday to demonstrate its solidarity and collective power. The society planned to proselytize among workers indifferent to or ignorant of the holiday's history and meaning. At ten in the morning Defense of Labor members visited workshops and invited artisans to participate in the festivities. At noon they encouraged a suspension of work "in commemoration of the date." At two o'clock the new Society of Tailors publicly approved its by-laws in collaboration with the carpenters and barbers. Later, the Defense of Labor celebrated the first issue of *Idea Roja,* its new newspaper. At three o'clock the society planned a "propaganda tour through the miners' neighborhoods to encourage the attendance of workers at the rally that night." A procession through the city's principal streets preceded the rally. Finally, at nine in the evening, the city's artisans and workers all gathered in the August 6 Plaza in a demonstration of unity.[48]

THE GOVERNMENT'S RESPONSE

Despite Bolivia's tardy industrial development, some viewed the republic as especially privileged for having avoided the class conflict that plagued other countries. Still, some reform advocates pushed for legislation based on laws adopted in neighboring nations, for they did not want Bolivia left behind by modernizing trends. Many also believed that progressive steps would prevent labor unrest. Oruro prefect Carlos M. de Villegas described the departmental capital in 1905 as a "city of Yankees" because of its industrial importance and its inhabitants' productivity.[49] Two years later a different prefect, Víctor E. Sanjinés, observed, "Those towns in which capital works to create industry are the ones that form the most solid guarantee of public peace, especially if they, as has occurred in Oruro, still have not experienced strikes, these turbulent laboring tremors that in other foreign capitals are a constant threat."[50]

Officials worried about the influence of Bolivia's neighbors. Chilean unrest, for example, could have significant repercussions; a strike in an important port city such as Antofagasta could paralyze Bolivia's international commerce. This concern was evident on February 8, 1906, when Oruro prefect Eloy de Castillo anxiously wrote Uyuni's subprefect, asking him to confirm or to dispel rumors about a strike in Antofagasta.[51] Foreign workers in Bolivia also made government bureaucrats anxious. During the construction of the Oruro-Cochabamba rail line in 1911, foreign workers in one camp threatened a strike, but police mediation prevented a work stoppage.[52] In 1911 officials generally still talked about class conflict as something unknown in Bolivia, but they feared its arrival. In January of that year Oruro's prefect, Constantino Morales, expounded on the topic during a speech at the University of San Agustín. "The present epoch has been characterized by the most savage struggles between capital and labor in the nations of the old continent," he observed. Morales admitted the working class's just grievances but rejected radical solutions: "At the root of these social problems there is always a question of justice. It is in vain to try and resolve these social problems—behind which there is always hidden some great sorrow—with the spilling of blood as the nihilists intend, or with the destruction of private property as the communists hope."[53]

If unrest did arrive, the government hoped to be ready. During the early twentieth century officials continued to fortify the institutions of domestic security—namely, the police and the military. In the nineteenth century mining companies had encouraged the creation of municipal police forces in towns close to their facilities. Despite these efforts, small mines frequently felt besieged by lawless neighbors and workers. In July 1897 the owners of the Santa Rosa mine of Poopó wrote Oruro's prefect requesting a stronger government presence, for they judged the area's police force insufficient. The mine's administrator related, "A few days ago some of this mine's workers were fired because of well-founded suspicions that they were about to join an incipient gang of thieves." The administration identified the company butcher, David Mealla, as the criminal boss. The firings, however, only aggravated the situation. Mealla armed the fired workers with "iron bars, dynamite, shotguns, and other firearms" and "obliged the Police Chief to come to this mine and charge false and invented wages, so as to make this company appear in arrears, thereby justifying ahead of time the robbery they [were] planning to carry out." The company requested reinforcements "because of the small and weak force" that the local police provided. The administration feared "an invasion," with the malefactors "attracted perhaps by a hunger for a few crates of refined mineral."[54] Such security concerns would continue for capital into the new century.

Mining companies sought to influence the police just as they sought to influence all levels of government. One such attempt occurred in July 1911, when the government planned a new police station in Morococala. A Penny and Duncan Mining Company administrator wrote Oruro's prefect, saying, "With great pleasure I freely cede a site in the mining camp of Morococala for the construction of a building to house the Police."[55] Other camps saw similar cooperation between officials and company administrators. Plans for a permanent police force in Condeauqui illustrate mine owners' influence despite the intentions of departmental prefects. In October 1916 Condeauqui's principal mine owners met with Oruro's prefect. Earlier that year the companies had established a private, one-man police force in the town. The mine owners hoped to expand the squad to two or three officers and regularize the body with the prefect's cooperation. The companies volunteered to fund the police until the end of the year, by which time the prefect hoped to secure a permanent stipend from the central government. In an attempt to insulate the police from private influence, the companies agreed to channel the officers' wages through the departmental treasury. Yet the police initially worked out of the Acensión mine's administrative building, until another mine owner completed a permanent building "away from the mining residences and installations."[56] Local officials—the *corregidores*—sometimes assumed the duties of the police, and the companies sought to influence them as well. In December 1916 the Penny and Duncan Mining Company of Morococala recommended Nícanor L. Gutiérrez as the settlement's *corregidor*. The company claimed to make the recommendation with an "impartial method of judgment."[57]

Despite the cooperation between government and the companies, hiring and training police officers in isolated mining towns was not easy. The companies often paid workers higher wages than the government paid the police. In 1907 Oruro's prefect, Víctor E. Sanjinés, complained of "the great difficulty in finding people to hire for Bs 1.20 a day here, where any laborer earns Bs 2." Sanjinés hoped to improve police pay, noting, "Otherwise we will have to use force to keep as police those who—because of their state of indigence—have to choose this means to earn a living."[58] In January 1911 Huanuni's police chief complained of not having the personnel to control the raucous mining town. Two of his jailers had just resigned to look for better-paying work. To hire replacements he had to offer "just, daily wages, asking loans from the mining companies."[59] In February 1912 Oruro prefect Constantino Morales expressed exasperation with Poopó's subprefect, who had complained that it was "difficult to organize in this [provincial] capital a good police force," because most agents were Indian and did "not have the good character necessary to ensure the order and safety of the population." The subprefect asked Morales to send instead five soldiers. The prefect responded with irritation: "I was much surprised by your note, to see that a leading authority in an important province cannot organize a small police force." Morales refused to dispatch the requested soldiers and admonished the subprefect to deal with the problem: "It not being true that in Poopó Province there are not ten men who might serve as police officers, I suggest that in the briefest time possible you organize said police."[60] The wages remained unappealing, though. In 1914 police officers in Oruro and Huanuni still earned only one boliviano per day. In Morococala and Negro Pabellón they earned eighty centavos a day, and in Poopó and Corque, only seventy centavos.[61]

Low wages did not attract high-quality applicants. Corruption became a common way to supplement a police officer's pay. In 1908 the prefect

Moisés Ascarrunz had to reprimand Huanuni's police chief because of the "constant complaints and protests" submitted to him concerning the chief's "abuses and extortions . . . , especially with the indigenous class." Ascarrunz fumed, "The police in this mining settlement, far from being a guarantee for its inhabitants, have become a constant menace." The most recent complaint had come from the town of Ventaimedia, near Huanuni, whose residents cited "invented fines, forced labor, [and] arrests of more than five days." The prefect warned the police chief, "The diverse abuses might produce a criminal suit against you that would be embarrassing and tarnish the authority of your office." Surprisingly, Ascarrunz gave the man one last chance: "If you do not dedicate yourself to the strict dictates of the Police Code, I will have to suspend you."[62] After this litany of complaints, there can be little surprise that the government frequently relied on the military to reinforce the police.

Ironically, although the government occasionally relied on the military to defend business, industry's need for young laborers could place employers at odds with officials seeking to enforce conscription and compulsory military service. A conscription law dated October 3, 1910, contained an exemption: "Railroad employees and workers will not be obliged to perform military service except in times of foreign wars." Bolivia's minister of war and colonization complained in 1911 that "a few conscripts who should have entered the army in January . . . , subject to the law of obligatory military service, have succeeded—through the convenient system of finding employment in the construction of the rail lines—in escaping from the fulfillment of their service."[63] Conscription tended to involve the government in the relation between employers and workers more than business might have liked.

Furthermore, the government sometimes dispatched military forces to the mining camps to display its authority even when the companies had no need for their presence. In September 1913 a Tin Company of Llallagua lawyer wrote Oruro's prefect, Alberto Diez de Medina, to ask why an infantry detachment had recently arrived. The company had received no warning, and the soldiers' arrival produced "great alarm." The prefect informed the lawyer that the detachment sought to "guarantee order in the mining camp, preventing subversive acts by workers in any one of the companies."[64] The deployment of troops to the country's mining zones became more common during the second half of the decade with the rise of worker activism.

Despite government's probusiness inclination, however, the police and military sometimes defended worker interests, as the police did when Oruro's tailors met to form a new industrial society on November 26, 1909. The local police chief actually proposed this organizational step to better keep track of and register the city's artisans. The department's prefect promised to "effectively cooperate with the progress of such a dignified association."[65] Despite the official origin of the tailors' association, however, the society's president, Luis J. Iraola, would emerge as a vigorous activist. He played a role in forming the Workers' Labor Federation of Oruro seven years later, in 1916.[66] In August 1914 Huanuni police chief Fausto López was dismissed when the mining companies determined that he was too sympathetic to workers. The outbreak of World War I had caused a temporary economic dislocation that spurred the departmental prefect, Alberto Diez de Medina, to dismiss López: "His continued presence in that town would have aggravated the subversive situation that has developed among the mine workers." The prefect cited incompetence, saying, "The lack of character and of action of Sr. López has made him absolutely inappropriate to fulfill the said position of police chief as this post is quite delicate taking into account the importance of the mining center of Huanuni," but the investigation into López's failings was headed by one Fermín López, a local "owner of tin properties."[67] The decision to remove this particular police chief favored the companies.

The government tasked the police with controlling the price of basic necessities in local markets and company stores. This was part of a tentative initiative to expand the government's supervision of mining. Officials hoped to prevent discontent and hence unrest. In October 1914 Huanuni's police chief, Alejandro Pacheco Pereira, complained to Oruro's prefect, "The merchants here (mainly Austrians) are trying to impose prices and carry out extortions using the excuse that their old stores of merchandise have been exhausted and that, at the present time, they have to bring in new imports, paying much higher prices." The police chief hoped for a new list of prices from the departmental capital to confirm the merchants' assertions.[68]

In general, the government sought a more active role in regulating living and working conditions for the country's miners, and some officials envisioned an aggressive supervision of industry as part of this. In September 1908 Oruro prefect Moisés Ascarrunz submitted a comprehensive proposal for a permanent commission to inspect the department's mines and mills. The prefect was especially concerned about the impact of industrial labor on women and children: "The miner's child begins working during his most tender years, and the women work, too, and this rude expenditure of labor consumes a whole family without the law ever arriving and offering them protection and succor." Ascarrunz first sought a statistical understanding of living and working conditions—the number of workers in the department's mines and mills, their wages, the hours of labor, the price of goods, the workers' debt load, and the quality of merchandise sold in company stores. The prefect proposed to inspect housing to discover whether living spaces were "hygienic and healthy" and to determine "their size and number in relation to the quantity of workers." Ascarrunz also wanted to examine the medical care provided to workers; he listed several concerns:

> If there is a permanent physician or in what form they attend to the sick, if there is a pharmacy or medicine chest, a hospital or a hall for the sick; what is the relationship that exists between pay and the quota a worker pays for medical attention, or is it free; what portion of the wage or benefit is given to the sick during their illness; and in the case of crippling injury that prevents work or in the case of death, what is the indemnity that is given to the family?

The prefect claimed that humanitarian and patriotic impulses animated his proposal. Ascarrunz wrote, "He [the mine worker] needs aid and resolute protection against speculation and greed; the worker raises a family, and he is obliged to maintain them and even educate them, and it is only natural that he be provided all the guarantees and advantages commensurate with the labor that he performs, almost always distant from population centers and many times without more elements of subsistence than those provided by the company store." The prefect hoped to include the mining settlements of northern Potosí—Llallagua and Uncía—in his program, since these towns lay closer to Oruro than to their own departmental capital.[69]

Although a lack of enforcement would constitute a perennial problem, reforms and inspections such as those proposed by Ascarrunz were eventually adopted. On July 14, 1913, for example, Minister of Justice and Industry José S. Quinteros issued a series of regulations for the mining industry. Quinteros claimed the power to issue the regulations based on the mining law of November 20, 1882, which authorized the Ministry of Industry to protect "both the businessman and the workers engaged in the exploitation of the subsoil's wealth." The minister identified a series of deficiencies in the mining industry, noting "the lack of personal security in the greater part of the mines; the deficient and costly medical attention; the employment of illiterate children in labors incompatible with their tender age; and the liberty that workers have to abandon a job despite the sizable advances in cash or merchandise that they receive, effectively annulling contractual obligations, to then be admitted without a single condition in nearby mines—simple practices that when taken together are contrary to the order, the moral discipline, and the management of mine labor." Quinteros blamed both the companies and inattentive government officials for the lamentable situation of the country's mine workers, observing, "There are few mining companies that know the duties that the law imposes and that the human spirit indicates; medical attention is scarce and expensive for the health of the worker, without means of easy access in rugged regions, threatening the life of the miner on all occasions, sending him to the tomb; the majority of the time [the workers are] ignored by the authorities, leaving proletarian descendents that grow up in the camps, beneath the rough labor of the mine, weak and sickly, subsumed in absolute ignorance, without a school to combat their illiteracy." Quinteros viewed the working class's physical and moral condition as a threat to national security and economic development.[70]

The minister issued a number of regulations to remedy these ills. Companies with more than twenty employees had to provide on-site medical services free of charge to their workers. Companies employing more than fifty had to maintain a co-ed elementary school in cooperation with local authorities, and Quinteros prohibited children younger than twelve from working in the mills. But the minister sought to regulate the mine workers, too; indeed, control of the working class was always a part of any workplace reform. Thus, all workers were to carry a government notebook recording their debts to the company store. Workers could not change jobs without first securing a "certificate of good conduct" from their previous employer. Workers also had to carry paperwork testifying to their completion of any obligatory military service. Finally, the names, origins, marital statuses, and job categories of all foreign employees were to be forwarded to the police in each departmental capital.[71]

By 1915 the Bolivian Congress and President Ismael Montes had taken an interest in labor issues. That November they passed a law sanctifying Sunday as an official day of rest, but the legislation was riddled with loopholes. The first article implied that the law affected only departmental capitals. The second article enumerated a series of exceptions: "jobs that are not apt for interruption because of the types of needs they satisfy, because of their technical character, or for reasons that it might do grave damage to the public interest or to industry." Labor on Sundays could also continue for "jobs of indispensable repairs or cleaning, so that weekday labors might not be interrupted in industrial establishments." However, when workers found themselves forced to work Sundays because of the exceptions, the law mandated a day of rest during the week. Children under the age of eighteen and women were never to be made to work Sundays in industrial establishments—except the law did not apply to "domestic service." For women this was the law's most glaring loophole. The law was scheduled to take effect in January 1916, and employers were to be fined Bs 100 for their first violation and Bs 200 with fifteen days' imprisonment for their second.[72]

Early twentieth-century Bolivia, however, suffered a disjuncture between law and practice. The labor movement arose more from a need to see existing legislation enforced than from a desire to secure new protective laws. In June 1916 Oruro's prefect, Melitón Lemaitre, warned that "illnesses of a pernicious character" were developing "in the various mining regions of this Department," and he feared "the impossibility of the Departmental Treasury to support fully the services of this city's Office of Public Health." Faced with a health crisis, Lemaitre ordered the department's various subprefects "to inspect the Mining Companies of this Province" with an eye to verifying whether they were "completely carrying out the regulations contained in the Supreme Circular Number 23 dated June 14, 1913"—that is, Minister of Justice and Industry José S. Quinteros regulations requiring mining companies to provide medical services to their workers. The prefect applauded the regulations' ethos "linking the pecuniary interests of the one [the employer] with the social guarantees of which the others [the workers] are creditors." Lemaitre recommended the decree's diligent enforcement, noting that ignoring the regulations negatively affected "working people and the whole country."[73]

The illness that so concerned Prefect Melitón Lemaitre was an outbreak of typhoid fever.[74] In the previous month, May 1916, the director of the department's public assistance office reported that 59 individuals had fallen ill with typhoid and 6 had died. To stem the outbreak doctors had vaccinated 245 people across the department. The director of the public assistance office hoped to establish a permanent office of public health so as to "eliminate the elevated mortality rate" found "principally in the small mining centers." The director felt that such a step was a "primordial duty of humanity." As for the disease's cause, he surmised, "The development and propagation of infectious illnesses is due to the terrible conditions in which the Indian and the mestizo live, due to their traditional habits that have not undergone any sort of alterations when it comes to hygiene." The doctor continued, "To this one must add the poor diet, the poor quality of the water—these being the medium in which microorganisms grow." He also remarked on the unwillingness of the department's Quechua and Aymara population to undergo treatment in the city's hospitals: "The indigenous class is no supporter of undergoing treatment in hospitals, preferring to do so in a town near to their homes or in their huts." In addition to criticizing Indian and mestizo living conditions and habits, the director of public assistance also criticized the stinginess of local mining companies. He complained that many of the ill had acquired the "dangerous disease in the mines of Conde-Auqui," where there was "no pharmacy or physicians that might attend them in the case of illness," even though the profitable companies could and should have provided funds for them.[75] Indeed, as he might have added, the companies had a legal responsibility to do so.

Even when the companies followed the law, workers were not always pleased with the quality of medical services. Such was the case with the Penny and Duncan Mining Company in the town of Morococala. On October 23, 1917, the company's workers organized a strike "asking for the removal of the doctor." At ten o'clock on the strike's first night, some two hundred workers attacked the home of Doctor Nícanor L. Gutiérrez. Morococala's police chief reported, "My opportune intervention with thirty men that I armed during the day asking for assistance from the townsfolk prevented an unfortunate incident of perhaps great magnitude." As the strike dragged on for two more days, the company finally agreed to remove the doctor.[76] In June 1921 the Cercado Province's subprefect made a trip to Morococala to hear worker complaints against another Penny and Duncan doctor. The workers lodged several complaints against this doctor: "[He] has no [medical] degree, . . . he is a despot, lacks respect with the women, is rough even with the children, lacks humanitarian sentiments, is ignorant in the fulfillment of his duties, and . . . because of his ignorance and his poor administration of medicines, some have died and some have become sick." The subprefect did not note whether the offending doctor was dismissed, remarking only that the mine's manager "took note" of the complaints.[77] Workers would soon have organizations strong enough to ensure a certain respect for their demands.

CHAPTER 3

Crisis and Organization

BOLIVIA CELEBRATES its independence on August 6. In 1916 Oruro's artisans planned to play an active role in the commemoration. A few days before the holiday, the Mutual Aid Society of Artisans, the May 1 Workers' Philharmonic, the Tunari Cooperative, and the Workers' Union of Bakers informed Oruro's prefect, Melitón Lemaitre, of their intention to participate in official events—and a few unofficial ones of their own. On the night of August 5 the societies would march in the "patriotic parade" with their own "allegoric float." On Independence Day they would participate in the civic procession before the "Patriotic Altar." Afterward, they planned to retire to the Mutual Aid Society of Artisans' reception hall for the distribution of "gifts among poor working families prepared by the four societies." On August 7 the artisans would inaugurate the new night school run by the May 1 Workers' Philharmonic. Prefect Lemaitre would attend the ceremony as a special guest and receive an honorary diploma in gratitude for his "valuable cooperation." On August 8 the artisans planned a picnic to be "made pleasant by a grand orchestra." finally, on August 9 the four societies would sponsor a series of athletic competitions at the local military base.[1] The itinerary illustrates the nationalist sentiment of Oruro's artisans and the educational, cultural, and athletic interests of early twentieth-century mutual aid societies. In the days following the 1916 independence celebration, the four societies plus a few others would form a new, more ambitious association, the Workers' Labor Federation of Oruro, which marked an important organizational and ideological advance for the region's popular classes.

The Liberal Party's political monopoly began to break down during the second half of the 1910s with the emergence of the rival Republican Party. Furthermore, the mining economy stumbled twice during roughly the same period—once at the outbreak of the World War I in Europe and a second time at war's end. These crises affected Bolivia's South American neighbors, too. Chile responded to these economic contractions by expelling thousands of Bolivian workers and their families from the nitrate fields and copper mines of the Atacama Desert. This domestic political and economic ferment, as well as the crisis of returnees from Chile, accelerated artisan and working-class organizing. The insecurity resulting from the rapid economic fluctuations and the incapacity of government and business to smooth over the rough patches compelled labor activists to seek a more powerful and unified voice.

World War I and the immediate postwar years were a formative period for working-class organization in Oruro and northern Potosí. In 1916, for example, artisans and workers formed the Workers' Labor Federation of Oruro, which immediately showed itself to be more aggressive than any previous labor association had been. Bolivia's labor federations generally began as offshoots of the older artisan mutual aid societies, but they rapidly developed more vigorous economic and political programs. Oruro's urban popular classes finally had an independent body to organize and lobby for the implementation of concrete reforms. The oligarchic Liberal and Republican parties continued to exercise a strong influence on artisans and workers, but the landscape of popular politics had changed. While the intensity of organizing and ideological ferment among the working class would oscillate for the rest of the twentieth century, Oruro's urban popular classes and their federations would remain a critical element of Bolivian politics and economy from 1916 on.

LIBERALS BECOME REPUBLICANS

The opposition Republican Party first emerged during President Ismael Montes's second term (1913–1917). World War I's economic dislocations caused immediate problems for the Montes administration, creating an opening for a new party to blossom. Dissident elements within the Liberal Party and remnants of the old Conservative Party began organizing in 1914, with plans for a national convention in August.[2] Domestic political ferment and international economic paralysis had provoked a sense of crisis. On August 8, 1914, President Montes declared a national state of siege. The minister of government and development explained the nation's "notorious situation of crisis" to the country's departmental prefects, writing, "Certain political groupings have degenerated into rebellious factions devoid of doctrinaire principles, of discipline, and of respect for the rights of others, and pursue as their only objective to introduce anarchy into the institutional development of the country."[3] The government shut down thirteen newspapers nationwide, including *El Industrial,* an opposition paper in Oruro.[4] To meet the political and economic difficulties, the Montes administration declared, "It is the highest duty of those that govern, of society in general, and of each honest citizen to unite in this emergency and to collaborate with generosity and patriotism for the improvement of the difficult situation that the people, and especially the working classes, are going through." The Liberal Party claimed that, in the past, it had promoted the "free exercise of public liberties" but that some opposition groups had "supposed that the respect for the law displayed by the Government implied weakness and a lack of energy to moderate unlimited abuse and criminal license."[5] Despite the repression, opposition politicians eventually succeeded in founding their new party.

Established in January 1915, the Republican Party included two personalities that would dominate Bolivian politics for the next couple of decades: Daniel Salamanca and Bautista Saavedra. Daniel Salamanca came from a wealthy, landed family in the fertile valleys of Cochabamba. Educated as a lawyer, he first entered politics in 1899 when President José Manuel Pando suggested that he run for Congress. A skilled orator, Salamanca became the early leader of the Republican Party. Also a lawyer, the La Paz native

Bautista Saavedra had an interest in history and sociology. He served as minister of education during the administration of Eliodoro Villazón (1909–1913), and he successfully ran for office as an independent in 1913. Between 1914 and 1920 Saavedra headed the La Paz section of the Republican Party, making him the most important party leader after Salamanca.[6]

The new party made purely political demands of President Montes and the ruling Liberals. It sought clean elections and a limit on the president's power over Congress and the judiciary. The party also suggested minor social reforms and greater economic nationalism—a preference for national business owners over foreign capital. The historian Herbert Klein sees the antagonism between the two parties as a "classic pattern of 'ins' versus 'outs.'" They shared a similar political philosophy and were run by politicians from identical economic and social backgrounds—the country's dominant classes.[7] Despite the similarities, though, the contest for power generated significant violence.

Physical clashes between party militants often accompanied electoral competitions. Elections during this period did not employ the secret ballot. Instead, voters cast their ballots in the main plazas of the country's cities and towns, a system that allowed all sorts of physical and psychological intimidation. Both parties maintained political gangs that sought to prevent the opposition from voting.[8] On the eve of Oruro's municipal election in December 1915, confrontations between supporters of the governing party and the Republican opposition led to a number of injuries and seven arrests. Republican leaders complained of police repression and intimidation. Oruro's police chief, Ángel del Castillo, responded by citing a litany of offences committed by Republican militants. The seven individuals under arrest had been detained for publicly insulting the "Government and the President of the Republic." The Republican Juan C. Zambrano had "made use of a cane, breaking it on the head of a defenseless citizen." Two others—Ismael Loaiza and Jorge Delgado—had "insulted in a vulgar manner" some of the Liberal Party's candidates. Other Republican militants had threatened their Liberal rivals' lives, swearing to "'blow their brains out' with their revolvers." Finally, the Republican Felipe Ortiz had stabbed Policarpio Daza, a Liberal, in the hand with a penknife. Despite the violence and arrests, however, Oruro prefect Melitón Lemaitre promised the Republican Party's leaders that the group might "continue exercising the right of suffrage" and that they were "also quite free to participate or abstain from the municipal elections."[9] Later elections sometimes saw more intense conflict.

In May 1917 the Liberal and Republican parties faced each other in a presidential election for the first time. Montes named José Gutiérrez Guerra as the Liberal candidate to succeed him. The Republicans chose José María Escalier, a physician and wealthy landowner, as their nominee.[10] A month before the May balloting the government circulated a series of recommendations to ensure a peaceful election. The Ministry of Government urged departmental prefects to "adopt measures prohibiting the entry and attendance of persons who [were] not citizens, such as women and children, in the polling place." The ministry noted that women and children often crowded the country's plazas and "made it difficult for voters to access the Electoral Tables." Additionally, nonvoters could still influence the election through intimidation and blockade. The government considered them "elements of disturbance."[11] Despite the precautions, both parties planned to employ the usual violence. In Huanuni the police arrested the Republican militant Quintin Pereira for "leading a march by a group of men from the Republican Party with gunshots from a revolver" on the evening before the vote.[12] The elections were violent, and the Liberal candidate Gutiérrez Guerra won by a wide margin.[13] The violence would continue during the elections of 1919 and 1920, and when the Republicans did finally defeat their Liberal rivals in July 1920, they did so not at the ballot box but in a military coup.

Two economic recessions book end the rise of the Republican Party and the defeat of the Liberals. First, mining experienced a serious contraction when World War I began. In August 1914 the Ministry of Government and Development reported that since the outbreak of European hostilities, Bolivia had suffered "the paralysis of European industry, the sudden suspension of price quotes for consumer goods, the alarming fall of exchange rates, and as a consequence, political and social crisis."[14] The recession eventually passed, and the wartime demand for minerals returned

Bolivia's export economy to health.[15] Between 1920 and 1922, however, the international price of tin dipped again. Stocks of metal accumulated in Asia during the insecurity of World War I began to flow into Europe and North America. The United States also started dumping some of its war reserves back onto the market, and economic difficulties in the United Kingdom aggravated the situation. Tin made a strong recovery in 1923, and the price remained high through 1927, but these economic fluctuations had a severe impact on the working class.[16]

A report composed by Negro Pabellón police chief Miguel Arzet in June 1914 documents the paralysis of mining and the sudden unemployment that afflicted Oruro and northern Potosí with the outbreak of World War I. Arzet originally wrote the document in black ink, but with the sudden collapse of tin's value, he went back and made corrections in red. The police chief wrote that Simón I. Patiño's Japo Mining Company had "suspended its labors because of tin's decline." The company cut its workforce from 120 workers to 14. Leonora de Toro's San Salvador Mining Company trimmed its workforce from an average of 80 to 100 laborers to just 8. Moisés Ascarrunz's Unificada Mining Company laid off all 30 of its workers. And the Santa María Company of Julio Foster, Atenor Martínez, and Juan Garafulich let go all 20 of its laborers.[17]

When the mining economy recovered and production resumed, the miners immediately resented the low pay and the long hours. They also remembered the callousness of the layoffs. Llallagua and Uncía in northern Potosí experienced significant tension during the war's initial crisis: "Because of the drop in the price of tin and the accompanying reduction in workers by the Mining Companies, two- to three-thousand laborers were left without employment, and the lack of a means of subsistence made them think of an attack on the commercial houses and company stores." The companies and the subprefect requested assistance from La Paz, and the government dispatched fifty soldiers. Later in 1915, when the mining companies resumed operations, "there was a kind of strike by all of the workers of the Llallagua Company, who, in a tumultuous and hostile manner, demanded an increase in salaries threatening to attack the Company's stores." The Llallagua Company's administrator, intimidated by the "violent stance" of the workers, authorized a 20 percent pay increase. The following day the workers, encouraged by the fact that they had "so easily achieved their objective," began demanding a reduction in the length of the workday and the right to exit the mine for lunch and dinner. This time the mine's administration and the police responded with force. When the workers sought to "exit the mine with shouts and threats," the police and a squad of company employees blocked the exit, "obliging them to continue in the interior until the customary hour." When the workers finally left the mine, the police "immediately captured the principal ring-leaders, placing them at the disposition of the justice system." The government would again reinforce its military presence in the region. The Bustillos Province's subprefect, too, requested additional funds to hire more police and jailers to cope with the zone's "frequent disturbances."[18]

Unpredictable swings in a mining town's fortune meant insecurity and migration for workers who had few economic alternatives. In 1917 several important mines in Huanuni suspended operations, leaving many without employment. Huanuni's police chief, Jorge Ardiles, noted a substantial decline in the town's population, which had been drained by an exodus of unemployed workers headed to other towns or mining camps: "As labors have been paralyzed in the Patiño, Talisman, and Rosarito shafts, the workers have been obliged to absent themselves in search of work in other mining centers that find themselves in better conditions than Huanuni."[19]

The instability of mining and the waves of unemployment could spark occasional chaos, especially when coupled with the rush to a new and promising mining camp. In 1917 Paria's *corregidor*, Marcial Vergara Rivas, wrote, "When the mountain of Conde Auqui began to reveal the wealth it hid inside, the flow of people, both to the mining camps and to this town, grew from day to day, and alongside this movement the complications that accompany the migration of all classes of people of varied nationalities have also grown." Vergara Rivas complained, "Murders, robberies, home burglaries, and duels between miners occur from one moment to the next, without the *corregidor*'s authority, for lack of positive force, being able to guarantee order to the town and its surroundings." The *corregidor* believed that crime was becoming endemic and highly organized: "It is widely believed that among the mining camps of Conde Auqui, the railroad work camps, and in this whole region, there is a strong group of desperados that probably surpasses a dozen in number who, with their raids and hair-raising crimes, keep the residents of this town in a state of constant alarm."[20] Vergara was also a mine owner. He held a concession outside Paria, and the insecurity surely hampered his profits.[21] Vergara's losses, however, paled in comparison to the life-threatening danger of unemployment that the economy's wild swings posed to working-class families.

World War I helped shape political developments not just in Bolivia but in neighboring Chile, too. Unemployment there and the expulsion of Bolivian workers would aggravate the tensions in Oruro and northern Potosí.

LABORING IN TWO COUNTRIES

The nitrate camps and copper mines of northern Chile attracted large numbers of Bolivian laborers in the early twentieth century. Officials in Oruro complained constantly of Chilean labor recruiters. The complaints emanated from a pair of concerns, not necessarily of equal weight. First, officials expressed concern over working conditions, pay, and unpredictable fluctuations in Chile's mining economy, for Bolivian citizens often sought repatriation at government expense when suddenly left unemployed. Second, bureaucrats worried about the impact emigration might have on Bolivia's industrial development. They feared that mining companies in Oruro, La Paz, and northern Potosí might suffer a shortage of laborers.

Work in Chile exposed migrants to the radical politics of the nitrate camps, but the economic dislocation of World War I had even greater repercussions for the development of organized labor in Bolivia.[22] In 1914 Chile expelled thousands of Bolivian workers and their families, and the newly unemployed laborers expressed frustration with the Bolivian government's inadequate and ad-hoc response. Immigration to Chile after

1914 became less attractive, and while some still made the journey, many chose to stay in Bolivia and push for domestic improvements.

Before World War I competition with employers from Chile sometimes left mine owners in Oruro and northern Potosí struggling to recruit dependable workers. Government officials understood industry's concerns and sought to restrict emigration. Some also worried about working conditions in the neighboring republic. Oruro prefect Moisés Ascarrunz complained in May 1908 that Chilean labor recruiters had already visited the department twice that year. In February the recruiters persuaded 80 to make the trip to the nitrate fields. In early May another group of 103 emigrated, "triggering the depopulation of Oruro and a scarcity of workers for the mines." Ascarrunz predicted that every worker leaving the country would soon "petition for repatriation complaining of poor treatment and a lack of work in the exterior." To assert greater control over the process, Ascarrunz ordered recruiters to send all potential emigrants to the prefecture. He wanted to ensure that all went "voluntarily and had been offered guarantees."[23]

The flow of workers changed in 1914, for World War I had an immediate impact on Bolivians living and working in northern Chile. The conflict caused mining and nitrate companies in the neighboring republic to reduce their labor force. Thousands of Bolivians suddenly found themselves without work. The unemployed clamored for government assistance in returning home, and an avalanche of repatriated workers overloaded Bolivia's railroad towns. Oruro's prefect in 1914, Eduardo Diez de Medina, estimated the number of repatriates at between 7,000 and 8,000.[24] The trains from the Pacific Coast carried whole impoverished families; just one train on October 2, 1914, carried 296 adults and 95 children.[25] Officials struggled to pay for their transportation and to feed them.

Bolivia lacked an established social welfare system, and the government had no contingency plans for this type of crisis. Workers and their families nevertheless demanded assistance. They interpreted emergency aid as a right of citizenship. In Oruro the prefect Eduardo Diez de Medina scrambled to satisfy the repatriates' demands. On August 24, 1914, one train arrived from Arica, Chile, carrying 340 returnees; the next day another train with 315 pulled into Oruro. The prefecture and the police supplied the unemployed workers and their families with food provided by the Ladies' Benefit Society. Diez de Medina hoped to speed the bulk of the workers on to their homes elsewhere in Bolivia—many came from the agricultural valleys of Cochabamba—but the railroad company balked at sharing the cost. The railroad's administrator instructed his subordinates in no uncertain terms: "Please take notice that we do not accept orders from the Government for tickets for repatriated workers; they must pay cash with a 50 percent discount in the Bolivian section. Proving that they are repatriates is a requirement for the sale of discounted tickets." Diez de Medina appealed to the central government to place additional pressure on the railroad to change its stance. He also requested funds for food, writing, "The workers have become demanding, swearing that they do not have a means of subsistence."[26] The minister of government, however, expressed frustration with the fiscal demands of repatriation: "The Government has been drained by the expenditures that the repatriated Bolivian workers demand, and it believes it has fulfilled its duty by placing them in the center of the Republic." Officials in La Paz sought to pass responsibility to Oruro's prefect, writing, "With as little assistance as you might give them, you should arrange that they be transported to the locations that best suit them, especially those who wish to travel to the Department of Cochabamba where they have employment."[27] A stressed Diez de Medina replied, "In light of this last telegram, I will arrange the transportation of the repatriates to their different locations, looking for the necessary means to do that."[28] Through the rest of 1914 Oruro's prefect continued to cobble together an ad-hoc program of assistance.

Oruro's relief programs relied heavily on individual philanthropy. In September 1914 Diez de Medina informed the central government that the city had established a rudimentary welfare program—a soup kitchen. The prefect wrote, "A great number of repatriates from the nitrate fields of Chile insistently demand that they receive aid during the days of their stay in this city," and "many of them remain here because they are from here or have the hope of finding some employment." Diez de Medina optimistically noted that the soup kitchen's first day of service produced "the most gratifying results." The Ladies' Benefit Society contributed Bs 300; the Bread of the Poor Society gave Bs 200; and the personnel of the prefecture, the departmental treasury, and the police contributed another Bs 100. The prefect hoped that private philanthropy might help the government by relieving some of the pressures of repatriation. He reminded tight-fisted officials in La Paz that Oruro's prefecture and police had "on several occasions been obliged to provide some very small means of subsistence, and that it was not possible that the fiscal resources [could] continue being employed in such a manner."[29] Despite Oruro's limited departmental budget, Diez de Medina continued to free up small funds to assist the growing ranks of the unemployed.

With the unemployment crisis, Oruro's prefect felt obliged to create a few make-work programs. Following an inspection tour of Carangas Province, Eduardo Diez de Medina authorized some small expenditures, "effecting in that way to assist the working element," who would thus "have employment in the repair of buildings like the jails, schools, etc."[30] The projects were unusual in that Carangas contained a significant Aymara population; government officials usually relied on Andean communities to supply involuntary and often unpaid labor for public works. Only rarely did Oruro's prefecture spend money on the construction and maintenance of buildings in Carangas. The danger posed by urban unemployment, however, caused the government to forgo its habitual exploitation of rural labor. The emergency also caused officials to suggest ideas to limit emigration.

Repatriation's costs caused some to contemplate the price of working-class mobility. Eduardo Diez de Medina recommended that in the future, the government take steps to prevent the "emigration of the lower classes." He noted that the current wave of repatriates had "made palpable the lamentable situation in which they returned—physically and economically." The prefect worried that the whole affair had impaired Bolivia's development: "This group of individuals could have offered useful and positive services inside the country; outside of it they have done nothing but waste their energy with no benefit, contracting vices and grave infirmities." Diez de Medina added, "Many of them returned overwhelmed by misery, which confirms that the meager salaries they received were not enough for even their daily subsistence. It is incumbent upon the Public Authorities to adopt measures that at least restrict the ease of emigration of our working elements, so that their services might be used for national activity." He viewed some returnees as dangerous because of their time abroad, writing, "Their presence becomes a danger to the towns where they settle because of the bad habits acquired outside of the country that impel them to commit criminal acts." The prefect claimed that he could "already cite bloody acts carried out during their new stay" in the area. He noted that a detachment of soldiers had recently traveled to Changolla—the railroad's end point in the department of Cochabamba—to "guarantee the life and property of the residents of that region."[31] Officials also worried about biological contamination. In August 1914 the Ministry of Government and Development issued a circular noting, "Unfortunately many of those who have returned are afflicted by contagious diseases." The ministry continued, "It is imperative to make an inspection of at least those who can be located so as to quarantine them in hospitals to avoid the spread of syphilis and tuberculosis."[32]

When export markets rebounded in 1915, Bolivians began again to migrate to Chile. While emigration never returned to prewar levels, officials still hoped to slow the flow. Government functionaries laced their correspondence with both humanitarian language and economic concerns. On November 18, 1915, the prefect Eduardo Diez de Medina wrote Oruro's local railroad office to remind the firm of restrictions on emigration: "[Do not] sell a ticket to laborers contracted to work outside of the Republic, unless they can show the required authorization written by the local authorities." The prefect also informed the railroad's administration that labor recruiters needed to show similar paperwork.[33] That same month the Bolivian vice-consul in Calama, Chile, Fidel Carranza, complained of the arrival of 115 laborers from Oruro and Potosí. Recruiters working for the North American Company of Chuquicamata had persuaded the workers to make the trip. Carranza wrote of the working conditions facing the recent arrivals in Chuquicamata's copper mines, saying, "They come to sacrifice their lives in the deadly labors of certain sections in which suffocating gases and dangerous electrical equipment provoke the instant death of workers with regular frequency." He even accused the recruiters of targeting workers without families, "which in itself is very revealing." Carranza closed with the suggestion that the government "adopt measures so as to avoid this disastrous recruitment," which, he said, "deprives our country of the necessary energy for its own development."[34] When Minister of State Arturo Molina Campero forwarded the vice-consul's letter to Oruro's newly appointed prefect, Melitón Lemaitre, the prefect responded by assuring the minister that he had "made use of all official means to avoid the emigration of Bolivian workers."[35] The focus on national industrial development in the correspondence explains why officials did not always express the same vigorous concern for worker safety in the mines and mills of Oruro and northern Potosí.

Workers and their families confronted corruption, long separation, and worrying uncertainties when they emigrated. They frequently looked to the government for assistance, and officials often fell short. One example occurred when the end of World War I produced a second, smaller repatriation. On March 14, 1919, the Bolivian consul in Antofagasta, Chile, reported a case of corruption that tainted the distribution of discounted train tickets. Two Bolivian citizens, Simón Villarroen and Ricardo Martínez, the president and vice president, respectively, of an immigrant social organization in the nitrate camp María, had volunteered to help the consul distribute government tickets to workers who "for lack of work wished to be repatriated," but the consul noted that Villarroen and Martínez, "far from deserving the confidence placed in them," had sold the 207 tickets.[36]

The travails of immigrant workers continued into the 1920s. Officials in La Paz and diplomatic representatives in northern Chile continued to worry about migration to the nitrate fields and mines of Antofagasta and Tarapacá. On November 3, 1923, the Bolivian consul in Antofagasta wrote the minister of government and justice to decry the terrible conditions in which immigrants lived and worked. He hoped that the government might publicize his warnings so that other Bolivians would "not enter into agreements with labor recruiters who deceptively hire them, making them promises that are never kept." The consul described the practices of one recruiter, Rodolfo Saavedra, who worked for a consortium of nitrate companies in Antofagasta. The companies paid him twenty Chilean pesos for every worker he delivered. From complaints and the local press, the consul learned that Saavedra had promised workers a daily wage of fifteen to twenty pesos. He paid for their railroad tickets and gave them a cash advance that was eventually subtracted from their wages. Once in Chile the workers discovered that the average wage was actually four to five pesos a day. The consul wrote that the work was "heavy and exterminate[d] the physical energy" of the Bolivian immigrants, who ended up "degenerating morally and materially." As for the wage, the consul noted that it "barely covered the cost of deficient food." The recruiter Saavedra typically sought workers in the agricultural valleys of Cochabamba and preferred hiring "married individuals with families." The consul noted that Bolivians were not the only ones to fall victim to this swindle: "The same thing happens with even Chilean workers who are hired in the countryside of the south" (they, too, earned the same disappointing salary). When Bolivian immigrants discovered the reality of their employment and sought to return home, they often solicited aid from the consul, but he lacked funds to cover the return tickets. The consul dwelt on the same themes of moral corruption and physical degeneration prevalent in previous discussions of immigration to Chile: "As for the moral aspect, our compatriots who are contaminated by the multitudinous bulk of Chilean workers acquire pernicious vices and customs." He added, "Bolivian workers are by nature subservient and rugged in their labors, no matter how heavy they are, but here they acquire vices like drunkenness and thievery, making them a danger later when they return to the agricultural towns of our country, where they become a danger to society; also, in general, the race degenerates because of the effects of heavy and extended labor and because of illnesses of social importance." The consul hoped that his observations would spur the government to adopt policies limiting the mobility of these workers, who, he felt, were "needed there [in Bolivia] for the cultivation of the extensive fields and in the labors of mining companies and others."[37]

While Chile's nitrate zone slowly declined in the 1920s, Chuquicamata's copper mines thrived, so these problems persisted. In December 1923, for example, Hugo Vargas—a concerned father—contacted Oruro prefect Aniceto Arce, asking him to inquire after the well-being of Vargas's sons Víctor and Guillermo. The young men had begun working for the Chile Exploration Company of Chuquicamata six months earlier. Vargas had heard rumors of a serious accident at the mine in early September with a number of fatalities. Since that time he had not heard from his sons, and telegrams to the Chilean police had produced contradictory reports. On October 23 the police informed Vargas that "there had been no accident" and that Guillermo and Víctor Vargas were "alive and well." On November 20 the same police station sent Vargas a second telegram that read, "Brothers Víctor and Guillermo Vargas Irrazabal voluntarily retired on September 12." Oruro's prefect asked the Bolivian vice-consul in Calama, Chile, to look into the conflicting telegrams and clarify the "whereabouts of the said Vargas [brothers]."[38] Despite occasional good intentions such as these, officials often lacked the resources to extend aid to workers moving back and forth between countries—a frustration for the mobile working class.

The influence of Chilean workers in Bolivia also deserves consideration given Chile's labor radicalism. Indeed, Simón I. Patiño sought to insulate La Salvadora mine workers from the perceived pernicious influence of foreign workers. At the end of March 1912 Patiño wrote Oruro's prefect, Constantino Morales, to complain about the arrival of "twenty or more Chilean workers" in Llallagua. The tin magnate viewed the men as a "threat to La Salvadora Mining Company," which he owned. Morales forwarded the complaint to the minister of state.[39]

The archive of Oruro's prefecture contains one well-argued and damning complaint, from September 1918, composed by Alberto Salinas Aldunate, a Chilean employed by the Mining Company of Llallagua. Salinas cataloged a series of abuses: "The mine shafts are in a terrible condition, and they offer no security to the worker; that is the reason for the daily accidents and deaths among the laborers, who often then leave their large families in poverty"; to families losing loved ones, the company supposedly offered only "twenty or thirty bolivianos' worth of merchandise from the company store." Further, Salinas complained, "All the workers live in windowless rooms without any comfort and lacking one of the necessities of life, which is water." The water available elsewhere in the mining camp was supposedly "filthy and unsanitary and posed a danger to the destitute working people." The Chilean judged the wages insufficient to "cover the necessities of life," especially given "the exaggerated prices at the company store," which he claimed, "completely absorb[ed] the worker's labor." When workers complained, the company "threw them into the street with the most outrageous violence." Salinas concluded, "'The Mining Company of Llallagua still maintains, in the midst of civilization, the odious customs of the colonial period, trampling upon constitutional rights, protected by impunity and distance."[40] As this litany of complaints suggests, Chileans could bring a refined sense of workers' rights to Bolivia's mining towns.

The flood of unemployed workers expelled from Chile during World War I, popular misgivings about the effectiveness of the government's response, and even the militancy of some Chilean workers in Bolivia number among the factors that contributed to the emergence of more sophisticated labor organizations in Oruro and northern Potosí. The artisans' long history of association, however, provided the framework on which to build.

THE WORKERS' LABOR FEDERATION OF ORURO

The last four years of Liberal Party rule witnessed an explosion of organization among Oruro's and northern Potosí's artisans and working class. The organizing impulse spread well beyond the departmental capitals; part of a larger national trend, mutual aid societies, craft unions, and labor federations sprang up across Oruro and northern Potosí. Many of these bodies, however, came to coordinate their activities through Oruro's pivotal Workers' Labor Federation, which had begun as a union of that town's principal mutual aid societies but quickly embraced the entire region's mining working class. The ruling Liberal Party repeatedly butted heads with the new federation and in 1920 sought to form a rival organization to check its influence, but no puppet association would succeed in rivaling the Workers' Labor Federation as the preeminent representative of the laboring classes.

The workers confronted companies continuously improving their own solidarity and their relations with the government. In March 1916 Oruro's mine owners founded a new coordinating body: the Mining Chamber of Commerce. The government in La Paz encouraged the new organization. A previous version, the Mining Defense League, had existed in Oruro, but that body was renamed and reorganized to conform to government instructions. The reorganization sought to ensure that mining's business interests formed a "juridical personage inside the national organism."[41] Arturo Loaiza was the president of both the new and old versions of the society and a representative of Simón I. Patiño's business interests.[42] Guillermo Gray represented the Penny and Duncan Mining Company of Morococala and was the Mining Chamber of Commerce's treasurer.[43] Francisco Blieck, the chamber's secretary, headed the Mining Company of Oruro.[44] The Mining Chamber of Commerce immediately named Oruro prefect Melitón Lemaitre an honorary member, following a practice often employed by Oruro's mutual aid societies. Lemaitre responded to the invitation, writing, "It will be my pleasure to collaborate with great enthusiasm in the development of the Mining Industry."[45]

Oruro's workers and artisans understood the bosses' solidarity and quickly countered with an organization of their own. In 1916 the city's principal mutual aid societies united to participate in the department's celebration of Bolivian independence on August 6. Less than a week later, on August 12, Oruro's artisans and workers announced to the prefect the formation of the Workers' Labor Federation—a body destined to guide the department's popular classes down a new and more radical path. The Mutual Aid Society of Artisans held a dominant position in the new society. Its president, José F. Avila, served as president of the new federation, too. The May 1 Workers' Philharmonic, the Tunari Cooperative, the Workers' Union of Bakers, and the Workers' Union FBC ("FBC" stands for "Football Club") also supported the new organization.[46] The federation immediately began a more vigorous political existence than that pursued by any previous labor association in Oruro.

The Workers' Labor Federation sought to represent more than just the artisans; its leaders hoped to improve the working and living conditions in the mines, too. On August 23, 1916, federation president Avila penned a complaint to Oruro's prefect about unsafe conditions in the mines and the seeming callousness of certain mine owners. Avila specifically mentioned a near-fatal accident involving a miner named N. Loaiza employed by the Socavón Mining Company. On August 21 a cave-in trapped Loaiza. Unfortunately, none of his co-workers or his supervisor noticed his absence; only "the insistent questions of the wife sparked the eventual discovery that Loaiza was still alive—buried in a place overlooked by the other workers." The company did not succeed in rescuing him until two days after the accident. Federation president Avila complained that the company did not "guarantee the life of its workers." The federation did not yet have the strength to put direct pressure on the company, so instead it asked the prefect to "intercede with said company, so that it might extend greater consideration to the working element and guarantee their lives."[47] In this case, the Workers' Labor Federation appealed to the prefect; in other instances, it sought to confront the national government.

Alcohol and drunkenness worried the nascent labor movement, but the abuse of government power alarmed it even more. On October 7, 1916, Julio Saavedra, president of the Workers' Labor Federation, and Nícanor Leclere, its secretary, penned a protest to six congressional representatives complaining that the police had abused Feliciano Mérida, an artisan. On the night of October 5 the police rousted a drunken Mérida from his home and carted him off to jail. The federation complained that Mérida was "cruelly punished en route by two officers." In framing the protest, the federation quoted Bolivian law: "The drunk should be extended all possible consideration by agents of the police, just as one who is ill." Saavedra and Leclere argued that officers violated the cited law: "The police, whether day or night, in full public view, carry off drunks with the use of blows and other abuses."[48] The congressmen asked Oruro's prefect to look into the charges and "to severely punish those who might be found to be guilty."[49] Within a few years, however, the Workers' Labor Federation moved beyond letters of protest and began organizing significant strikes and work stoppages.

The trend toward greater organization and affiliation continued into 1917. In February 1917 a new association of carpenters and a new cobblers' union appeared in Oruro.[50] That same year saw the birth of a mutual aid society closely linked to the Catholic Church in Oruro: the San José Workers' Society. Oruro prefect Melitón Lemaitre wrote the new society's president, Ezequiel Aguilar, expressing his pleasure that the new society would pursue "ends eminently religious and of mutual protection, seeking the education of the worker and his moral and material well-being."[51] Soon, however, the Liberal Party would no longer welcome the organizing trend and its political implications.

The organizing impulse among workers and artisans affected small towns throughout the department of Oruro, not just the capital. In January 1916 individuals in Pazña announced to the prefect the formation of the local Workers' Union. The new organization declared a series of civic objectives. It expressed the typical provincial concern that local interests had been "much abandoned" and announced that it hoped to "promote public works of absolute necessity." The society also sought to improve the popular classes' "moral education" and to defend the "individual rights and constitutional guarantees many times vitiated and truncated by a few provincial authorities." The cross-class Workers' Union highlighted the broad resentment provoked by the mining companies' arrogance and power in the hinterland of the Altiplano. The new organization's leaders decried those "mine owners and managers who, relying on their wealth, [took] advantage of poor and defenseless workers as well as small industrialists and merchants."[52]

Workers, artisans, and their allies had good reason for concern. New laws regulated the mining companies, but managers continued to govern their businesses as if those laws did not exist. In February 1917 Cercado Province subprefect N. Murgia conducted an investigation of nearby mines, including the Mining Company of Oruro, the San José mine, and a handful of smaller operations. Murgia focused on issues mentioned in recent legal decrees: the medical services offered to workers, schools, female and child labor, and the safety of mining operations. The subprefect discovered that some local mining companies deducted 1 percent from their workers' paychecks for medical attention. Oruro's prefect had actually prohibited that practice in June 1916. The Mining Company of Oruro stopped collecting the 1 percent deduction after the prefect's injunction but also cut back on the medical services provided to workers and their families. "Putting into practice this new system of free service to the ill has prejudiced the families of employees and workers who had received medical and pharmaceutical attention; now they only extend these services to the worker," wrote Murgia. The Mining Company of Oruro administrator Francisco Blieck hoped to reinstate the deduction and informed the subprefect, "If the prohibition against charging this one percent continues, the company will continue limiting itself to attend[ing] only to the workers, denying services to their families." At the San José mine the administration continued to impose the 1 percent deduction despite the prefect's decree.[53] The new labor associations that emerged in 1916 and 1917 would seek to close such gaps between law and practice.

The Liberal Party felt threatened by the Worker's Labor Federation and sought to establish a rival organization. In early 1920 the pro–Liberal Party and antisocialist Workers' Democratic Institution appeared in Oruro. An earlier incarnation with a different name already existed, but the group was reorganized in March 1920. The institution's president, Juan Béjar, explained the need for the reorganization, asserting that the group's previous work had been "interrupted by an opposition that claimed to be Socialist." Béjar promised Oruro's prefect, "This Assembly will always act within the bounds of our laws, which means respect and moral adhesion to our leaders and Authorities."[54] While the association hoped to enlist "competent personnel from the working element," it primarily sought to steer workers away from socialism and opposition to Liberal Party rule. Béjar planned to give a public conference on socialism on March 21, 1920, so as to "guide" the many who, he felt, called themselves socialists but were actually followers of a nineteenth-century anarchism, which had caused "much bloodshed in all the countries of the world." He continued, "In our country a few discontented individuals—who have no reason for being such—want to impose this semisavagery of a past era." Béjar sought to "inform the workers as to the duties of conscientious citizens toward the Bolivian Fatherland."[55] During another conference, Béjar discussed foreign relations and international politics. Despite the talk's declared topic, he stressed domestic tensions, declaring, "It is the duty of the workers to leave things to our leaders, who define international affairs through diplomatic channels, and we, as Bolivians, should remain alert waiting for the alarm signal from our

Leaders, so that we are united to defend our National sovereignty." Béjar saw his talks as an opportunity to state that "not all Bolivians [held] anti-patriotic and traitorous ideals"; many Bolivians, he said, "love our Father-land, and . . . support the Government that currently guides internal and external order."[56] Despite the Workers' Democratic Institution's progov-ernment stance, though, even it encountered a growing indifference to working-class concerns among the Liberal Party leadership in La Paz.

The Liberal Party's alienation of working-class supporters would even-tually prove fatal. In May 1920 the Workers' Democratic Institution wrote the Ministry of Development and Industry to complain about the prefer-ential treatment accorded to Chilean workers at the Antofagasta-Bolivia Railroad/Bolivian Railway Company. The minister, César M. Ochávez, penned a scathing reply. The ministry, he declared, "has always been and continues to be actively concerned with addressing all justified complaints that have been presented whenever our citizens truly suffer an offence on the part of the railway companies." Nevertheless, despite the high-minded declaration, the minister proceeded to criticize the "notoriously deficient" Bolivian worker:

> Sincerely, many Bolivian workers do not satisfy their superiors in the exe-cution of their labors, and as in the railroad business, the attention must be efficient and constant, because if it were any other way, the lives of the passengers would be in immediate risk; there is reason then that the bosses concern themselves with the selection of the personnel that they have as their dependents, because the responsibility for any accident might justly fall on them as those responsible for supervising the traffic. In these cir-cumstances one cannot but approve of the methods of internal discipline and order adopted by the Bolivian Railway Company.

Ochávez did propose that the railway company establish a machinist's school in Uyuni for training maintenance personnel to address the per-ceived lack of skilled Bolivian technicians.[57] Just two months later, how-ever, in July 1920, the Liberal Party fell victim to a Republican Party coup. The Workers' Democratic Institution disappeared from Oruro in the wake of that political defeat, and Bolivia's independent labor movement would have a schizophrenic relationship with the new ruling party.

CHAPTER 4

Strikes and Contracts

ON JULY 12, 1920, Republican Party militants and several military units rose in rebellion against the Liberal Party presidency of José Gutiérrez Guerra. The insurgent Republicans triumphed with little bloodshed.[1] A month later mine workers in Oruro and northern Potosí decided to test the new political environment. In August 1920 Oruro's interim prefect, Demetrio Canelas, informed the Republican junta in La Paz, "During the last couple of days, worker agitation has completely occupied the attention of the prefecture." The movement began in Huanuni. "The workers of Huanuni were the first to organize a delegation demanding a pay raise, a reduction in the company store's prices, and other points," wrote the prefect.[2] On August 14 Canelas and Cercado Province subprefect Adolfo Ceballos presided over a conference that brought together the administration of Huanuni's most important mining company and various worker representatives. Pablo Pacheco represented Simón I. Patiño's business interests, and Melchor Quiroga, the manager of the company store, attended to represent his own. The workers sent four men to the meeting: Jacinto Arias, Telésforo Tapia, Máximo Tóvar, and Conrado Molina. The workers advanced two principal demands: that wages be raised by twenty to thirty cents per day and that "the company store sell its merchandise at the same prices as the Huanuni market." The mine's manager, Pablo Pacheco, initially resisted, while Melchor Quiroga insisted that the company store sold important products such as sugar at Huanuni's usual market value. Quiroga complained of his own business costs, lamenting that he paid a "a high rent" to the company and that he gave jobs to the several people who worked in the company store, and he highlighted the "frequent losses occasioned by workers suddenly abandoning their jobs." Under pressure from the prefect, the company agreed to a twenty-cent raise. In addition, Quiroga promised to keep the company store's merchandise at market value, and the prefect set up a system to check local prices. Every two weeks local officials and company managers would "survey market prices and post them on chalkboards hung on the doors of the company store and the local police station." Prefect Canelas empowered workers to double-check the prices and weights of goods in the company store. Finally, Canelas extracted a promise from Pablo Pacheco that "the workers who attended this session should be guaranteed in their jobs."[3] But this was far from the end of things. From Huanuni the agitation of August 1920 spread to mines in the city of Oruro and companies in northern Potosí, as workers and artisans deftly exploited a political window opened by the Republican coup.

REPUBLICANS IN, LIBERALS OUT

By 1920 Bolivia's tin mines employed just under 22,000 workers—a group so numerous that their discontent had national political repercussions.[4] The Liberal Party had lost support among the urban popular classes, however, and the Republicans who replaced them had an erratic relationship with the working class. Artisans and the workers hoped for major reforms; initially, at least, the Republicans supported moderate improvements. Bautista Saavedra, the first Republican president, became a focus for the popular classes' hopes and aspirations, and the workers and artisans of

Oruro and northern Potosí rejoiced at the Republican victory and Saave-dra's ascendancy. The euphoria lasted just three years.

The usual political violence between Liberals and Republicans marred elections in 1919 and 1920. Oruro's municipal elections on December 14, 1919, produced a clash between Republican militants and the police that left three men dead: David Irahola, Simón Astorga, and Fermín Rivero—all Republicans.[5] Oruro's municipal police actively defended the interests of the Liberal Party. The animosity continued into the next year. In May 1920 Oruro's prefect, David Ascarrunz, deployed a significant military presence to control that month's vote. José María Escalier and Bautista Saavedra's wing of the Republican Party opted to abstain from the congressional elections. In Oruro and Potosí, where Daniel Salamanca's faction held sway, the Republicans participated.[6] Oruro's prefect eventually had to explain to La Paz his use of two army regiments during the May 2 elections. Ascar-runz insisted that he subscribed to the philosophy that "military detach-ments should not get mixed up in political affairs, except in those cases when it is necessary to preserve public order." He reported that in meet-ings before the election, "the representatives of the Liberal and Republi-can parties insistently solicited that military detachments intervene on election day"—a proposal, he maintained, that he "flatly rejected." The prefect added that Florián Zambrana, the president of Oruro's electoral commission, requested command of the army regiments on election day —another request he denied. Ascarrunz explained that he called on the two regiments as a last resort, "when the clashes began in a manner that suggested eventual deadly consequences." Zambrana and representatives of both parties supposedly requested military action; despite the preten-sion of impartiality, however, Republican militants bore the brunt of the intervention. The prefect was most alarmed by a "planned assault by a Republican group on the police." Ascarrunz closed his defense by explain-ing the delicate situation: "The bulk of the opposition considers the police force biased, and this belief has grown more pronounced with the lamen-table events of last December; any intervention by agents of the Police provokes openly hostile resistance."[7] The Republicans lost the May elec-tions, but just two months later the opposition party overthrew the ruling Liberals.

Strikes and Contracts

Republican victory did not come through the ballot box; it came instead at the point of a bayonet. The unwillingness of Escalier and Saavedra to participate in the May election indicated that some Republican leaders believed electoral struggle futile, and the election-day beating administered to Salamanca's supporters in Oruro and Potosí tended to confirm the conspirators in this belief. They began exploring extralegal means to oust the Liberals, and Bautista Saavedra rose to a preeminent position in the party because of his central role in plotting a coup. With an upswing in labor activism having already weakened the Liberals, on July 12, 1920, Republican militants and sections of the military overthrew Liberal president José Gutiérrez Guerra with little fighting.[8]

Workers and artisans greeted the Republican "revolution" with hopeful anticipation. In particular, they expected significant reform from Bautista Saavedra. While three personalities jostled for control of the Republican Party—Salamanca, Saavedra, and Escalier—Saavedra dominated the interim junta, and the Republicans elected him president in January 1921.[9] During the first five months of junta rule and the early years of Saavedra's presidency, the Republican Party sent a series of mixed signals to the country's urban popular classes. The Bolivian scholar and Marxist politician Guillermo Lora writes that Saavedra's administration so deceived the expectations of the working class that "it fortified among the laboring vanguard the need to give birth to a revolutionary party belonging to the workers."[10] That political development, however, was still several years away.

The Republicans viewed the department of Oruro as essential political real estate (one of the party's most important power brokers served for a time as Oruro's prefect: Hernando Siles, who eventually sat as the country's president from 1926 to 1930).[11] Party members in Oruro thus sought to strengthen the party's following among the mine workers. The region's mining companies, however, sometimes resisted the politicization of their labor force. On July 21, 1920, for example, a commission of Republican Party members from the towns of Pazña and Hurmiri traveled to the nearby mining town of Avicaya to "explain to the workers of the Totoral and Avicaya mining camps the glorious movement of July 12 and to unify and consolidate the membership of the Republican Party, forming committees in both mining settlements." The Republican activists informed both mining companies of the planned political meeting and asked that they give their workers a one-hour break. Pazña and Hurmiri's Republicans were infuriated when the Avicaya company's administrator, Sr. Abelli, put up "marked resistance" and gave their petition a "resounding no." The activists judged Abelli to have given them only "empty and tendentious pretexts" and claimed that his refusal damaged "the liberty of the workers and frustrated the patriotic goals of the party."[12]

Despite such occasional roadblocks, the Republicans continued to consolidate their hold on Oruro. The region even had its own pantheon of party martyrs, for, once in power, the Republican Party celebrated the memory of its activists killed on December 14, 1919, by Oruro's then Liberal police force. On the killings' one-year anniversary, the Republican Party's leadership in Oruro requested that the prefect order the Fourth Infantry Regiment to provide a band to honor the memories of Irahola, Astorga, and Rivero. During the commemoration, Republican Party members planned to "visit the tomb of these defenders of free suffrage."[13]

As the Republican Party consolidated its power, it hardened its response to discontent among the popular classes. Urban workers, however, were not the first segment of Bolivia's population to feel the repressive side of Republican rule; the rural, Aymara population of the department of La Paz suffered the first blow. Even before the coup, the Aymara community of Jesús de Machaca had long chafed under the economic exploitation of local merchants, and the expansion of hacienda property at the expense of Aymara communities aggravated the region's tensions. Callous government officials further irritated local sentiments. As a result, important Aymara leaders supported the Republican coup of July 1920. Merchants not affiliated with the Aymara community tended to support the fallen Liberal Party. Nonetheless, despite Aymara support for the Republican government, President Saavedra dispatched an unpopular *corregidor*, Lucio T. Estrada, to the region; he favored the town-dwelling merchants. Incensed, members of the Aymara community attacked the town on the morning of March 12, 1921. The insurgents killed the *corregidor*, along with his wife and son. In response, Saavedra dispatched the military to quell the rebellion and allowed local merchants to participate in the repression. The killing spread to neighboring Aymara communities accused of complicity. Several hundred died in the government assault; seventy Aymara were imprisoned for the rebellion.[14]

Mining recessions provoked by international economic cycles eventually presented difficulties for the Republican Party's relationship with the country's working class. As mentioned in chapter 3, the international demand for tin softened significantly between 1920 and 1922. The owners and managers of Oruro's larger and more affluent mining companies felt especially threatened by unemployed mine workers in 1922. In March of that year, for instance, the Mining Company of Oruro's manager, Jorge Wiessing, requested special authorization from the prefect so that a company guard, José Domínguez, might "carry a firearm for the strict vigilance of this company's properties threatened by unemployed operators."[15] Workplace tensions provoked by these economic swings continually undermined any understanding between the government, business, and the workers.

THE UNCÍA STRIKE OF 1919

In October 1919 a powerful strike shook Simón I. Patiño's northern Potosí mining company, but the Liberal Party government stifled the movement. The close bond that had seemingly once united Patiño and his workers at the beginning of the twentieth century no longer existed. Industrial growth had killed paternalism's effectiveness. The bosses began to rely more and more on open violence and unflinching government support to maintain their dominance. The Liberal Party's blatant favoritism for capital's interests had eroded the government's popular support.

A peaceful strike in Huanuni in September 1919 stimulated the October strike in Uncía. Simón I. Patiño owned both companies involved. On September 5, 1919, Huanuni's police chief reported that a "peaceful strike" for "moderate demands" had occurred in the mining town.[16] The strike began at seven in the morning with an energetic protest march through the town's principal streets. The workers eventually arrived at the gates of the Santa Elena mill. Attracted by the march's noise, the police chief questioned two participants about the reasons for the protest. Assuring the police chief that they had no "sinister motives," the workers told him that they had "complaints about the hours of entry and exit and also the prices at the company store"; they wanted to begin their workday at seven in the morning. The mining company's administrator, Pantaleon Dalence, received the protesters' complaints and agreed to a six o'clock start. The workday would then end at four-thirty in the afternoon. The workers eventually assented to the compromise schedule. Dalence informed the police chief that he agreed to a change because of the "intensity of the winter and the scourge of illness." As for prices at the company store, the workers "secured a reduction in the price of basic necessities." The workers promised to return to work immediately, as long as they were not docked pay for the morning's protest. The manager swore that no retaliation would occur. The strike agreement covered only the shaft workers, however, and the next day the company's mill workers also mobilized to secure concessions. The administrator adjusted the mill's hours to begin at six in the morning and to end at five in the afternoon. The police chief concluded his report on the strike by noting, "The incident occurred, according to my judgment, in a spontaneous manner without there being a single leader."[17]

Simón Patiño's managers and the Liberal government responded quite differently to a strike in northern Potosí just one month later. The strike in Uncía provoked a significant confrontation involving workers, the company, local merchants, the police, and the military. A final police report about the strike recorded three dead, sixteen wounded, and twenty-two arrested.[18] The strike began in the Patiño shaft, just uphill from the company's Miraflores mill on Wednesday, October 8, 1919. Workers in that section disagreed with calculations on their previous paychecks and despised their overseer, José Soruco, who often came to work armed with a sinew whip.[19] The morning the strike began, Víctor Silveti, president of the Miners' Protective Society, supposedly addressed a provocative speech to the disgruntled workers as they headed to the mine. The police reported that Silveti said, "Turn right around and demand a reduction in the hours of labor, a pay raise, and the closure of the company stores; how much longer are you going to suffer the owners' deceit?"[20] When the company's administrator, Máximo Nava, saw the workers descending the hillside, he equipped himself with a pistol and went to meet them accompanied by a squad of armed men. The police reported that Nava had "promised to attend to all their concerns" when, "unexpectedly, he was hit (in the middle of talking) by a rock in the left temple, and because of the blow, he fell to the ground wounded, and in self-defense, seeing himself wounded and attacked so suddenly, he drew his pistol and fired a shot." Nava's bullet hit two workers; Tiburcio Quispe was shot in the left shoulder, and an unnamed teenager was wounded in the hand. The teenage worker was shot because "when Sr. Nava was drawing his pistol, he [the youth] attempted to disarm him, and that is when the shot occurred." After the confrontation with the administrator, the workers stormed the company store, "opening the doors with blows." Several store employees attempted to defend the location, but "seeing that the defense was useless, they fled to save their lives, which were seriously threatened." The pitched battle at the store killed Conrado Enrique, and the police could not determine "where this bullet came from or who fired it." In sacking the store, the workers hoped to find crates of dynamite, but they instead found only "two boxes containing powdered milk." That night, "the striking workers entrenched themselves on a small rise in front of the mill, where, armed with slings, they threw dynamite in the direction of the mill with the intention of blowing it up." The struggle that night produced a second death—Macedonio Abendaño died of a gunshot wound.[21]

On Thursday, October 9, the striking workers continued to besiege the mill. The company reinforced its own guards and succeeded "in capturing three of the principal strikers." On seeing this, the workers "attacked with greater violence seeking the freedom of those captured." To confront the better-armed company guards, the workers descended on the town of Uncía to "arm themselves with rifles and revolvers." When the owners of several commercial establishments refused to sell and "locked their doors," the workers, "seeing their intentions frustrated and armed with iron bars and dynamite, broke down the doors with force." Frightened by the vandalism, some merchants opened and "handed over their revolvers and money to buy ammunition." Nine different merchants reported stolen or extorted goods and money; the stolen items included two revolvers, an automatic pistol, and sacks of dynamite with fuses and blasting caps. While the workers scoured Uncía's small commercial district, a man back at the mill was killed in an accident. One of the company guards, Guillermo Ayala, died at the hands of another guard—"the shot had escaped from the rifle of Honorato Alegre, who did not know how to operate it."[22]

The government responded to the strike by dispatching troops to the region. On October 9 Oruro prefect David Ascarrunz advised Huanuni's police chief to expect an express train carrying forty-five soldiers to "prevent any sort of conspiracy or violent strike that the miners of the diverse mining companies in the region might try to carry out." The police chief was to cooperate with the commanding officer of the expedition, but he was cautioned always to be guided by "the law and by equity."[23] Two police officers from Oruro, V. B. Sandoval and V. M. Zubieta, accompanied the army detachment to northern Potosí. The expedition arrived there around noon and began an overland march to Uncía. En route, the army learned that "strikers were committing all kinds of outrages on the local commercial houses, and that there were a few dead and wounded." At five in the afternoon the police and military arrived in Uncía, where the two police officers reported seeing a "great multitude of stirred-up people." The striking workers came out "in mass" to greet their arrival, "believing that it was their comrades coming from Llallagua." The soldiers immediately made their way to the Miraflores mill, where "they dispersed the strikers with great tact, without employing a single violent method." Tensions were hardly allayed, however; the police reported, "[The workers] agreed to retire, but as they withdrew, we heard them insult Sr. Nava with offensive words." The police closed their report to Oruro's prefect with contradictory observations. "Currently we have left the workers laboring in their ordinary duties," they told him, but they added, "The workers say that they intend to continue the attack once the army withdraws."[24]

Government officials worried that the Uncía strike might involve a greater political conspiracy, but informants among the workers dispelled that worry. Oruro prefect Ascarrunz informed the minister of state: "I had asked the [police] delegation if, among those subversive ideas, there was any sign of something related to politics, and they told me that no, their whole point was a pay raise." Ascarrunz also asked whether prices in the company store had contributed to the strike, and his informants reported, "The workers complain about the low weight of articles but say nothing about the price."[25] In the strike's wake the Liberal government dispatched an "investigative commission" to the region. The commission consisted of senior officials from the Ministry of Justice and the Ministry of Industry, as well as two labor activists from La Paz, José L. Calderón and Macario Murillo. The government hoped to use the commission's findings to formulate "the most appropriate general policies to ensure the right of property and the liberty of labor consecrated by the Political Constitution of the State."[26] Uncía's workers, however, saw few tangible improvements.

The mining zone that stretches from Huanuni to Uncía continued to experience heightened tension through the rest of the year and into the next. In January 1920 another strike developed among Huanuni's mine workers. Oruro prefect David Ascarrunz dispatched twenty men to reinforce Huanuni's police. He warned the police chief to remember that the soldiers should be used not "in the service of a company or private individual, [but] only to safeguard the order and tranquility of the town." The police and military needed to take care "not to commit abuses of any kind."[27] Despite this prefect's restraint, the relationship between workers and the Liberal government had reached a nadir. When the Republican Party launched its coup in July 1920, many workers and artisans sympathized and hoped for more from the new government.

THE ORURO LABOR CONTRACT
OF AUGUST 1920

Politics and economics converged in August 1920 to create a propitious—or at least encouraging—moment for labor action. During the first half of the year, tin exports reached new and dizzying heights, and workers sought a share of that prosperity. The Republican "revolution" of July temporarily disrupted the government and the oligarchy, and labor activists believed the Republicans and their leader Bautista Saavedra would be more accommodating to workers' demands than the fallen Liberals had been. For its part, the new governing party felt the need to shore up its political base in the wake of the coup, and many officials leant a sympathetic ear to labor's demands.

The department of Oruro's first movement for improved labor conditions occurred in Huanuni. As described in this chapter's first paragraph, Huanuni's workers swiftly won a pay raise and checks on prices at the company store. The movement became generalized throughout the department and even spread to neighboring regions in northern Potosí. Newly empowered Republican officials sought to placate the workers and calm the agitation.

In August 1920 workers employed by Oruro's four principal mining companies—the Mining Company of Oruro, the San José Mining Company of Oruro and Alantaña, the Tetilla Company, and the Santo Cristo Mining and Agricultural Company—used disciplined strikes and the threat of more to bring their bosses to the table. Once there, the two sides reached an agreement that touched on almost every aspect of mining employment. Workers from all four companies submitted similar and coordinated petitions. The San José Mining Company's workers punctuated their demands by carrying out a short, "peaceful strike."[28]

Oruro's prefect, Demetrio Canelas, presided over the meeting that resolved the conflict on August 16, 1920. Worker delegates from all four companies attended, as did the principal leaders of important local labor associations.[29] Rómulo Chumacero, a major promoter of Bolivia's early experiments with unionism and anarcho-syndicalism, represented workers at the Mining Company of Oruro; his participation in these negotiations indicates their national importance. Chumacero would eventually serve as president of both the Second and Third Workers' Congresses, in 1925 and 1927. By the 1930s Chumacero had developed into a declared Marxist-Leninist. Ricardo Perales, a tailor and a lawyer with a history of representing poor clients, also advised the workers.[30] Perales was a founding member of the Workers' Socialist Party in Oruro and a future representative to the Bolivian Congress. Donato Téllez and Justo Montaño attended the meeting as representatives of the Workers' Labor Federation of Oruro (Téllez was a leader in the Workers' Socialist Party as well). This conference produced the first comprehensive and detailed labor contract ever won by mine workers in the department of Oruro.

The session began with a consideration of the workers' petitions. Eventually, those in attendance came to an agreement on twenty-three points. The companies accepted the attending delegates as legitimate representatives of the workers "in all that relates to the defense of their rights." The companies also promised to reverse recent retaliation: "All those workers who have been fired because of the current petition will be returned to their jobs." On the traditional issues of schedules and pay, the workers won significant concessions. Between seven and eight in the morning workers had an hour to prepare for the day. This included the traditional *aculli*— the practice of chewing coca leaves before a hard day of labor. The workers then toiled from eight o'clock to eleven-thirty. They had a ninety-minute break for lunch and then returned to work until four-thirty in the afternoon. This schedule meant that workers would spend nine and one-half hours in the workplace "with seven hours of actual labor." The negotiators also won a 5–10 percent raise "in proportion to the needs of the workers." A council of workers would have a say in the award of raises.[31]

The agreement also addressed traditional worker concerns about the company stores. The companies accepted three points limiting their power to manipulate the stores to the detriment of workers. These points also prevented managers from regulating public markets in the shadow of their mines. First, prices in the company store had to reflect Oruro's market prices. Second, a workers' council was granted the power to "control and test the weight and price of goods." Workers engaged in these regulatory inspections enjoyed a guaranteed leave from work to complete the task. Third, the managers agreed to the "liberty of commerce in the established encampments," swearing that their companies "could not, under any circumstances, obligate their workers to make their purchases in the company stores."[32] This final concession benefited more than just workers and their families, for it protected the segments of the urban popular classes engaged in petty mercantile activities—activities the companies traditionally sought to regulate or even abolish.

Despite measures adopted during previous presidential administrations, workers returned to issues of health care and workplace safety in their negotiations. The new contract spelled out regulations protecting workers and their families in the cases of illness, injury, and death. The companies pledged to take "all efficacious steps to guarantee the life and health of the workers with the strengthening and reinforcement of the galleries, shafts, etc., as recommended in the mining law." Obviously, lax implementation left workers struggling continually to close the gap between written legislation and enforcement. The companies acknowledged their obligation "to protect the worker victims of accidents on the job." The workers demanded consistency in the medical services provided by the four companies, to which the companies acceded: "In the case of illness, the workers will have a right to medical attention and a pharmacy paid for by the company plus a half-day's pay, except in instances of illness brought on by drunkenness." The contract continued: "In cases where there is a dispute over the type of illness involved, a doctor employed by the office of Public Assistance will subject the sick worker to an exam whose certification will stipulate the company's obligations." Finally, in the case of fatal injury caused by "falls, cave-ins, or any other professional risk," the companies would pay the unfortunate worker's family an indemnity of one year's pay, "in conformity with the mining law," plus "the cost of funeral expenses."[33]

The mining companies retained a diversity of employment arrangements and contract practices. The agreement of August 1920 contained improvements for both wage laborers and contract workers. The negotiations promised miners a double wage when they worked legal holidays. The companies agreed to pay wage laborers every fifteen days and to abolish "valueless tokens that cannot serve in commercial circulation." The contract further allowed workers with *kajcheo,* or ore-sharing, agreements to conduct independent assays of their ore: "The companies are obliged to provide the contractors a packet of ore, so that they might, of their own account, assay and establish a control over the measurements conducted by the companies." *Kajcheo* workers also secured a certain protection against runs of bad luck in the mines. When contract workers lost money, the bosses agreed to compensate *kajchas* at the rate of Bs 3.50 per day.[34]

Workers also demanded and obtained greater job security, more respect in the workplace, and better housing. "No worker or laborer can be fired or suspended from their employment by lower-level management," the agreement read. "They must limit themselves to informing their superiors of the infractions that might have occurred, and only the manager or the administrator might decree the dismissal after hearing from the accused, and when it might be necessary, from the Council of Workers." The limitations on management continued: "When a worker's dismissal has been declared, they will give him a fifteen-day warning or a salary indemnity equivalent to said time, except in cases of grave negligence." The companies agreed to abolish fines and corporal punishment—practices the workers considered insulting to their honor. The Council of Workers also won a voice in regulating overseers and foremen so as to prevent a trampling of workers' rights: "The abuses committed by middle-management employees harmful to workers can be reported by them, or through the Council of Workers, to the management or administration respectively." The workers also won the abolition of corporate security forces that were "not recognized by the government" and "duplicate[ed] existing officials." Finally, workers sought and obtained an improvement in their housing: "The mining companies are obligated to provide hygienic housing to the workers in relation to the size of their families."[35]

The mining companies extracted one concession—a reform with which some labor leaders actually agreed. The workers acceded to a prohibition on "the sale of alcoholic beverages in the established encampments, especially in the company store." The bosses also won the right to fire workers who showed "symptoms of drunkenness."[36] In general, however, the Oruro labor contract of August 1920 was a substantial victory for the departmental capital's working class. Workers throughout Oruro and northern Potosí sought to impose similar accords on their employers with mixed results.

Activism in the mines inspired the Bolivian Railway Company's employees to walk out. The company's traffic office initiated a sudden strike at noon on August 17, 1920. The striking workers immediately involved the prefect, Demetrio Canelas, "bringing to the Prefecture the keys to their respective offices." Canelas summoned the railroad's administrator and "succeeded in pacifying the impatience of the employees with the promise that their demands would be attended to." With the prefect's intervention, "the employees agreed to return to their respective labors." Canelas recommended to his superiors that the government enter into conversation with the railway company to see what concessions might be made to the employees, for as he said, "It is evident that the salaries that some of them earn are extremely deficient."[37] The workers had correctly judged the interim prefect to be an official sympathetic to reform.

In northern Potosí officials answering to different authorities shrugged off the influence of Oruro's conciliatory prefect; they even collaborated in killing five striking workers. Military men stationed in the region initiated an aggressive persecution of labor activists to prevent potential mobilization, displaying a side of the Republican Party that would strengthen over the next couple of years. Lieutenant Colonel José Gonzales and Bustillos Province subprefect Eduardo Inarra launched a midnight sweep of Uncía on August 11, 1920. Soldiers stormed a "bar where people were drinking to excess and shouting death to various personages and praising others." Gonzales reported, "To avoid even greater uproar and disorder, we resolved to take these people to the police station."[38] The measures failed. On August 13 Oruro's prefecture received an urgent message from northern Potosí. "Tonight, there has occurred in the Llallagua Company an uprising of sizable proportions." The communiqué requested that Oruro's prefect dispatch "two machine guns and all the men necessary to save the situation." Lieutenant Colonel Gonzales was trying to pacify the region with "part of the urban guard maintained by the Patiño company"—the military and police, that is, were using company mercenaries to repress the workers.[39] These clashes had fatal consequences for the workers. A message from Patiño's company to Oruro's prefect on August 14 noted, "In Uncía everything is tranquil; but in Llallagua they have not yet resolved the strike, and this afternoon the strikers are burying the five that died." The missive continued, "Because of this there it much anger in Llallagua, including dynamite blasts in the hills surrounding it."[40] Colonel Gonzales eventually identified Trinidad Aguilar, a tailor, as one of the principal labor leaders in northern Potosí. The region's workers demanded that Aguilar be made subprefect. The colonel reported to Oruro's prefect, writing, "Happily the Governing Junta, listening to a telegraph message and understanding the danger posed by this individual, determined his deportation to one of the provinces of the Department of Cochabamba."[41] The killings had few national repercussions, however, and were soon overshadowed by the Uncía Massacre of 1923.[42]

Prefect Canelas had better luck imposing his will on smaller mining towns within the department of Oruro. On August 23, 1920, Canelas received word that workers in Avicaya were planning to initiate a strike, and so he asked that a delegation of Avicaya's workers visit him. He hoped to extend the accord that he had negotiated for Oruro to the smaller mining camp. Canelas noted in his report to La Paz that already in Morococala "the company [had] spontaneously implemented the improvements with great satisfaction on the part of the workers."[43]

Oruro's Demetrio Canelas eventually sought to extend his moderating influence more vigorously to the neighboring department. Specifically, Canelas tried to impose Oruro's labor agreement on northern Potosí, where the recent killings had taken place, but he encountered significant resistance. On August 24, 1920, in a report to the Republican junta in La Paz, he wrote, "I have sent a copy of this agreement to Uncía, instructing the subprefect to summon the management of the two mining companies in that town and to convince them of the need to enter into concessions." The inflexible stance of the Tin Company of Llallagua particularly frustrated the prefect, in part because the company's Chilean ownership and management provoked Canelas's nationalism. The prefect informed his superiors that the company had "denied, in full, the petition formulated by the workers, even though most of it" was "worthy of consideration." The company's stance placed the prefect in the uncomfortable position of having to "silence with the force of arms the demands of working people."

Canelas continued, "It is essential that the companies realize their duties at this moment. No government in the world guarantees business against strikes, now less than ever." Press coverage of the dispute in Chilean newspapers annoyed the prefect: "I see in the newspapers of Chile that they have made the most capricious and depressing comments, presenting the strike in Llallagua as an attack on Chilean interests and explaining that the [Bolivian] government has been thoroughly pleased with the 'outrages' committed." Canelas noted that the company's management had been in contact with the Chilean Ministry of Foreign Relations during the strike. The prefect concluded by declaring, "All of this demonstrates a lack of loyalty and consideration for our nation."[44] Laborers in northern Potosí eventually won concessions, but their gains did not match those in Oruro.

The implementation of the labor accords faced several difficulties even in the city of Oruro. On August 19, 1920, Prefect Demetrio Canelas wrote the Itos Mining Company's administration, saying, "The labor federation of this town sent me a report yesterday that informed me of the suspension from their jobs of the workers Romelio Peñaloza and Aniceto Canedo, who were representatives to this office of the Itos Mine belonging to the company that you manage; they worked to resolve the list of grievances composed by the workers." The prefect gave the company the benefit of the doubt, suggesting that perhaps an employee "ignorant of the extent of the agreed-upon stipulations" had dismissed the workers. Canelas pushed for the men's reinstatement.[45] A few days later a commission of seven workers wrote Canelas with another complaint. When they had visited the office of Francisco Blieck, the manager of the Mining Company of Oruro, to confirm the new workday schedule, they were rebuffed: "Sr. Blieck refused to approve it, responding that he did not accept a stay of nine hours in the mine, only ten, and that those who did not submit to his determination should leave their jobs and abandon the mine." The workers informed the prefect that if the manager did not "satisfactorily comply" with their "polite and respectful petition," they would "collectively suspend labor." They requested Canelas's "paternal intervention" in resolving this "conflict between capital and the workers."[46] This incident was only one of many in which the bosses continually probed the government's dedication to the enforcement of legislation and labor accords.

By 1921 Oruro had a new prefect, Adalid Tejada Fariñez, and workers found themselves forced to revisit issues seemingly resolved just a few months earlier. In February 1921 the Santo Cristo Mining Company, a subsidiary of C. F. Gundlack and Company, wrote to Tejada to explain the operation of its company store, for workers had complained to the prefect. The mine's administration asserted that the prices of goods in its store matched those in Oruro's markets. The company claimed adherence to the agreement of August 1920, insisting that its workers had "the right to check the weights and to make complaints personally or through the Workers' Council recognized by the company." The administration claimed that it "did not profit from its store": "Since various concessions were made to the working class, the store limits itself to covering its operating cost." As for the accusation that the company sought to control commerce in the Santo Cristo camp, management wrote, "The sale of any article or food is free to all; the company has not imposed barriers of any kind." The mine's administration noted that goods sold in the camp by outside merchants cost nearly the same as those sold by the company store, "except the products of the countryside (potatoes, mutton, etc.), which are a bit cheaper than in the city of Oruro." The administrators noted, "The company does not sell these products in the company store." Finally, the administration denied accusations of debt peonage, writing, "The company makes loans according to the wages earned by the worker."[47] For a time, even with new officials in place in Oruro, the companies felt compelled to adhere to—at least publicly—the 1920 accords.

Indeed, some companies paid a price for failing to abide by the government-sanctioned labor accords. Oruro's prefect had imposed the contract of August 1920 on the companies of Morococala. In September 1921 Cercado Province subprefect J. Alvéstigui visited Morococala to look into complaints of fraud directed at the Penny and Duncan Mining Company's store. The complaints centered on the weights used there. The subprefect eventually determined that the one-pound weights were three to four ounces light and fined the company Bs 500 for the infraction.[48] Direct action had earned the working class some temporary consideration from government officials.

RAILWAY WORKERS, SOCIALISM, AND POLITICS

The ideological advance of labor and its allies underwent a similar acceleration during the same period. Self-proclaimed socialists sought to rival the dominance of the oligarchic Liberal and Republican parties. The Socialist Party emerged as a national party in November 1921, but its activists had a longer history in Oruro. The Workers' Socialist Party first appeared in Oruro in 1919.[49] The party participated in most departmental elections between 1919 and 1923. An alliance between Socialist Party militants and labor federations even began to produce politicized strikes that disturbed mainstream politicians.

Socialist candidates first ran for office in Oruro during the violent municipal elections of December 1919. While confrontations between the Republicans and Liberals dominated official concern, politicians in some small towns listed the new Workers' Socialist Party among the upstarts undermining Liberal rule. A pronouncement issued on December 1, 1919, made clear the Socialists' intention to function as an independent workers' party:

> The laborers have grouped themselves around the red banner; those who have taken bread to the victims of Uncía; those who have succored the miners of Huanuni, Monte Blanco, and Colquiri; those who have asked for labor laws from the Legislature; those who have established a night school to educate working high school students; in total, those who have dedicated their lives to the service of labor's cause, they have sworn a solemn oath in the name of God, the Homeland, and Honor to unite and call together their brothers to defend the sacred banner of the proletariat.
>
> Workers: you who are still blindly devoted to the bourgeois parties, you should think upon the harm you do to your class and your cause.

Workers: Are you on the side of the rich or that of the poor?
If you are poor, unite with us![50]

In the town of Poopó, home to the Mining Company of Oruro's Alantaña mill, the municipal council's Liberal president, Fernando Frontanilla, claimed that the mining company's Chilean management sponsored the local Republican, Radical, and Socialist Parties, "damaging in this way the dignity of the country; for we are not talking about a national politics, but the meddling of a Chilean Company pursuing ends favorable to its own interests."[51] Such accusations of antipatriotic behavior were the final, desperate recourse of a decaying party.

The Republicans, not the Socialists, emerged triumphant from the Liberals' collapse. One principal promoter of the Workers' Socialist Party in Oruro, Ricardo Perales, initially viewed the Republican coup of July 12, 1920, and Bautista Saavedra's rise to power with enormous hope. In this Perales followed the political inclinations of artisans and workers, many of whom believed Saavedra's Republicans truly represented their interests. Yet Perales and other Socialists soon began to express disappointment with the new administration, and elections in November 1920 amply illustrated Republican hostility. During the vote Perales sought a seat in Congress. Donato Téllez, of the Workers' Socialist Party, requested that Oruro's prefect, Luis Calvo, restrain incessant attacks on the Socialist campaign. "For several days now groups of drunken individuals have threatened with hostilities our party's supporters, especially our candidate, Sr. Ricardo Perales," wrote Téllez. He called upon the prefect's sense of duty: "In the face of these threats that represent an imminent danger to our persons and homes, we come to you, so that you might order the implementation of precautionary steps to protect the life and health of citizens."[52] Perales later wrote of the election, "What a great deception we have suffered in witnessing the election in which the Republican Party debuts in power; deep bitterness we have felt at seeing Republican workers, urged on by their candidates, pursue and persecute independent citizens."[53] For some workers a break with the Republicans took time, yet it would come. Bautista Saavedra hoped to make workers and artisans a docile segment of his political movement, but workers eventually asserted their independence. The government blamed the Socialists.

Railway workers illustrate the political vibrancy of working-class movements during the early years of Republican rule, a dynamism encouraged by the Socialist Party. Oruro's and Potosí's railway workers struggled with the intersection of class and nationality. Workers organized the League of Railroad Employees and Workers in La Paz on August 3, 1919. Less than one year later the Railway Federation of Oruro and Potosí emerged from a schism in the earlier organization. The split occurred because of difficulties in organizing across companies and across international borders. The original League of Railroad Employees and Workers sought a national union incorporating workers from several railway and trolley companies. A strike in Chile led to the league's fracture and the emergence of the smaller Railway Federation. In December 1919 league members employed by the Antofagasta-Bolivia Railroad/Bolivian Railway Company—a multinational corporation with offices in both Bolivia and northern Chile—requested that strike funds be sent to workers in Chile. The league's leadership in La Paz denied the petition, citing the union's poverty.[54] As a result, workers in Oruro and Potosí sought the league's reorganization to allow for greater local autonomy. Eventually, workers at the Antofagasta-Bolivia Railroad/Bolivian Railway Company abandoned the national organization and formed their own body, the Railway Federation, in Oruro on March 6, 1920—"removing ourselves from the association and subsequently breaking it."[55] Company pressure also played a role in fracturing the league. The new Railway Federation's president, Luis Herrero, informed the faltering League of Railroad Employees and Workers' president, Héctor Borda, that the railway company had refused to negotiate with the league because it was not an association purely of company employees and laborers.[56]

The schism killed the League of Railroad Employees and Workers. In June 1920 league leaders in La Paz received a disheartening letter from Uyuni, Potosí:

> In response to the letters that have arrived addressed to the President of the Committee of the League of Railroad Employees and Workers, I must

inform you that said association no longer exists here since the organization of the Railway Federation. By unanimous agreement League members have decided to extinguish the League and form a new association with new statutes and a different constitution, without a dependent relationship on any other body, with an exclusive membership of this company's employees and rail workers. If you wish a relation with the Railway Federation, please direct yourself to its Secretary General.[57]

The original union faded from the scene soon after receiving this rebuke. The league closed out its existence with a recommendation that former members organize associations similar to the new Railway Federation, "as this is the only solution for members of the proletariat, so as to guarantee in some way their rights."[58]

Despite a somewhat inglorious beginning—sabotaging a national federation in favor of a local union—the Railway Federation of Oruro and Potosí emerged as a progressive working-class force. Indeed, railroad men pioneered the use of the political strike in Bolivia, and such politicized work stoppages angered some among the Republican Party's governing faction. In late January 1921 several labor associations paralyzed Oruro's industry to protest insults exchanged between two rival politicians in La Paz. Oruro's workers leapt to the defense of Ricardo Soruco Ipiña, a member of Daniel Salamanca's wing of the Republican Party, when Abel Iturralde, an ally of Bautista Saavedra, assailed his character during a session of the convention organizing a permanent Republican government on January 20, 1921.[59] Soruco had a close relationship with the Railway Federation, which led the strikes that followed. In December 1920 he had attended its first convention, a meeting of eighty worker delegates from across the country.[60] At the convention Soruco declared, "If the Republican Party wishes to throw itself against the rights of the working class in a hostile manner, I prefer to abandon my obligations to the Republican Party and become nothing more than a railway representative, taking my seat in Congress on the extreme Left."[61] Angered by the attack on a political ally, the Railway Federation paralyzed Oruro's rail traffic. Writing to his counterpart in Cochabamba, Oruro's prefect, Adalid Tejada Fariñez, reported, "Yesterday at 5:00 p.m. the railway workers declared a work stoppage. Railroad lines on the Machacamarca-Uncía route as well as some services to La Paz are on strike."[62] In solidarity with the Railway Federation, several other organizations in Oruro suspended labor. Donato Téllez and Ricardo Perales, of the Workers' Labor Federation and the Socialist Party, informed Tejada of the result:

> A resolution approved in a great assembly of the working class held last night: a general strike has been decreed by a unanimous decision of all the artisan associations that have a pact of solidarity with the Railway Federation, which finds itself today engaged in a work stoppage until the congressman Sr. Iturralde makes the asked for apology for his slanders directed at the working classes in the person of Dr. Ricardo Soruco. The decision was that we begin today a general work stoppage among the artisan associations; it will be conducted in an environment of culture and respect for society and the authorities.[63]

The prefect feared that the conflict, if not resolved quickly, might spread to the mining companies, where, he said, "popular feeling is already tense because of the suspension of pay in some [mines], and the reduction of personnel and salaries in others."[64]

The work stoppage angered some officials. The movement's political aims clashed with some bureaucrats' conception of the limited, "legitimate" circumstances in which the working class might strike. La Paz's prefect, Óscar de Santa Cruz, declared, "The working class has cast shame on the principal object of the right to strike, taking as their cause for declaring a stoppage of the railroads an incident that occurred between Honorable National Representatives in one of the sessions of the Convention."[65] Despite the frustration of some, mediation quickly resolved the dispute. On January 28, 1921, striking workers, the two politicians involved, and Oruro's prefect reached an understanding. Abel Iturralde agreed to send Ricardo Soruco an apology stating that "in the congressional incident dating to the twentieth of this month, it was not his intention to offend the Railway Federation or the national proletariat in the person of the Honorable Congressman Sr. Ricardo Soruco." The government promised to release those "workers who, because of their solidarity with the railway men's strike, [had] been arrested." Officials swore not to initiate any further action, "either civil or criminal, against the President, Secretary, committee members, or railway men associated with the stoppage of railway traffic and the damages that they might have caused."[66] In the wake of January's successful strike, the railway workers sought to expand their influence.

In July 1921 the Huanchaca Mining Company's workers initiated a strike that eventually involved the Railway Federation. The conflict began in Pulacayo, Potosí, when the company fired some fifteen to eighteen workers in its machine and electrical shops. The manager, Leonardo Ball, pointed to the company's precarious financial situation "caused by steep losses" over the previous couple of years that, "because of diverse economic factors," had "restricted labor in the mines." Ball justified the layoffs as part of a "strict economizing plan adopted by his company"; the workers had a different explanation. They argued that the "real motive for the firing of their comrades" was their role in forming the Mining Federation of Pulacayo, organized in June of that year, which was "disagreeable to the Manager, Bell." Enrique Mallea Balboa, a government representative dispatched to resolve the dispute, judged that "between these two contradictory assertions," there was "much truth and a bit of exaggeration."[67]

Mallea's report contained a comprehensive narrative of the strike. In late May the company's interim manager, a Sr. Lott, had fired César Zúñiga, who belonged to a small trade association among the company's mechanics, the Mechanics' Society. His fellow mechanics eventually negotiated his return to work. Mallea believed that "a few agitators took advantage of this first collective success to easily inculcate among the miners ideas somewhat subversive and socialist, suggesting the need to organize a Federation affiliated with the railway workers of Uyuni," who, he said, had "the support and solidarity of others throughout the Republic to impose themselves on businessmen everywhere." Mallea reported that "the propaganda spread rapidly, and at the end of June they had a list that included all kinds of men and of every age." He judged the list illegitimate, because it included "many minors and illiterates who could not read or write." With their list of potential members, Luis Carrazano, Guillermo Pozo, César Zúñiga, Ricardo Carrazano, and a few others traveled to Uyuni to consult with the Railway Federation. The men returned with representatives from the Railway Federation and formed the Mining Federation of Pulacayo. When the company dismissed more than a dozen workers from the machine and electrical shops, the federation called a general assembly. A majority at the meeting decided for an immediate strike. The federation's leaders then submitted a list of demands to the company. Mallea could not secure a copy of the document but believed it was written "precipitously and without adhering to the laws of courtesy that are usual in all relations of modern life." He added, "It revealed the morbid state of being of its authors, and they undoubtedly worked under the pressure and influence of hate and anger. It was no more that a declaration of defiance and an insolent ultimatum—a form in which the procedure of a strike has never been employed." The company rejected the ultimatum, "occasioning a rare strike, in violation of the procedure established by the decree of September 29, 1920." This decree by the Republican Party government sought to limit the flexibility and spontaneity of strikes. Mallea estimated that the strikers numbered between 150 and 200. He also asserted that 90 percent of the company's workers remained on the job. The Mining Federation of Pulacayo supposedly "attempted to drag them into the strike with threats, insults, promises, and violence, denying them their rights and their liberty to work." Mallea lamented in his report that "simple and innocent people had been pushed and influenced by agitators and leaders of bad faith—those truly responsible for the situation that Pulacayo experienced." The striking workers eventually reduced their demands to just two: that the company return the fired men to their jobs and that management recognize the Mining Federation of Pulacayo. The company refused both points, and the strike was defeated. Mallea, the government mediator, concluded, "The imprudent and brusque strike of 10 percent of the workers has been peacefully resolved in this manner."[68]

Despite the defeat in Pulacayo, the Railway Federation continued to push its agenda in other ways. In December 1920 the federation issued a call to labor associations across Bolivia to meet in Oruro. The labor movement would remember this as the "First National Congress of Workers." The meeting, however, failed to create a durable framework for coordinating the country's various local labor associations. Militants of the oligarchic parties, especially the Republican Party, disrupted the congress.[69] In February 1922 the railway workers supported the Workers' Labor Federation of La Paz and that city's taxi drivers when they called for a national general strike—the country's first.[70]

The Railway Federation also played a pivotal role in consolidating May Day as a national holiday. Workers imposed May Day or Labor Day on their employers and on the government. Oruro's workers first celebrated the holiday in the mid-1910s, and by 1926 it was an official national holiday. In April 1922 a conflict developed between the Railway Federation and the Antofagasta-Bolivia Railroad/Bolivian Railway Company's administration over the holiday. The federation planned to paralyze railway service on May Day, and the company vehemently opposed the idea. On April 26 Oruro prefect Adelid Tejada Fariñez wrote the Railway Federation's president that the government had negotiated a compromise with the company's administration. The company agreed to a traffic stoppage on May 1 from six in the morning to six in the afternoon. The holiday principally affected the international train from Antofagasta, Chile, which was scheduled to "arrive Monday the first in Oruro at six in the morning." Tejada continued, "It will remain here until six in the afternoon; at that hour, it will continue its trip to La Paz so as to arrive Tuesday in the morning, or even that same night, depending on what the company decides." In exchange for his intercession on the federation's behalf, the prefect asked that "the working classes observe decorum and discipline during their rallies, without propagating ideas of a subversive character against the established order." If the rallies got out of hand, Tejada threatened, "The authorities would find themselves forced to employ repressive measures—something to be avoided."[71] The concession irritated the railway company, whose administrator vented his anger in a final letter to the prefect: "Permit me to inform you that the agreement is completely in deference to your suggestion without the Company feeling itself legally obliged to adopt this measure."[72] Four years later the government completely legalized the holiday.

The labor movement's growing power during the early years of Republican rule encouraged Socialist politicians to aim for public office. In turn,

Socialist Party activists further stimulated the working class. The story of one such activist illustrates this dynamic. Ricardo Perales, the tailor, labor activist, Socialist Party politician, and lawyer from Oruro, won election to Congress in 1921. In January 1922 he began a short but vigorous congressional career, pushing legislation favorable to the workers and seeking to fortify workers' job security and living standards. In addition to cooperating with Oruro's labor movement, Perales frequently represented poor clients in the courts and in the prefecture. This practical experience informed much of the legislation he presented in Congress. On August 9, 1921, for example, Francisco Chávez, one of Ricardo Perales' clients and a twenty-year employee of the Mining Company of Oruro, met in the prefecture with company managers to protest his dismissal. Various witnesses declared Chávez an experienced and reliable employee. One worker, Francisco Lazo, recounted the incident that had led to Chávez's dismissal, relating that a foreman had "wished to force him [Chávez] to labor in a gallery where Chávez declared work to be impossible, because no one had yet done preparatory work." Lazo continued, "Because of this negative reply, they fired him immediately." The company refused to return Chávez's job, but Prefect Adalid Tejada Fariñez felt that he deserved compensation. "It is strict justice to have a certain consideration for an employee who has grown old in the service of an enterprise; the Mining Company of Oruro should pay him an indemnity of one month's salary," Tejada determined.[73] Such incidents led Ricardo Perales to pursue legislative means toward increased job security and improved living standards for workers.

While in La Paz, Perales proposed the creation of militant unions in all the nation's mines. Ideally, the unions would maintain a strong bargaining position vis-à-vis management. He even suggested that workers control pricing in the company stores and regulate the assay of minerals, the quality of which affected the compensation of contract workers. Perales sought to break the power of mine administrators in company towns; in his view, liberty of commerce should reign, and civil authorities should replace company police. Perales proposed collective bargaining, union control over the firing of workers, and two weeks' pay as compensation for all dismissed workers. The reform legislation sought double pay on holidays and the elimination of company fines for worker infractions. Perales proposed a separate law promising a secure retirement and pensions. Congress rejected the legislation wholesale, even though the reforms were substantially the same as those already won from Oruro's mining companies just two years earlier, in August 1920; Congress's failure to approve these reforms indicated the growing moderation of President Bautista Saavedra and the Republican Party and the rapid adaptation of the mining companies to the political shake-up of 1920.[74]

Ricardo Perales served only one term in Congress and failed to win reelection. In May 1923 the Socialist Party's executive committee announced that both Perales and Donato Téllez would run in upcoming elections. The party hoped that "political guarantees would be a reality" during the campaign and asked local authorities to adhere to "the official word of the Supreme Government." Despite a hardening of Republican rule, Perales and Téllez expected that "the Socialist Party would enjoy complete liberty" and promised to acknowledge and thank "the authority who knows how to do his duty."[75] Just one month later the Republican government repressed the Socialist Party. This followed serious labor unrest in northern Potosí and the military's killing of striking workers—the Uncía Massacre. The Socialist Party disappeared from Oruro, but former members continued their activism without a formal organization.

CHAPTER 5

The Uncía Massacre, 1923

ON MAY 1, 1923, some five thousand workers and artisans from the most important mining towns in northern Potosí gathered on the soccer field of the provincial capital Uncía to organize a march celebrating Labor Day (i.e., May Day). At two in the afternoon, the workers began their procession through the town's principal streets to the cries of "Long live Labor Day! Long live the First of May! Glory to the Martyrs of Chicago!" and occasionally, "Long live the Labor Federation of Uncía!" The march finished in the Plaza 6 de Agosto, where the workers listened to a number of speeches emphasizing the transcendent importance of the holiday and its history. After the speeches the congregation engaged in a symbolic act of charity: they distributed clothing to the children of deceased comrades. The afternoon of ceremony culminated with the official foundation of the Central Labor Federation of Uncía.[1]

The Central Labor Federation sought to unify the whole of the region's working class. While not the first federation of its kind, the Uncía organization posed a special threat to capital in the all-important mining industry, for the Uncía region contained the country's richest and most productive tin mines, and the area's companies thus exercised enormous influence over both local and national government. In 1923 the tin magnates refused to tolerate the creation of a regional labor federation uniting all the area's workers—a process that presciently anticipated the consolidation of capital—and on June 4 of that year, the military opened fire on Central Labor Federation supporters protesting the detention of union leadership. The gunfire killed four immediately, with two to five others dying of wounds in the following days. The federation's leaders endured arrest and deportation. Working-class Bolivians and intellectuals remember the episode as the "Uncía Massacre." While not the first time the government had employed deadly force in dealing with the working class, the massacre marked a symbolic beginning, for it inaugurated the twentieth-century struggle between labor and the forces of capital for control of Bolivia. Ultimately, the Uncía Massacre constituted a moment of conjuncture between working-class experience and descriptions of capitalism as presented by socialist, Marxist, and anarcho-syndicalist activists.

ORGANIZATION

The Central Labor Federation of Uncía emerged suddenly in May 1923, but activists had long talked of organizing. The workers and artisans of northern Potosí took heart from the labor movement's successes following the Republican coup of July 1920, and workers there could look to the nearby department of Oruro for inspiring, recent success. In Huanuni workers challenged one of Patiño's companies in February 1923. Political connections between the ruling Republican Party and workers played a central role in bringing the incident to a rapid conclusion. Following a series of firings on February 16, Huanuni's police chief, Miguel Ramos, organized a conference between labor and the company. On February 19 the mine's manager, Herman Brehem, met with twelve worker delegates. The meeting began with the police chief reading an earlier labor agreement signed in 1919; both sides reaffirmed the document with a few minor additions. Brehem agreed to rehire laborers "suspended without sufficient cause." The workers also secured the return of the popular doctor José Arzadum Aramayo, whom they judged to have "carried out his mission with determination and generosity" accompanied by "undeniable competence." Labor made one concession to management: "laborers who miss work without a just cause" would pay a fine equivalent to a half-day's wage. Another point, this one conceded by both parties, directly involved the government. Patiño's company agreed that "conscripts returning from their military service" would be "rehired to their old jobs," but the men had to return any previous severance pay in regular installments. One final point hints at the reason for government willingness to mediate the dispute: the company agreed to pay Hermógenes Iraola the equivalent of seven days' wages (a standard severance package) as a "special bonus for his years of service in the Company."[2] At the end of 1923 Iraola would emerge as the head of the Republican Workers' Party in Huanuni, a branch of the ruling Republican Party designed to harness working-class political support. Another delegate at the conference, Pablo Salas, became the new party's secretary.[3] The intimacy between some labor activists and the country's dominant party typified the early years of Saavedra's presidency. The labor federation that developed in northern Potosí just a few months later provoked a wholly different response.

The dismissal of one worker, Pedro Gutiérrez, triggered the creation of the Central Labor Federation of Uncía. Gutiérrez was a longtime employee of the Tin Company of Llallagua and a foreman in the company's Cancañiri shaft. After his firing, Gutiérrez visited the mine's administrator, a Sr. Lahay, to demand his back pay. Lahay denied him the money and—according to Gutiérrez—assaulted him. Gutiérrez then took his complaint to Llallagua's police chief, Gerardo Tórrez Ruiz, a captain in the Bolivian army and new to the position. Tórrez ordered Lahay to his office. The administrator initially refused and appeared only when escorted by a police officer. Lahay mocked the police chief's authority; Tórrez responded by jailing the administrator. The company's manager, Emilio Díaz, quickly received news of Lahay's imprisonment and called on the police chief. Tórrez ordered Díaz to give the fired Gutiérrez his back pay. Díaz agreed to comply, but only if Lahay was released. The police chief refused, citing the administrator's disrespect for authority. The manager then made a quick trip to nearby Uncía to visit Bustillos Province subprefect David Michel and to request the police chief's dismissal. Michel, however, supported Tórrez's authority. With this rejection Díaz began plotting the downfall of both the police chief and the subprefect, hoping to see them replaced by more compliant officials—something to which the companies were more accustomed.[4]

The dispute prompted northern Potosí's workers to mobilize. On April 30, 1923, four workers interrupted a meeting of the May Day committee with news that the Tin Company of Llallagua had asked the government to remove the two sympathetic officials. The region's workers and artisans looked to the activists of the May Day committee to defend the two and confront the company. The committee resolved to support the embattled officials and dispatched emissaries to the region's various mines to inform workers of the decision. The committee's leaders viewed the conflict as a propitious moment to organize a local labor federation.[5]

The Central Labor Federation of Uncía started life on May 1, 1923. After May Day's march and speeches, the workers and artisans of Uncía and Llallagua met in a "grand popular assembly" to inaugurate the new federation. "By unanimous agreement, all those in attendance resolve to found the Central Labor Federation of Uncía for the ends of patriotism, struggle, and worker solidarity, expelling from its bosom political rancor and disagreement that only contribute to the dilution of the working element's strength," they wrote.[6] While the federation's founders sought to minimize political divisions, the union was not completely apolitical. Ideas promoted by the traditional oligarchic parties, such as nationalism and patriotism, permeated the federation's membership, and the workers held an especially dangerous belief in the benevolence of the Republican Party.

The Central Labor Federation of Uncía immediately identified labor's friends and enemies in northern Potosí. The federation singled out the subprefect David Michel and the police chief Gerardo Tórrez Ruiz for a "vote of applause" because of their "patriotic and just stance in defense of the rights and prerogatives of abused and oppressed workers." The federation identified two principal enemies: Emilio Díaz, the manager of the

Tin Company of Llallagua, and that company's lawyer, Germán Noya. The federation's leadership vowed a letter of protest denouncing "the unqualified abuses and outrages frequently committed by said Company against the national working element": "We hereby declare the previously mentioned Manager an unwanted person by the laboring element, and, in consequence, we request his immediate deportation from the Republic so as to avoid future abuses that might provoke disagreeable consequences for the tranquil development of the mining industry." The federation emphasized nationalist language. Díaz was Chilean, as was the company for which he worked. Northern Potosí's artisans and workers sought to use nationalism to bridge the chasm separating them from high-ranking officials. The federation hoped that President Saavedra would react with outrage at Díaz's "reiterated campaigns of violence against the national labor movement."[7]

On May 2 Díaz fired twenty-six workers. The dismissed men claimed that the firings were retaliation for their participation in the May Day parade and for joining the new federation, and the union dispatched a commission to investigate the firings.[8] The federation sought an official escort for the commissioners' visit; the Central Labor Federation of Uncía president Guillermo Gamarra wrote Subprefect David Michel, asking that he grant "the necessary support so that the commission dispatched to the Catavi Mill—for the purpose of collecting succinct information about the abuses and humiliations inflicted upon . . . workers—not be molested by the arbitrary Manager Emilio Díaz."[9]

In addition to launching a campaign against the Tin Company of Llallagua, the federation set out to test the disposition of the region's other substantial mining concern: Simón Patiño's La Salvadora Mining Company. On May 3 the federation offered assurances to Patiño's company: "The Directory of this new grouping is composed of persons that constitute an effective guarantee for the mining companies, that at all times will find respect and guarantees for their interests—looking for, on your part, mutual concessions." The federation's president, Guillermo Gamarra, closed out his letter by writing, "I believe and hold out hope that you will know how to encourage and lend your moral support to the recently founded Federation."[10] La Salvadora Mining Company's manager, Francisco Blieck, did not reply until five days later. Laying out the argument that companies would employ throughout their struggles with the federation, Blieck wrote Gamarra, "I must inform you that this Company excuses itself from entering into relations with the organization that you represent, in view of the fact that it cannot tolerate the interference of private persons foreign to it in its internal affairs."[11] The argument was particularly ironic as Gamarra was a carpenter employed by La Salvadora Mining Company.

The federation never let slip an opportunity to respond directly to a company's arguments. On May 11 union president Gamarra penned an energetic reply; "You assert that the Company that you represent declines to enter into relations with the Federation, alleging that 'it cannot tolerate the interference of private persons foreign to it in its internal affairs,'" he wrote. "I suppose there is some misunderstanding," the federation's president said; "in my first letter, I explained to you that the Federation was made up of workers from the two Tin Companies and by the individual workers of this city and Llallagua, in other words, a coalition of all of the workers in general, without professional distinction, under one idea, one banner: THE FEDERATION." Gamarra and the federation's secretary, Ernesto Fernández, continued, "You, better than anyone, are capable of judging the character of a legal organization that seeks nothing more than to improve its class, as is done in all the most advanced countries of the planet, under the protection of laws that authorize citizens to think, write, and associate freely, with no more limit than a respect for the beliefs and interests of others." Gamarra concluded with a note of defiance, writing, "I believe, Sr. Manager, that in my name and in that of the proletarian class, that instead of an encouraging word, you have issued a challenge, a depressing slight of which the Federation will take note."[12]

Despite the bitter correspondence between Simón Patiño's company and the federation, the Tin Company of Llallagua remained the union's primary target. Two days after the retaliatory firings by Emilio Díaz, a five-man federation commission arrived at the company's Catavi camp to investigate the dismissals and examine living and working conditions there. An officer of the local police, Nicolás Sánchez, accompanied the workers.

The manager and the company lawyer, Germán Noya, agreed to negotiations and a cursory inspection only when they realized a police official was in attendance. The commission requested the reinstatement of workers recently dismissed; Díaz and Noya agreed to the return of workers who had not closed out their accounts with the company, arguing that replacements for the fired men had already been hired. The commission agreed to the compromise but requested that the company buy train tickets for those who would not be returning. Díaz and Noya refused. The unemployed workers reconciled themselves to the company's intransigence, complaining of years of service wasted on an ungrateful employer. After the negotiations the company invited the commission to visit some of its installations. During the tour Noya was thrilled that no workers complained of their treatment; in fact, however, many signaled to the commission behind the lawyer's back that they would talk freely during the noon break. At that meeting, free of company intimidation, numerous workers swore their allegiance to the new union.[13]

Following the visit, the Tin Company of Llallagua hardened its resistance. Díaz and Noya closed Catavi to individuals not employed by the company and limited workers' liberty to leave the camp. Finally, they continued firing federation laborers and expelling their families from company housing. The union could not dispatch a second commission, as Díaz had deployed a cordon of security guards.[14]

On May 7 the Central Labor Federation of Uncía received a surprise letter from a new, "rival" organization in northern Potosí: the Union of Llallagua's Workers. Díaz and Noya had established a company union to counteract the independent federation. "Please permit us to inform you that today the 'Union of Llallagua's Workers' has been organized—composed of the most distinguished laboring elements among those who live in the Llallagua Canton and work for the Tin Company of Llallagua—with a membership of 2,500 men," they wrote. The yellow union claimed that its formative objective was to "prevent speculators without consciences, alien to the industry and to the work, from seizing their representation and defaming them before the Nation and the World, attributing to them indecent, greedy, and personal intentions and goals unbecoming of conscientious and honest elements." The insults continued for several paragraphs. "We protest with all the energy of our convictions as honorable and free men against your iniquitous attitude"; "[you are] . . . a tiny group of heterogeneous individuals—a conglomeration of bourgeois persons of diverse type—who have no more in common than their invented self-interest, their incapacity to support themselves, and their desire to prosper by snatching the workers' honorable salary," the company union wrote. The recent visit by the Central Labor Federation of Uncía commissioners had stimulated the anger. The false union railed against the "indescribable audacity" of the federation for "intruding" on the work camp at Catavi "to ask for donations and dues with lies and criminal propaganda." They closed one paragraph with an insult designed to offend the sensibilities of the urban popular classes, accusing federation members of coming to Catavi to "beg for a glass of beer." Friendly socialization lubricated by alcohol was an ingrained part of Andean culture, both urban and rural.[15]

The yellow union's leaders proclaimed themselves a labor aristocracy and derided the artisans among the Central Labor Federation of Uncía. "We who earn high salaries, who enjoy well-being and comfort, we cannot entrust our interests to townsfolk who are country lawyers, barbers, cobblers, typographers, and tailors, who earn much less than us and lead lives of misery because of their own incompetence," they wrote. The company union also issued threats against workers who might seek the federation's representation: "If there is some traitor among us who goes back on their word and seeks to find assistance from you or from any element foreign to the 'UNION,' he will be dismissed, and we will orchestrate his firing from work."[16]

The vitriol did not intimidate the Central Labor Federation of Uncía, which composed a scathing reply. "In response to the nasty flyer that you, our fellow countrymen, have signed—the fruit of a passionate rant by the proletariat's executioners—let us respond by informing you that the tenor of the mentioned flyer has been conveyed, along with a related complaint, to the public prosecutor's office." The federation defended the honor of its artisan membership: "Barbers, typographers, cobblers, and tailors, as you call us, we prefer to taste the black bread of misery before insulting our comrades in labor and sacrifice." It labeled the company union a servant of foreign interests and an affront to national dignity. The federation warned against "the smile of a foreign executioner that yesterday trampled upon national sovereignty, who is snatching from us the richest and most exuberant bits of our Father Land."[17]

Throughout early May the Central Labor Federation of Uncía continued to consolidate its membership. By May 15 the union claimed around 1,800 members.[18] It continued a sustained letter-writing campaign to inform labor organizations and newspapers across the country of its struggle. The union also wrote the central government in La Paz but never received an acknowledgment. President Saavedra was monitoring the situation but corresponded with the companies, not the union. Subprefect David Michel and Police Chief Gerardo Tórrez Ruiz had inclined toward the federation, but a new wave of officials favored the companies.

NEGOTIATION

Sympathetic officials such as the subprefect and the police chief stoked the urban popular classes' hope for impartial government mediation. Unfortunately, Michel and Tórrez were exceptional in their treatment of the working class. As negotiations advanced, the federation encountered only indifference and deceit, with the rejection going all the way to the presidency. In the wake of this battle over unionization in northern Potosí, socialist, Marxist, and anarcho-syndicalist activists employed the memory of Uncía to illustrate their arguments about ingrained government perfidy, and there was plenty of perfidy in the negotiations between President Saavedra's administration and the Central Labor Federation of Uncía.

On May 12 a representative from La Paz arrived to investigate the situation in northern Potosí. Although the visit would eventually frustrate and anger the federation's members, they were initially optimistic, with 3,000 workers and artisans meeting the delegate Nícanor Fernández at Uncía's train station as an expression of their faith in the government's intentions. Fernández spent the first night in Uncía; the next morning a car from the Tin Company of Llallagua ferried him to Catavi. The federation organized a commission to Catavi as well. In Catavi, Fernández disappeared into Emilio Díaz's personal residence. As Díaz entertained the government investigator, plying him with alcohol, the federation had unrestricted access to the Catavi camp. Union leaders from Uncía accepted new declarations of membership and swore in a Catavi subcouncil. The federation also sought to carry out an impromptu march. When word of the intended march reached management, the government delegate appeared and asked the workers to refrain from a public demonstration. Federation leaders acceded to the request, hoping to make a good impression. Fernández then disappeared once again into the manager's residence, and the assembled workers waited in vain for him to reappear. Eventually, one of the representative's assistants informed the crowd that Fernández was feeling ill and that testimony would be taken the next day in Uncía. The federation worried that Díaz might fire workers making the trip to Uncía to testify, but the assistant assured them that no one would be fired. At five in the afternoon the federation's commission and a group of witnesses returned to Uncía after a fruitless day of waiting.[19]

Despite the assurances, federation members from Catavi feared that Díaz might take advantage of their absence to suspend them. The workers returned to their homes that night.[20] At ten o'clock in the morning on May 14, the federation sought to call on the government delegate and could find no sign of him. They received word that Fernández was still in Catavi; he had spent the night with Díaz. Even worse, four federation witnesses had been fired.[21] The Uncía leadership received an urgent letter from Catavi workers soon thereafter: "We arrived at the place where the sign-in sheet is circulated this morning, but we discovered that time cards belonging to four members of the Directorate of this Subcommittee had been retired. We were notified to present ourselves before the Shift Captain; they told us that he ordered our firing." The suspended men immediately brought the situation to the attention of Fernández, who supposedly approved the firings. The workers also expressed dismay with Fernández: "Instead of carrying out his mission, he informed us that we should present ourselves as witnesses on behalf of the Manager Díaz, and that afterwards, we would immediately be reinstated in our jobs." The workers refused; "As it was impossible to tolerate such an inequity, we responded to him that we were ready to declare as witnesses, but not in his [Díaz's] favor, because we would have to say the whole truth," they wrote. Catavi's workers informed the federation's leadership that the delegate appeared not to be leaving and asked for a commission to assist in presenting testimony.[22]

Federation men immediately set out for Catavi, but they had traveled less than a half-mile when they happened on the government delegate. Fernández shamelessly asked why they had not presented any testimony that morning. The activists promised to soon have witnesses. In Catavi they found over one hundred men prepared to walk to Uncía to testify but took only twenty-five. After two days of evasion, the federation finally pinned down Fernández. They presented him a copy of their demands and a battery of questions to guide their witnesses' testimony. The delegate—after much arm-twisting—interviewed four men. He did not use the federation's questions and refused to record any testimony hostile to Díaz and the Tin Company of Llallagua. Fernández then declared that he was feeling ill and returned to Catavi and the Chilean mining company.[23]

Infuriated by the government investigator's obvious bias, the federation resolved to send its own commission to confer directly with President Saavedra. The delegation consisted of Gumercindo Rivera, a federation vice president; Marcián Arana, representing La Salvadora Mining Company workers; Juan L. Sotomayor, a delegate from the Tin Company of Llallagua; and Melquiades Maldonado, representing Llallagua and Uncía's artisans.[24] Despite the dispiriting experience with Fernández, the commission's instructions showed a surprising faith in liberal-democratic institutions. They read, "We have faith in the justice of our cause and more faith in the acts of our Government."[25]

The union delegates left northern Potosí by train on May 16. They arrived in La Paz the next day and met with the president on May 18.[26] The men placed a copy of the union's demands directly into President Saavedra's hands. The eight-point petition sought to defend the federation's right to organize in the face of unrelenting company persecution. In addition, the union continued to push for Emilio Díaz's deportation; the petition identified him as an inveterate opponent of unionization and labeled him "an unwanted person by the laboring element." Among Díaz's offenses the union cited "his despotism, his abuses, and his depressing outrages against the national labor movement." The federation also criticized Germán Noya, the Tin Company of Llallagua's lawyer. Unlike Díaz, Noya was Bolivian, and the union attacked him for defending the interests of a Chilean company over the "national dignity of his compatriots." The federation also assailed Díaz's underlings as "blind instruments of abuse and tyranny." The workers singled out three security guards, accusing them of "brutal and dishonest words" directed at workers' wives. In the petition's final points, the union laid out steps it hoped the government would take to ensure labor's right to organize in northern Potosí. The activists sought the reinstatement of fifteen workers fired from the Tin Company of Llallagua. They called for unmolested access to that company's dependencies for the "free development" of their "ideas, organization, and negotiation." They demanded legal recognition by the Tin Company of Llallagua and La Salvadora Mining Company. They sought guarantees against "hostilities" and demanded "legal meetings inside the camps." Finally, the federation assured the government that it sought only the "improvement of the working class," that the propaganda accusing the Central Labor Federation of Uncía of "pernicious political goals" was nothing more than "calumnious and biased accusation."[27] The meeting with President Saavedra lasted around fifty minutes, and Gumercindo Rivera reported a positive reception by the country's chief executive.[28]

After meeting the president, the federation delegates visited Francisco Iraizós, the minister of government. This meeting and subsequent encounters left the commission with a poor impression of Iraizós. Rivera reported that the minister did not know what a mining camp looked like or how one was managed. The commission met again with Iraizós on May 19; the minister was evasive. A third meeting on May 21 again resolved nothing, and the delegates were asked to return the next morning. The commissioners informed Iraizós that they could no longer extend their stay in La Paz and would seek to return to Uncía the following afternoon.[29]

When the commissioners visited the Ministry of Government again on the morning of May 22, they insisted on a written resolution of their petition. The insistence angered Iraizós, but his office drafted a biased document and sought to force the activists to sign. The men objected. The "resolution" denied the deportation of the Tin Company of Llallagua's manager; "It is not yet time to apply the law of residence to Sr. Emilio Díaz, but the Government will exercise its influence to improve relations between him and the workers," it read. The minister agreed to seek the firing of security guards responsible for abusing workers, and he promised to pressure the company to rehire fired workers. On the critical point of recognition of the federation by the mining companies, the government disappointed by adopting management's position that the companies would accept the formation of only those workers' federations "with elements belonging to each mining camp." The government, that is, denied the federation regional unity and unity across company lines.[30]

The ministry prepared a document for the delegates to sign. The scripted response read, "On the different points of the petition that we presented in our capacity as commissioners of the Central Labor Federation of Uncía, it is our pleasure to inform you Sr. Minister our absolute agreement with the accords reached." The commissioners stood in total disagreement with the statement. Forced to sign, they wrote just above their signatures, "We sign under duress, making it known that we completely reject this resolution."[31]

As soon as the commissioners left the building, police detained them. The police released the men but required them to check in twice a day at the La Paz police station, once in the morning and once in the afternoon. The commissioners immediately went to the home of José Paravicini, a senator from the department of Potosí, to complain. The senator promised to talk with the president. The delegates then returned to the Ministry of Government to demand an explanation and to request that the government pay for their extended stay in the capital. Minister Iraizós rejected the request—both parties now despised the other. Finally, at nine in the evening, the commissioners received word that President Saavedra had retired the "higher order" keeping them in La Paz. They made the return trip to Oruro the following day, May 23. By then, government support of the companies had made some kind of conflict inevitable.[32]

CONFRONTATION

While the Ministry of Government imposed bureaucratic delays on the federation's delegates in La Paz, the union's position in northern Potosí deteriorated. The military began a substantial deployment to the region. In La Paz the federation's commissioners received only limited instructions from northern Potosí. Gumercindo Rivera later claimed that someone was intercepting and suppressing the correspondence.[33] Conversely, the federation in Uncía found itself cut off from its delegates, with the silence creating suspicion of the government's motives.

A call from La Paz for more union negotiators and the arrival of troops stimulated the federation's paranoia. On May 19 union president Guillermo Gamarra issued a circular to the country's labor organizations, writing, "I inform you in the name of the Federation that the Government has resolved to expel from the breast of the Fatherland the principal leaders of our Directory, slyly calling them to La Paz." Gamarra continued, "Today an armed detachment from Challapata should arrive. As soon as our leaders are imprisoned, we will call a general strike, advising you of the act so that you might cooperate in the defense of labor's cause that is unfortunately at the mercy of the caprice and influence of the Llallagua Company, especially Emilio Díaz. The town in general and the working element are indignant about the hostile disposition against the Federation."[34] A telegram dated May 21 elaborated on the union's misgivings, but federation delegates in La Paz never received the missive: "Please contact the Minister of Development and ask him why Secretary Fernández has been called there [La Paz], as you have broad powers to discuss the petition. We believe it is a trap." The federation continued, "If you note evasiveness on the part of the President of the Republic, return immediately. At this moment two military squadrons are arriving."[35] The government had begun maneuvering to protect the mining companies.

As the federation struggled to understand the government's intentions, Minister of Development Adolfo Flores made a surprise appearance in northern Potosí, staying as a guest of the Tin Company of Llallagua. The visit gave Emilio Díaz a chance to stage an elaborate production with obedient and seemingly happy workers. When federation leaders visited Minister Flores, he seemed not to know that Catavi and Uncía were different towns. The federation eventually convinced him to travel to Uncía; during the visit workers met with Flores in the city's municipal theater. After the gathering the federation's leaders invited the minister to the Francia Hotel for a drink. Flores declined, explaining that he had an engagement with Francisco Blieck, La Salvadora Mining Company's manager. Flores's final report led to the deployment of additional troops to the region.[36]

A collection of telegrams from La Salvadora Mining Company preserves the maneuvering of northern Potosí's mining companies with the government. La Salvadora company's administration began a series of telegram conferences just as Central Labor Federation of Uncía delegates were making their trip to La Paz. On May 17 Pablo Pacheco, in the company's Oruro offices, exchanged telegrams with the company manager in Uncía, Francisco Blieck. Pacheco was also in contact with Emilio Díaz of the Tin Company of Llallagua. Díaz reported, "The laborers are completely disorganized in Catavi; the workers occupy themselves with meetings and constant correspondence with the Uncía agitators." Díaz also complained that several Uncía merchants were supporting the workers with money, and he asked Pacheco to contact the president and request soldiers from Challapata, Oruro. If the chief executive failed to provide "government protection," Díaz proposed "suspending operations" until all was peaceful and "reorganizing with other elements." Blieck reported that La Salvadora Mining Company workers continued "in their labors without apparently concerning themselves with the Federation" but believed that, were the federation to order an uprising in Llallagua, they would "probably participate." Blieck also reported rumors about ulterior motives: "There are merchants in Uncía that support the Federation with their money because of personal animosity toward Díaz with whom they are involved in a lawsuit." Blieck did not yet favor suspending operations—some federation leaders were in La Paz, and the danger of violence was low. He did favor the increased security of the army.[37]

On May 18 Pablo Pacheco and Francisco Blieck discussed the impending visit of Minister of Development Adolfo Flores. Pacheco had hoped to escort Flores from Oruro to Uncía but could not because President Saavedra had summoned him to La Paz. Instead, Blieck planned to travel from Uncía to Huanuni to meet with Flores and accompany him. The mining company furnished the minister with cars to make the trip. Pacheco recommended to Blieck that he "do everything possible" to help the minister "understand . . . the situation," especially "the hostile propaganda of the union and its leaders": "Make him take note of the necessity of stationing a cavalry squadron for some time." As Pacheco prepared for his trip to La Paz, he laid out the company's official response to federation demands: "It has to be fought, accepting only that which is reasonable and does not cause difficulties for the Company."[38]

Two days later Pacheco and Blieck communicated their satisfaction with President Saavedra's and Minister Flores's resolve to crack down on union activism in northern Potosí. The minster of development impressed Pacheco. "He seemed determined to take the necessary steps to repress the type of subversion that Federation members seek to carry out and to capture and expel the agitators," Pacheco reported. The president also showed himself sympathetic to company concerns and ordered a cavalry company from Challapata to northern Potosí. Both men agreed to keep secret the army's imminent arrival.[39] The federation eventually learned of the reinforcements but could do little to prevent their deployment.

With government reinforcements, La Salvadora Mining Company developed a more confrontational stance. In turn, the federation began employing more forceful language. On May 21 Pacheco informed Blieck, "The members of the federation, seeing that the Minister has not listened to them, are threatening a strike." He noted that the federation continued to insist on Díaz's dismissal, a demand that Pacheco categorized as "absurd." Blieck responded by observing that a strike might end up "producing divisions" inside the federation. Pacheco concurred and added, "I do not believe that said federation would succeed in influencing our workers. It would be a movement of just a few who could then be identified; the good people would not tolerate a strike of one or two days, and I hope that the troublemakers would then be isolated." Blieck concluded that he was "disposed to force the situation then, informing the workers of the Company's firm resolve not to be influenced by the threats" that the federation had made.[40]

On May 22 the army began its deployment to northern Potosí. With no word from their delegates in La Paz and the failure of negotiations, the Central Labor Federation of Uncía began seeking allies in case of an attack. They wrote the Workers' Labor Federation in Oruro to complain of certain points in the government's response: "the unprecedented stance of the Government that has come to sow nervousness among the laboring element of this mining settlement, sending military units of distinct types as if they were trying to repress a movement for rebellion." The federation's leaders added that the companies were trying to "dissolve this Federation with all the means that money and political influence place in the hands of [the workers'] eternal class enemies." They claimed to know of a government plan "to exile from the bosom of the fatherland the principal members of the Directory of this Federation, . . . to suffer nostalgia for the Fatherland, and to taste the bitter bread of ostracism." Despite the threat, they asserted a stout resolution: "Our comrades are resolved not to renounce their opinions even in the face of the traitorous noose that the hand of Capital has raised against this Institution. It does not matter. We will continue firm in our duty." The union warned its Oruro allies, "As soon as they detain some member of the Labor Federation here, we will raise a voice of alarm: 'Strike,' as a sign of protest."[41] The federation sent a similar missive to the Railway Federation, this one containing a darkly prophetic observation: "The honor and determination of our comrades to defend their rights has, and will have, the strength of granite, and only machine-gun fire could silence our voices of condemnation."[42]

May 22 was a busy day for the companies and the military. La Salvadora Mining Company's Pacheco and Blieck corresponded several times to make arrangements to receive the army in northern Potosí. The government had activated the Ballivián Regiment in Challapata to seize control of the situation. A special train left Oruro on the morning of May 22 to pick up the regiment and transport it to Machacamarca, where the soldiers switched trains, traveling through the night to arrive in Uncía on May 23. The company expected 18 to 20 officers and around 220 soldiers and servants. Pacheco advised Blieck to prevent the federation from "discovering much" about what was going on.[43] The company was also coordinating closely with the Tin Company of Llallagua's Emilio Díaz. Blieck and Díaz agreed to divide the soldiers equally between Catavi and Uncía to better protect both companies.[44]

The companies sought to receive the military in relative luxury and worked to win the sympathy of officers and soldiers assigned to the region. Díaz ordered Catavi's schools emptied so that soldiers might be housed in the buildings. Díaz informed his subordinates, "For the lodgings of the officers, I have today purchased eight cots and five complete beds, sheets and blankets, a lavatory set, chairs, etc. that I am transporting. Add to the furniture in each room a washbasin, taking them from the employees' houses. Assign the necessary personnel to do a detailed cleaning of all of the mentioned bedrooms." The company did not skimp on food. "The company store should take care of the troops' food, and everything should be of the highest quality and abundant," ordered Díaz. "The commanders and officers will eat in the administration's dining room; you shall order a cook and servants to be ready to attend them," he continued. Díaz ordered one of his subordinates, a Sr. Scott, to "accompany them at the table and to attend to them personally at all times," leaving aside his usual work. For the enlisted men, Díaz ordered company carpenters to construct thirty to forty bunks, two or three outhouses, and three large washbasins. He also ordered the broken windows of the schools housing soldiers repaired.[45]

Pablo Pacheco, at La Salvadora Mining Company, wanted to make sure that Díaz did not show him up. He noted, "Díaz is sparing no expense; he has given orders to treat them [the soldiers] like kings." Pacheco feared that, given the division of the troops, there would "surely be a comparison made between how one company or the other treats them." Pacheco advised Blieck to house the troops in a local school, since a warehouse used in the past had generated complaints: "The officer of the guard that was there before had complained that the warehouse is very humid and that two soldiers became ill." As for the officers, Pacheco wanted to house them in the company offices or the Hotel Miraflores. Blieck responded that the warehouse really was the best location for the soldiers. For the officers he had reserved the administration's offices. Blieck observed that the soldiers could "sleep on the ground covered with hay and blankets." Pacheco worried about relations with the military and ordered the construction of 100 bunks, even if the carpenters had to work "night and day."[46] The attention paid off. Officers deployed to northern Potosí came to sympathize with the companies.

On May 23, the day the military arrived in northern Potosí, the federation's delegates to La Paz returned to Oruro. They immediately had to defend their negotiations to federation members in the departmental capital. The press, especially those papers allied to President Saavedra, had published edited versions of the "agreements" composed by the Ministry of Government. The four commissioners explained that they had been forced to sign but had done so noting their complete disagreement with the accords. The delegates also confronted the fact that fired union members had not yet returned to work.[47]

While in Oruro the delegates wrote politicians and union leaders about the issue. One telegram went to Ricardo Soruco Ipiña, the congressman from Cochabamba once closely associated with the labor movement but now more inclined toward President Saavedra. Gumercindo Rivera wrote, "Our fired comrades are without means. I beg you to meet with the Minister of Government and ask that he carry out the agreed-to accords and order the companies to return their jobs."[48] Congressman Soruco met with Minister Iraizós and responded, "The return of fired comrades is guaranteed, and you can return to your jobs with this security. Additionally, the Political Constitution and Government protection guarantee the freedom to organize. There is no need to thank me, as all I am doing is carrying out the duty that my proletarian convictions demand."[49] The congressman obviously did not know what was really happening in northern Potosí.

The commission returned to Uncía on May 25. A large crowd of workers and artisans met the delegates at the train station and accompanied them to the municipal theater to hear their report. In the following days another government investigator arrived in northern Potosí, but this official produced nothing substantial for the union. Despite the return of the federation's commission, the union's position continued to deteriorate.[50]

With the military ensconced in northern Potosí, the companies began discussing means to dismantle the federation with a minimum of collateral damage. A telegraph conference between Pacheco and Blieck on the morning of May 24 focused almost exclusively on Guillermo Gamarra, the federation's president. The managers expressed embarrassment that Gamarra worked for La Salvadora Mining Company, and Pacheco had felt government pressure to do something about his leadership. Pacheco wrote Blieck, "I believe it appropriate that you inform the president [Gamarra] that it is inconvenient for the Company that one of its workers is directing these movements; that he should renounce his position, or we will be obliged to suspend him." Pacheco claimed to oppose not Gamarra's membership in the federation but only his leadership, and he wanted Gamarra's name to disappear from federation correspondence with the government. In the event of a strike, Pacheco wanted to clean house: "Let it be understood that if they declare a strike, there will be an expulsion of all the bad elements that we can no longer tolerate." He added, "If Gamarra does not accept your insinuation, we will be obliged to fire him on the spot." The manager felt the company looked weak. He complained, "We are giving them reasons to treat us as very weak; that we are accommodating them."[51]

Blieck was not yet ready to take such an aggressive stance with Gamarra. He reported that the situation was "tranquil" but worried that "it could become something else" were the government to implement "its plans for intervention." Blieck agreed that the company "should not tolerate that the federation president continue his threatening propaganda against the Company" and that it was "time to stop his activities inside the Company." But he counseled patience, writing, "I already know that an invitation to leave the presidency will not be accepted by him. Then it would be necessary to suspend him, but then the Company would lose its advantageous position in the present conflict, giving them a reason for a strike, something that they have threatened up until now but will not carry out." Blieck wanted to wait and see how the federation responded to the government intervention, adding, "Only then will I take the necessary steps to fire the Federation president."[52]

Pacheco deferred to Blieck and asked him to counsel "the aforementioned president to think about the damage that he is doing to the Company." Pacheco suggested employing paternalism—"ask him to look at it as a good worker of Sr. Patiño's Company; the damage that it could cause him [Gamarra]. It would be most appropriate for him to renounce the presidency without leaving his membership in the Federation, something that the company does not prohibit, and that another person from outside the Company assume leadership and responsibility for what might happen." Pacheco also believed that a strike would cause only a minimum of damage: "In the event of a conflict, I do not think that the Company will suffer more than a work stoppage, because this is a conflict fomented by those in town, and they have to support the Uncía Company's interests, because they will be the first to suffer in any case."[53]

Pacheco and Blieck again conferred later in the day, with Blieck sharing the results of his meeting with Gamarra. Blieck reported, "This afternoon, I had a long conversation with Gamarra, hinting at the grave responsibility he would bear for leading the federation's activities, and I tried to persuade him to renounce the presidency." According to Blieck, Gamarra "was disposed to do it but was afraid that his comrades might take vengeance on him, believing that he had been bought with money to renounce his office." Blieck continued, "I made him understand that it is quite likely that the Company will not accept the principal points in the petition presented, and that in that case, the Company will find itself obliged to fire those elements which have made common cause with the group from the town, whose only goal is to disturb the tranquility of the Companies." Gamarra gave Blieck the impression that much of the federation's rhetoric was a bluff. "Speaking of a general strike, which Gamarra had threatened in a telegram sent to the General Administration, he told me that he did not think it possible for the Federation to carry it out, in light of the fact that their number of followers would be insufficient," Blieck wrote. Pacheco closed the conference by expressing his regret that their "gestures of reconciliation" had "not produced results."[54]

The two administrators again conversed by telegraph on May 25. More upbeat than the day before, Pacheco reported that the federation was having difficulty crafting alliances: "I must inform you that the crescendo of support they expected from other federations is escaping them, and I have learned that the Railway Federation of Oruro and that of Uyuni have decided not to take part in the invitation made by the federated workers of Uncía, and that it is becoming clear to all that the group in Uncía is made up of townspeople and not the Company's miners."[55] The federation lost allies in northern Potosí, too. At that same time, the government summoned Subprefect David Michel to La Paz and replaced him. Llallagua police chief Gerardo Tórrez Ruiz was also stripped of his authority.[56] The companies delighted in any dip in the federation's prospects.

The giddiness did not last. On May 26 Pacheco and Blieck again conferred but expressed frustration with a situation that showed no improvement. The two complained of federation inflexibility, yet the companies never modified their own stance. Pacheco and Blieck still refused to recognize the federation. "The leadership of the aforesaid Labor Federation are townspeople from Uncía that live dependent on the earnings of the miner and his transactions with the town of Uncía," Pacheco wrote; "I judge that we are like we were at the start, without having advanced in absolutely anything, and with the enormous cost to the Company of attending to the contingent of troops." The failed negotiations between the government and the federation confused the mining company. Pacheco and Blieck apparently did not know that the minister of government's "agreement" with federation delegates was a one-sided imposition, leading Blieck to complain of vacillation. The two thought that the federation commission had agreed to break the union in two and purge the artisan element. "In light of this," Blieck reported, "I made note of this in my response to Minister Iraizós, that there was not agreement among even the workers." The manager insisted that the company would "not recognize a Federation made up of elements foreign to it." It wanted only a union the company could control. Blieck wrote, "The Company rejects a federation made up of foreign elements, but it would not oppose the formation of an internal grouping made up of its own elements, being protected against anarchist agitation by means of statutes that should have the approval of the Government and should have the positive consent of the Companies." If future negotiations occurred, Blieck wanted them held in La Paz or Oruro, "but under no circumstances in Uncía, where the Federation is under the influence of the mutual fear and distrust which reigns among elements of this class."[57] The companies were determined to dismember broad solidarity among the urban popular classes.

With the entrenchment of capital and labor, the government took the next decisive step. At five in the evening on May 30, Uncía's police chief, Nicolás Sánchez, sought to capture the federation's secretary, Ernesto Fernández, escort him to the train station, and deport him from northern Potosí. A handful of nearby workers confronted the police and demanded to see a written order of arrest. When Sánchez failed to produce the paperwork, the workers forced Fernández's release. The police chief informed the military, and a squad of soldiers began searching for the secretary.[58] The night of the bungled arrest, La Salvadora Mining Company's Pablo Pacheco and an underling named Naeter discussed the incident in a telegraph conference. Naeter noted that the reaction of the popular classes was immediate: "Town and workers have opposed the detention of Fernández; they protested after leaving work." Gumercindo Rivera called for a general meeting of the federation to discuss the attempted arrest.[59]

Despite the manhunt, Fernández attended that evening's meeting.[60] The gathering drafted a short telegram to the Workers' Labor Federation of Oruro and the Railway Federation. "Just now the authorities of this location have committed abuses without name; they have tried to arrest the Secretary General of the Federation, comrade Fernández, and judging from the hostilities that have just begun, we believe that we will be the victims of despotism and injustice," they wrote. The workers and artisans closed their message with a plea for solidarity: "In the hope of powerful assistance from you, our sister Federations; we are comrades."[61] The federation also dispatched a delegation to meet with Potosí's public prosecutor, then staying at Uncía's Francia Hotel as a special representative of the government. The official refused to recognize the union, claiming that the federation's statutes had never received government approval. He also expressed anger at the popular classes' refusal to submit to government authority.[62]

Tensions rose following the attempted arrest. On the evening of May 31, Pacheco and Naeter again conferred; this time a company lawyer named Iporre joined the conference. Naeter and Iporre informed Pacheco that they had submitted a legal petition "making concrete accusations, soliciting an order of arrest." "Given the gravity of the case," they said, "we suggested to the Judge that he imprison the leaders." They wanted the government to employ the full force of the police and military to avoid what had happened the previous day with Fernandez.[63] The federation also sought to fortify its position. The body empowered two emissaries to seek solidarity with labor federations across Bolivia. The union named Melquiades Maldonado ambassador to federations in Oruro and La Paz. Ernesto Fernández was appointed to carry out the same mission in Cochabamba, Sucre, Potosí, and Uyuni.[64] Maldonado's and Fernández's instructions empowered them to sign "a PACT OF UNION AND WORKER SOLIDARITY with similar Federations." The emissaries were to formulate "a special code with each of the allied Federations to give mutual warning of an emergency or a declared strike."[65] The union also sought to make one final overture to the national government. For this they nominated trusted local notables not affiliated with the federation: Uncía's priest, Fernando Gonzales, and the subprefect of Potosí's Charcas Province, Trinidad Aguilar. All four emissaries left Uncía on June 1—the very day President Saavedra declared a state of siege to smother the union movement in northern Potosí.[66]

The president's declaration covered the departments of Potosí, Oruro, Cochabamba, La Paz, Chuquisaca, and Santa Cruz—that is, almost the entire country. The government wanted to prevent inconvenient expressions of solidarity with the embattled activists in Uncía. Saavedra explained the need for the temporary suspension of civil liberties, proclaiming, "Some parts of the Republic have presented evident symptoms of deep political commotion that are involving working elements in a movement for the general alteration of public order." The president attributed radical political motives to the Central Labor Federation of Uncía, mentioning the "manifest intervention of anarchist agitators and revolutionary politicos." The government veiled its intervention in terms that implied the paternalist protection of nonunion workers. Saavedra declared, "It is necessary to succor the rights of laborers who wish to work tranquilly and the interests of Companies of undeniable industrial importance."[67] The state of siege stifled the ability of labor federations elsewhere to respond to the crackdown in northern Potosí.

On June 2 the military began patrols through Uncía's streets.[68] The state of siege prohibited federation gatherings, but the interim subprefect, Lieutenant Colonel José Villegas, invited union leaders to a meeting on June 3. The officer reportedly assured the activists that he believed them to be honorable men fighting for a just cause and promised to forward his opinion to the central government. In private, the military and the companies sought to persuade federation leaders to abandon their comrades. Major Guillén invited federation vice president Gumercindo Rivera to La Perla Pastry Shop to discuss the tailor's activism. The officer knew Rivera from the artisan's time as an army conscript; Rivera had served in Guillén's regiment. The major wondered at Rivera's position of leadership in the federation, considering his relative prosperity as a tailor. The subprefect, Lieutenant Colonel Villegas, eventually joined the conversation. The two officers advised Rivera to take a vacation—visit Cochabamba for a couple of months—and return to Uncía when things had settled down. Rivera refused the suggestion. As for federation president Guillermo Gamarra, La Salvadora Mining Company promised him money and a letter of recommendation if he would abandon the union. Gamarra, too, declined.[69]

The military and police began arresting federation members and suspected sympathizers at 9:45 a.m. on June 4. They first detained a local lawyer, Gregorio Vicenti. Five minutes later they seized Gumercindo Rivera. The government also arrested the local Republican Party president,

Meltión Goytia, and Silverio Saravia, a judge. At 11:00 a.m. two military officers and La Salvadora Mining Company's manager visited Guillermo Gamarra at his place of work in the company's machine shop. The three invited Gamarra to the subprefecture to talk over federation demands. Numerous workers counseled their president not to go, but Gamarra dismissed their suspicions. Once in the subprefecture he discovered the four men already arrested. The detained men insisted on composing telegrams of protest to President Saavedra, the minister of government, their senators, and several congressmen, but acting subprefect Villegas suppressed the telegrams. The military then locked all five men in an interior room of the subprefecture.[70]

When news of the arrests spread, workers began gathering in the Plaza Alonso de Ibañez before the subprefecture. At four in the afternoon Emilio Díaz arrived; the Tin Company of Llallagua's manager was escorted by a cavalry detachment flying small Bolivian flags from their lances. The crowd reacted with catcalls and indignation. At five o'clock the day-shift workers finished their labors and flooded the plaza, adding their numbers to those already gathered. The growing body of men, women, and children continued to demand the release of the detainees, shouting at the soldiers: "Shameless men, you have sold out to the companies!" To calm the workers, the military forced Guillermo Gamarra and Gumercindo Rivera to address the crowd. The two issued defiant declarations. Soon after, the shooting began.[71]

Major José V. Ayoroa submitted a report to President Saavedra two days after the massacre. In it he claimed that he had addressed the gathered workers on the night of the killings—but he made no mention of Gamarra's and Rivera's speeches. Major Ayoroa claimed to have assured the crowd that the government sympathized with them: "The Government is always desirous of caring for the interests of working people, constantly working to attend to their needs and demands, proposing to Congress a law about workplace accidents that will be approved in the next legislative session." The officer said that he twice ordered the crowd to disperse, but to no avail: "As night fell, they grew more spirited and sought to defeat us and take the prisoners from us." The major claimed the workers attacked the subprefecture with "bullets and dynamite." According to Ayoroa, his soldiers fired over two thousand warning shots into the air over the course of a half-hour: "Because of that, the people reinforced their attack with greater energy, and before seeing ourselves totally defeated, I was obliged to make use of my machine gun, much to my own dismay." The major estimated that the gunfire killed four and wounded eleven. Of the wounded he wrote, "Two of these latter died, and, according to the doctors, three more will die; the others will heal enough to return to work, except one made handicapped because they amputated his leg."[72]

Ayoroa's account differed somewhat from that of Gumercindo Rivera, held prisoner in the subprefecture at the time of the shooting. According to Rivera, he and Major Ayoroa were exchanging heated words in the government office when a pistol or revolver shot sounded outside. Hearing the report, Rivera claimed, Ayoroa rushed out and ordered his men to open fire on the crowd. Initially the soldiers fired into the air, but Ayoroa commanded them to target the people. According to Rivera, the major himself operated the army's only machine gun. The crowd rushed into the side streets, seeking cover in whatever homes might let them in. With the workers scattered, the military ordered all doors closed until morning. Rivera acknowledged that the subprefecture was bombed and had its windows blown out, but he said that the explosion occurred after the crowd had dispersed. The union vice president suspected a conspiracy—specifically, that the initial shot was a signal by company provocateurs and that the bombing was a postmassacre justification. Despite this suspicion, Rivera noted that the violent events surprised and terrified company managers and lawyers in the subprefecture. Rivera confirmed Major Ayoroa's account of four killed in the plaza. The bodies were brought into the subprefecture, where union leaders might see them. Rivera identified the dead men as Manuel Leiza Tapia, Daniel Palomino, Víctor Mendoza, and Pablo Montaño.[73]

News of the massacre reached Oruro at 10:00 p.m., when representatives of La Salvadora Mining Company cabled their superiors in the departmental capital. Their telegram read, "At seven o'clock we were attacked in the Subprefecture; also there, the military commanders and the managers of both Companies. They attacked with dynamite and bullets. Foresee situation dominated by army troops." The telegram continued, "Major Ayoroa indicates that the dawn will find him in Oruro with his troops escorting prisoners, and with that, he has completed his mission."[74] Ayoroa ended up spending several days in northern Potosí cleaning up after the massacre.

At 2:30 a.m. on June 5 a truck from La Salvadora Mining Company arrived at the subprefecture to transport the four dead men for clandestine burial.[75] Major Ayoroa later wrote that "the night of the combat the cadavers were buried to avoid further angering the town." But the bodies did not remain hidden for long. As the commander explained to President Saavedra, "The next day they were exhumed by the workers who then reburied them with ostentatious ceremony in the presence of workers . . . from Llallagua and Catavi." Ayoroa saw a conspiracy in the funeral, with federation members trying "to make it look like Uncía had sacrificed itself for their fellow comrades as a kind of seed of reciprocity for the future."[76] Gumercindo Rivera further detailed the honors rendered to the four fallen workers. After exhuming the bodies, he said, the workers moved them to the reception hall of the Albina Patiño Society, a mutual aid society sponsored by La Salvadora Mining Company. That night the federation held a vigil for the four men. On June 6 the union organized a massive funeral attended by workers and artisans from all over northern Potosí.[77]

As for the prisoners, after the massacre the military moved the five men to a room in the Francia Hotel. At 3:15 a.m. soldiers took the prisoners at gunpoint to a warehouse being used as an informal barracks. At dawn a train took the men to Machacamarca. From there another train took them to Oruro. On the outskirts of Oruro the military put the prisoners into cars rented by La Salvadora Mining Company. The five eventually arrived in Corque, Carangas Province's capital, on June 6. The government planned to use the provincial town for the long-term detention of union leadership.[78] The companies and President Saavedra's administration would smother the Central Labor Federation of Uncía's remnants in northern Potosí.

AFTERMATH

Major Ayoroa remained in Uncía for several days following the massacre, his presence meant to stifle the federation's simmering anger. On June 5 the union declared a general strike, but the government sought to break the strike and impose a resolution favorable to the companies. Major Ayoroa and Lieutenant Colonel Villegas continued in their unflinching support of capital. In a June 6 report to President Saavedra, Ayoroa parroted the companies' arguments about the federation. "Even though there exists a majority of workers with the spirit and desire to work, there is a group of instigators that induces them to subversion without themselves [the instigators] being miners but townspeople . . . belonging to other trades," he wrote. The military man sought to pin events on the federation's secretary, Ernesto Fernández. "Before the month of May the workers did not have the idea to federate; that began with the arrival of this Peruvian citizen whom the Manager Díaz fired from his job, and that is when the campaign against this latter man began," Ayoroa argued. The officer judged the previous "resolution" imposed by the government—he labeled it a "friendly accord agreed to by the workers and the Companies"—dead. "Only energetic action will here end . . . the topic of strikes," he wrote. Ayoroa further claimed that the workers sought "to form something like a soviet with obvious Bolshevik tendencies."[79] President Saavedra supported the military in its pacification of northern Potosí.

In fact, the government imposed only cosmetic concessions on the companies. On June 6 the Tin Company of Llallagua's Emilio Díaz telegraphed his superiors in Santiago, Chile. The strike had idled the company's facilities, but Díaz expected to resume operations in a couple of days. He informed his bosses, "On the President of the Republic's instructions, the company has accepted three points from the Uncía Federation's list of demands: those that refer to the firing of three watchmen, the return of expelled workers, and permission to federate inside the company." Despite recent events, Díaz continued to argue that the federation appealed only to a minority. "There are workers that wish to work, but those federated with Uncía threaten to attack them," he wrote. The manager believed necessity would swiftly swing events in the company's favor. "Strike tranquil until now, calculating that workers cannot maintain it more than two days, that is until the eighth," Díaz reasoned.[80] La Salvadora Mining Company also embraced the government's proposed concessions. Pablo Pacheco and Francisco Blieck informed their own superiors on June 6 that they had "addressed themselves to the town and a gathering of miners in the same vein, [emphasizing] the victory won by the town," which had seen "the acceptance of the majority of its demands."[81] The strike continued until June 9, but the government had torpedoed the federation's principal demands. Authorities split the association in two, prohibiting a union of workers at La Salvadora Mining Company and the Tin Company of Llallagua. Artisans were expelled from both bodies. And Emilio Díaz remained in control in Catavi.[82]

Government persecution of the federation's leadership continued after the massacre. From Corque union sympathizers Gregorio Vicenti and Silverio Saravia were exiled to Arica, Chile. Meltión Goytia was released. In Oruro the prefect Aniceto Arce arrested federation members Primitivo Albarracín, Néstor Camacho, and Ernesto Fernández when they appeared to inquire about the imprisoned Rivera and Gamarra. The prefect labeled Albarracín, Camacho, and Fernández "professional agitators."[83] Another union leader, Melquiades Maldonado, fled the country for Buenos Aires, Argentina. The government sent Albarracín and Camacho to Corque; Fernández was deported to his native Peru. Until late August the four union leaders in Corque were kept locked in the subprefecture and allowed only occasional walks around the town's plaza. They were not permitted to leave Corque until the end of December.[84] President Saavedra sent the four men a telegram on December 28, 1923, offering them a provisional release: "If you prefer not to leave the country, you can settle in Oruro without the right to return to Uncía or Llallagua under any circumstances."[85] The president sent a similar telegram to the Carangas subprefect but added, "If they prefer to leave the Republic, put them immediately on the Chilean border."[86] In January 1924, Oruro prefect Aniceto Arce allowed Gumercindo Rivera, Primitivo Albarracín, and Néstor Camacho to return to Uncía for fifteen days to "gather their property and arrange their business." The provincial subprefect had instructions to "keep an eye on the indicated workers" and ensure that they left "once their time [was] up."[87] Despite the continued persecution, the four men returned to activism in years to come.

Back in northern Potosí the mining companies worked to rebuild their former control. La Salvadora Mining Company sought to bribe and administer loyalty oaths to the Central Labor Federation of Uncía's new leaders. One document composed by company lawyers and presented to Mariano Beltrán and N. Balcázar read:

> The undersigned . . . in our capacity as leading members of this city's federation of workers: Over and done with are the questions maintained between the workers and La Salvadora Mining Company as a result of the strike that occurred on the fourth and the following days of the present month. As an express condition debated and agreed to with the Delegate of the Supreme Government, for our own persons and as representatives of the federation, so as to maintain order and mutual respect between the workers, the representatives of La Salvadora Company, and the professional personnel and the administration of it, we promise to be on our best behavior and guarantee not to meddle in any future issues like those currently being debated, and most importantly, we promise not to take part in workers' movements that go against the interests of the Company and its professional personnel.

Managers could not guarantee that Beltrán and Balcázar would sign but hoped to bribe them into doing so: "In case they do sign, we will give each one of them one month's salary."[88]

One month after the massacre the situation in Uncía had begun to stabilize in a manner favorable to the companies, but union activists had not completely given up. La Salvadora's Francisco Blieck reported on July 5 that, during the most recent payday, no one "collected dues for the Central Federation." But he added, "According to information that I have, they must have collected them in the town of Uncía, primarily by the tailor Julio Vargas." Tensions continued in the workplace. On July 4 one of the company's mechanics exchanged heated words with his supervisor. Blieck ascribed the argument to "the antagonism . . . between strikers and those employees who remained loyal to the Company during the recent strike." When the company suspended the worker, the chief of mechanics, Patricio Álvarez, immediately protested, "giving rise to another incident." Blieck intervened in support of his underlings, "calming tempers, but giving the definitive order that employees must maintain discipline in a strict and just manner." In Oruro Pablo Pacheco approved of Blieck's handling of the incident, which he thought demonstrated "the little respect" that the working people had for other employees, "much less for superior personnel like the administrator." Pacheco added, "[Blieck] should warn the chief Álvarez to avoid, from now on, incidents like the one" involving the suspended mechanic.[89] Álvarez eventually emerged as a worker firmly loyal to the administration despite the incident.

Because of lingering animosities, La Salvadora Mining Company hoped for a continued military presence, but the government inclined toward withdrawing the troops. The new commanding officer in the region, Major Guillén, had visited Francisco Blieck to inquire whether "the companies wished the presence of the military for more time." Blieck told the major that he did not "consider the situation completely tranquil" and "could not calculate the amount of time" before the outbreak of another strike. Pablo Pacheco made similar observations but had tired of repeated overtures to the government: "The companies will leave the decision to whatever the Government resolves, being tired of making continuous petitions to the authorities for the maintenance of the military in these places." Pacheco judged a precipitous withdrawal to be folly given the circumstances: "The situation is not tranquil, and . . . at any moment there might be an outbreak of another movement with worse consequences." Pacheco concluded by observing, "If the Government does not extend us aid with the presence of troops, we are going to have to take steps that we think prudent for security in the defense of our interests."[90]

Although the military and the companies insisted that the crowd had provoked the shootings, some correspondence in the massacre's wake indicated that a few officials worried about potential legal repercussions. In July 1923 Major José Ayoroa wrote La Salvadora Mining Company requesting a report on the violence composed by company lawyers. The officer also inquired after "any lawsuits that might have been filed against [the troops] in Uncía." Francisco Blieck promised to send Ayoroa the report, but the query about lawsuits confused the manager: "As far as I know, there has been no suit against the officers."[91] No one in the military was ever punished for the massacre.

The embers of discontent died slowly. At the end of July 1923, fears of a resurgent federation continued to haunt the companies. As Independence Day (August 6) approached, rumors that some workers were "threatening to carry out acts of violence, taking advantage of the holiday," worried La Salvadora Mining Company. Pablo Pacheco fulminated against "those bad elements" who remained to direct Uncía's labor federation, calling them "those who have caused us so many difficulties." Rumors suggested division among the workers. "They fear that a conflict might break out among the workers themselves, because these bad elements are hostile to those that have left the federation," Pacheco reported. Francisco Blieck tried to calm his colleague, writing, "The rumors about disturbances during the patriotic holiday have also come to my attention, but I have not given them any importance, because I consider them the gossip of idle people." Blieck did worry, though, that a new company union was slow to take shape. "I was informed about a certain antagonism that exists between the members of the new federation and the rest of the workers," he reported. Some workers did not trust the company union's leadership and refused to join the new federation, "alleging that the money charged for dues to the sum of Bs 1 every two weeks [would] benefit only the leaders." The workers had complained to the departmental prefect, and the prefect had barred the union from charging dues until receiving government approval of its statutes. The yellow union's president, the previously mentioned mechanic Patricio Álvarez, noted that a similar body in the Tin Company of Llallagua was already collecting dues. La Salvadora Mining Company eventually provided the company union's leaders with "copies of statutes of similar federations so that they might craft their own."[92]

During the 1920s the tin-mining region saw an enormous consolidation of capital, a consolidation that labor presciently attempted to parallel with its own organizing. In 1924 Simón I. Patiño revealed his ownership of the Tin Company of Llallagua. The announcement was the culmination of Patiño's secret, nine-year plan to buy a controlling stake in the rival company. In July Patiño created a new holding company, the Patiño Mines and Enterprises Consolidated, Inc., that officially merged the Tin Company of Llallagua, La Salvadora Mining Company, and the Machacamarca-Uncía Railway.[93] This union of northern Potosí's most important companies illustrates the consolidation of capital during the first few decades of the twentieth century. Yet when workers attempted a similar unification, they met with the bullets of the Bolivian army.

The creation of the Central Labor Federation of Uncía, the appeal to President Saavedra, and the workers' disbelief at the violent repression of their movement illustrate labor's ideological and organizational development during the first two decades of the twentieth century; the events of 1923 drove home the need to strengthen labor's independence and ideology. In Uncía's wake workers began to express a growing skepticism of traditional oligarchic parties and the government. The violent confrontation between miners and the military established a pattern of relations that would dominate Bolivia's history for the rest of the twentieth century. The workers never completely extirpated oligarchic liberal-democratic thought, but after 1923, the appeal of alternate ideologies—socialism, Marxism, and anarcho-syndicalism—grew stronger.

The government and the mining companies occasionally unleashed sudden assaults on the working class, but the campaigns were never thoroughgoing or prolonged. Union activists could move and reestablish themselves elsewhere. Some three years after the Uncía Massacre, federation president Guillermo Gamarra wrote a La Paz newspaper to criticize the paper's interpretation of the event: "Your newspaper labels us 'agitators,' fine. There will be agitators in Bolivia as long as the working people suffer misery and hunger; there will agitators if no one puts a stop to the indescribable abuses of capitalist gentlemen."[94] The work of activists such as Gamarra continued throughout the 1920s.

CHAPTER 6

The Vicissitudes of
Republican Rule

ON APRIL 7, 1924, Oruro prefect Aniceto Arce wrote the Antofagasta-Bolivia Railway noting that the Railway Federation had complained about an "overseer in the north workshop" who harassed workers in that section, "giving the example of the employee Nícanor Terrazas, who was suspended from his job for the reason that he left his labors for a few minutes to drink a cup of tea." The prefect asked the company to use greater diplomacy and tact. "These incidents might provoke a protest and maybe even grave reprisals by the working elements because the spirit of solidarity might take them to the extreme of declaring a strike," Arce wrote. He asked the company to "issue instructions to remedy these rigorous measures and to avoid them in the future."[1] The government had violently repressed a drive for unionization in northern Potosí in 1923; now, in the Uncía Massacre's wake, the government sought to repair its relationship with organized labor. Officials attempted to avoid confrontation, especially over minor incidents that threatened to shut down critical industries such as the railroads.

Elements of the Republican Party repented the naked use of violence in Uncía and sought to win back working-class political support. The strong economy of the mid- to late 1920s helped; the mining industry experienced steady growth until the economic collapse at the decade's end. Despite the Republicans' courting of organized labor, however, the workers continued to suffer from a pervasive disconnection between the written law and its haphazard enforcement. Thus, although the vigorous economy of the mid-1920s minimized discontent, labor organizations continued to expand, and not all working-class activists were willing to forget the lessons of Uncía.

REPUBLICAN PARTY REFORM

Despite its heavy-handed response to the strike in Uncía, the Republican Party continued to court artisans and workers, charting a more diplomatic course after the massacre. Bautista Saavedra and Hernando Siles, the two Republican presidents during the 1920s, when tin was booming, both introduced legislation favorable to labor. The strategy met with some success until the economic bust at the decade's end.

Bolivia's mining industry reached staggering levels of production in the mid- to late 1920s. Following a downturn between 1920 and 1922, the value of tin rose steadily from Bs 2,421 per long ton in 1922 to Bs 3,989 in 1926. From that peak the mineral's value fell over the next five years to the Great Depression level of Bs 1,593 per long ton in 1931. The value of Bolivia's tin exports peaked at Bs 151,912,576 in 1927. After that the industry sought to compensate for tin's declining value with an increased production volume that reached 47,081 long tons in 1929. The bottom fell out of the industry in 1930, when Bolivia produced only 38,733 long tons, worth a meager Bs 72,713,341.

While tin's value was rising, the mining industry continued an extended process of consolidation. By 1925 ten large companies accounted for 81 percent of Bolivia's tin production, yet even this statistic does not completely capture the level of industrial concentration that mining had reached by the mid-1920s. Mining companies owned by Simón I. Patiño in the Llallagua-Uncía region and in the settlement of Huanuni accounted for one-third of Bolivia's tin exports. The progressive consolidation of mining continued into the 1940s.[2]

Despite a fierce political rivalry, Presidents Bautista Saavedra and Hernando Siles pursued similar policies toward the mining industry and the labor movement. Immediately after the Uncía Massacre and during the related state of siege, President Saavedra clamped down on his opponents. In 1924 he crushed several minor political rebellions and eventually succeeded in calming the anger, if not erasing the memories, of the urban popular classes with a series of modest social reforms. During the final months of his presidency, he engineered the victory of a seemingly pliant successor in the election of May 1925. When the president-elect José Gabino Villanueva began to espouse an independent political line, Saavedra had the election annulled. This sparked a crisis within the Republican Party. Eventually, Saavedra accepted the elevation of a party rival, Hernando Siles, to the presidency and agreed to a comfortable exile in Europe. Hernando Siles, born in 1881 in the department of Chuquisaca, had studied law and eventually became rector of the state university in his native Sucre. Siles joined the Republican Party in 1920 and immediately allied himself with Saavedra, who was engaged in a power struggle with Daniel Salamanca for control of the party. Siles enjoyed an important following among younger party members and the military, and he played a pivotal role in imposing labor peace in northern Potosí in 1923—a peace hostile to the workers. Eventually, Saavedra came to resent Siles's growing popularity. When the 1925 election began to fall apart, a majority of the Republican Party imposed Siles's presidency on Saavedra. Siles took office in early 1926.[3] The new president would confront significant challenges and eventually failed during the Great Depression; no oligarchic politician had a sensible solution to the economic collapse.

Bautista Saavedra and the Republican Party legalized the right to strike in 1920, but only after organized labor had used the weapon to paralyze the economy in August of that year. Saavedra's laws sought to regulate and control strikes. In September 1920, therefore, the Republican Party junta, led by Saavedra, issued decrees legalizing the right to strike and establishing a system of labor arbitration. The junta also empanelled a committee to study potential labor reforms, though nothing came of the initiative. The historian Herbert Klein suggests that Saavedra initiated these policies primarily to create a base of support among the working class so he could outmaneuver his political rivals. In fact, however, the decrees followed powerful strikes that had unsettled the new Republican government. Saavedra's laws mainly sought to regulate worker activism and extend government control over the process. Once firmly entrenched in power, President Saavedra suggested even more reforms to Congress in September and November 1921. Congress substantially watered down the legislation before eventually adopting it.[4]

The way in which Bautista Saavedra's legalization sought to limit and regulate the strike can be seen in a 1922 confrontation between the Machacamarca-Uncía Railway Federation and Simón I. Patiño's company. Oruro prefect Tejada Fariñez wrote the federation's president on May 18, 1922, noting its decision to "declare a strike" if the Patiño company did not "favorably resolve the three points submitted for their consideration." The prefect continued, "It is not yet the moment to debate the justice of the petition to which you allude, for there exist established formalities to which one must adhere." Tejada explained the logic behind the government's limitation of the right to strike: "A strike, as you very well know, has consequences that affect not just the companies and the employees; no, there exists another entity named the public, which is the part that suffers the most and, as such, is the most interested in a favorable solution to conflicts that might occur." Tejada made reference to the Supreme Decree of September 29, 1920, which mandated, "Railway workers must announce to the political authorities with eight days anticipation their intention to declare a strike." The prefect noted, "In the current dispute between the Machacamarca-Uncía Railway Federation and Simón I. Patiño's company, that had not occurred." Tejada declared that both sides had eight days to form a council of reconciliation, and if that did not "produce an understanding," then an "arbitration court" would hear the matter and "pronounce a binding decision." The prefect proceeded to chastise the federation: "I hence see that the Machacamarca-Uncía Railway Federation is ignoring the Regulatory Decree whose precepts I have cited, placing itself at the margins of the law, and occasioning a labor movement that disturbs the harmony and order of its neighbors, a stance that one cannot tolerate and which will be repressed according to the law." Tejada then reassured the federation of his benign goals, saying, "It is not my intention to in any way harm the workers"; he wanted only, he claimed, to "remind the railway workers that they should adjust their actions to the already indicated dispositions." The prefect concluded: "As for my part and carrying out my duty, I have resolved to send a commission to which you should name a Delegate to immediately form a Council of Reconciliation."[5] Here as elsewhere, then, the government wanted to circumscribe labor's autonomy.

A populace increasingly versed in protest tactics pioneered by organized labor disturbed the country's oligarchic political parties. Surprising social groups sometimes employed the strike. Just before the violence in Uncía, Oruro's authorities confronted a strike by secondary students that tested their patience. On March 11, 1923, the Federation of Secondary Students informed Oruro's prefect, Ramón Rivero, of their intent: "A spirit of solidarity that dominates the student element of this locality has compelled us to go on strike with our comrades from La Paz." The students were protesting the imprisonment of three youth leaders in the capital. Despite promises to return to their "daily labors" after one day of protest, the strike dragged on for several days.[6] On March 16 the director of a local kindergarten, Ofelia G. de Aguirre, wrote a harsh report to the prefect. "This morning at ten o'clock a group of students arrived," she recorded. "They were primary school students, who banged on the door of the establishment, and hearing the disorder they were making, I leaned out the window of one of the classrooms, and hearing that they wanted to take the little students out to enroll them in the strike, I energetically scolded the troublemakers, succeeding in getting them to renounce their intentions." The kindergarten administrator held a low opinion of the "scholastic strike" and judged the leaders to have been "delinquent elements and opponents of the government."[7] Enrique Quintela, the director of Oruro's

Model Public School for Children, a primary school, also objected to the strike and the secondary students leading it. On March 16 he reported that four secondary students from Bolívar High School had entered his school as the children were preparing for recess. The director immediately "addressed all the students of the school, recommending to them good behavior and a definitive prohibition against participating in the strike." Quintela claimed that the secondary students "produced panic in the children of the school, who fled because of their instincts for self-preservation, some into the classrooms and some into the street."[8] With the tactics of labor activism becoming so ingrained among the urban population, government repression—such as that employed in Uncía in June 1923—had its limits. The country's oligarchic parties had to employ diplomacy as well.

Officials in Oruro's smaller towns often saw political opportunity in local labor federations.[9] The Liberal and Republican parties both frequently recruited working-class clients. For example, a July 1923 report by a Poopó interim subprefect, J. Vera P., indicated that the local labor federation inclined toward the old Liberal Party, but Vera felt that astute diplomacy might induce many to swing to the Republican Party's camp. The subprefect's exploration of the labor movement began with the return of a controversial local political figure: the priest Juan L. Rojas, a member of the Liberal Party. During a previous election, Rojas had found his citizenship rights temporarily suspended because of his involvement in a court case. The priest had returned to Poopó after judges in Oruro had reinstated his rights. Rojas planned to run in the upcoming congressional elections, and the subprefect noted that he had "occupied himself in visiting his political friends, most especially the Labor Federation of this location, an institution of which he [had] been an Honorary President, a recognition for his having been an initiator and founder of the already mentioned Federation." The federation invited the subprefect to attend a get-together for Rojas, an invitation that Vera accepted to "get to know personally the leaders of this society," whom he characterized as the government's "main opponents." Vera reported that federation members treated him cordially at the gathering. He also observed that the "principal leaders" of the federation were "completely foreign to the workers of the Alantaña Company" (the Alantaña mill was a substantial industrial installation connected to a tin company in Oruro). Vera reported that the federation's rank-and-file membership was "easily swayed and could be brought to [the Republican] side with a little skill."

In addition to perceiving splits among workers and their leaders, the subprefect thought that creating barriers between the town's artisans and the Alantaña Company's workers would serve the interests of the Republican Party: "It would be wise to reach an agreement with the Alantaña Mill's Administrator to prohibit his workers from supporting the indicated Federation, so that they do not admit into their breast private individuals who do not belong to the Company; this would be an easy means by which we could undermine the pretensions of these Liberal elements that, until now, have sought to be the representatives and leaders of the federated workers."

Like other party officials, Vera believed Poopó's working class to be a valuable electoral demographic. "Their numbers—they are more than one hundred—deserve some consideration, especially for having political importance," he wrote.[10] Despite the crackdown on labor activism in northern Potosí, Bautista Saavedra's Republican Party could still rally significant support among the urban popular classes, an ability that did much to keep the party in power through the end of the 1920s.

Many Republican officials struck a pose of benevolence and reconciliation in the wake of the killings in Uncía. In November 1923 Antonio Carvajal, the president of the Workers' Labor Federation, had been arrested in Oruro and transported to La Paz because of his labor activism. The federation immediately protested Carvajal's detention to Oruro's prefect, Aniceto Arce. The prefect wrote to the federation, explaining his inaction: "The active appeals by telegraph made by this Prefecture to the Supreme Government requesting the liberty of Sr. Carvajal have not produced any results because said gentleman has been implicated in disturbing the public order according to evidence collected in the city of La Paz." But Arce assured the federation that he would act in their behalf: "in light of the claims of innocence by Sr. Carvajal, I will submit a new complaint to the Government to obtain his liberty, which will no doubt be granted in La Paz."[11]

This reconciliation sought to control and harness the working class's strength for the Republican Party's benefit. In February 1923 the activist Hermógenes Iraola had helped to win concessions for Huanuni's workers from Simón Patiño's company. By the end of 1923, however, Iraola was the president of Huanuni's Republican Workers' Party, a branch of the Republican Party designed to harness working-class political support.[12] Iraola was clearly working as a government agent to control and pacify Huanuni's workers. In January 1924 Oruro prefect Aniceto Arce wrote a letter to Iraola thanking him for informing the government about "the existence of a few workers in this district with subversive tendencies." The prefect further informed Iraola that authorities had warned the workers "to abstain from disturbing the tranquility of this settlement" and that the Patiño Company's administrator had "given them a similar warning with the threat of separating them from their jobs." If the suspected workers did not improve their behavior, "the Prefecture would take the necessary repressive measures."[13] Three of the men that Iraola denounced were Vicente Guzmán, Celestino Mendoza, and Ramón Bellot —all members of Huanuni's municipal council. Iraola accused them of being the "principal leaders" of a subversion that "daily" threatened to "incite the working class." Iraola sought their exile from Huanuni.[14] Eventually, in July 1924, Oruro's Supreme Court would reprimand the three, suspend them from the municipal council for four months, and fine each of them Bs 40.[15]

Despite the darker side of the Republican Party's overtures, unions understood the benefits of having a sympathetic ear in the halls of government. Labor associations continued to court the good graces of important officials. In June 1924 the Workers' Labor Federation expressed to Oruro prefect Aniceto Arce its interest in participating in planning sessions for the one-hundredth anniversary of Bolivia's independence. Arce responded by "congratulating the distinguished Federation for its very laudable patriotic fervor." The prefect looked forward to the participation of the federation's delegates in the planning process.[16]

The rapprochement paid dividends for workers, as sympathetic officials once again intervened on labor's behalf. On July 19, 1924, for example, Poopó Province subprefect Casto Eyzaguirre reported that the El Salvador

Mining Company had laid off 233 workers without the necessary warning or severance pay. The situation was brought to the subprefect's attention when a commission of ten workers visited his office, "complaining of the unjustifiable separation from their jobs of the majority of the personnel from El Salvador." The subprefect immediately appointed a commission to look into the situation.[17] In his letter to the El Salvador Mining Company, in Antequera, Eyzaguirre employed forceful language to condemn the company. First, he transcribed the pertinent law adopted on August 16, 1920: "A dismissal must follow a warning of fifteen days . . . , and in the case of an involuntary and final firing, each former worker will be indemnified with a sum of Bs 200." The subprefect continued in a personal, excoriating tone: "This Company has always harassed the working class, imposing upon it a subordination akin to slavery, depriving it of all rights to organize, making it swear off all association to carry out abuses that are prohibited by the laws of the Fatherland, but this shall not be; it [the working class] is free and independent of all foreign groups, and has in its heart decided amiability which will make way for its progress and well-being."[18] By July 22 Eyzaguirre reported many of the fired workers had returned to their jobs with an indemnity covering the three days that they had been suspended. Another forty workers refused the offer and "signed their voluntary withdrawal, receiving the corresponding bonus for their inconvenience and for transport to wherever they wish[ed]." Ultimately, the subprefect doubted the long-term solvency of the El Salvador Mining Company: "It is common knowledge that this Company is in a bad economic position due to the lack of production, and they emphasize that they will suspend their work for the lack of capital, which their investors refuse to give more of."[19]

Not all officials practiced Eyzaguirre's vigorous defense of the working class. Many understood that much of the legislation adopted by President Saavedra sought to control rather than benefit the working class. With continued organizing in the department of Oruro, the Cercado Province subprefect Zevallos hoped to extend government surveillance over the working class in his jurisdiction. He wrote the prefect in September 1924 that there were "constant rumors of a possible labor action that might take on the characteristics of a strike against the mining companies; it might be a political movement." Zevallos was especially concerned with "the presence of foreign and dangerous elements in the mining companies and factories near the city." To track these perceived dangers, the subprefect proposed to carry out a "precise control of the employees and workers entering and leaving the mining companies and factories that surround the city."[20] The official circulated an order among Oruro's industrial enterprises directing them to send to his office, "every Saturday, an exact list of the employees and workers entering and leaving" their companies' properties.[21] Zevallos hoped that the prefect would approve of his plan, which, he said, conformed "with the legal methods that preserve public order that should be adopted by the authorities."[22]

This inclination to regulate the working class extended to all levels of government. One series of proposals that straddled the line between improving the working class and regulating workers' private lives were laws seeking to restrict the consumption of alcohol. On November 13, 1923, President Saavedra issued a decree prohibiting the sale of alcohol in mining and industrial districts from noon on Saturdays until noon on Mondays. The president explained the decree by arguing that "it is urgent to attend to the well-being of the laboring classes that dissipate the fruit of their labor and the integrity of their health in the consumption of alcoholic beverages on days that are destined for rest to recover their personal energies and with grave prejudice to the dignity and economic comfort of their families."[23] The labor movement was not completely averse to restrictions on alcohol. Two years earlier, in April 1921, the president of the Railway Federation of Oruro had asked the local prefect to "completely close" establishments selling alcoholic beverages "on May 1—known as Labor Day."[24] The union hoped to avoid "disagreeable excesses."[25] Yet some provincial authorities thought that rank-and-file workers might react adversely to the new measures. On November 27, 1923, Poopó subprefect H. Achá Panoso wrote the prefect that he agreed with the measures "seeking the extirpation of debauchery in the mining camps" but estimated that he would need "at least six police officers to contain the workers and to impose the closure of bars and shops" that sold alcoholic beverages.[26] In 1924 the government imposed even greater controls. On February 20 President Saavedra ordered that all "Theaters, Cinemas, Bars, Casinos, Clubs, Restaurants, Hotels, and other analogous institutions" close at 12:30 a.m. each night so as to prevent "the propagation of gambling, drunkenness, and other vices."[27] Like many Bolivian laws, the new regulations were not always enforced.

Sometimes, however, the labor movement reminded government officials of the laws' existence and requested their enforcement. On April 17, 1928, the Railway Union Mutual Aid Society (Sports and Recreation) of Machacamarca requested the effective enforcement of the four-year-old prohibition of alcohol sales on the weekend. The society noted, "Unfortunately until now, the cantonal authorities charged with the execution of these regulations have not been effective, tolerating the open sale of all kinds of alcoholic beverages during the prohibited days with grave prejudice to the working element." In explaining alcohol's dangers, the leaders of this particular mutual aid society employed arguments and images more often associated with government officials than with labor activists: "And the worker's situation is even more grave if you take into account that in these places he spends the meager surplus that is left after using his salary for necessities, leaving, in consequence, his family in the most frightening misery, and what is even worse, giving the Fatherland sick children, stigmatized by vice, who in the future will be useless elements for the society in which they live." They hoped that eventually the government would completely prohibit the manufacture and sale of alcohol within a five- to ten-kilometer radius of "railroad, mining, and industrial centers of all types."[28] Working-class leaders, then, sometimes shared the cultural predilections of the upper and middle classes.

Some of President Saavedra's reforms unambiguously benefited the working class, and the labor movement genuinely appreciated the legislation. In January 1924 the government adopted a popular workplace accident law that mandated financial compensation for work-related injuries and deaths. Soon thereafter, Huanuni's police chief, Juan Zuleta, reported that the town's workers had composed a note of thanks and organized a march "carried out in good order, that traveled the principal streets; the workers, who numbered more than 200, shouted enthusiastic support for Doctor Bautista Saavedra and the Grand Republican Party."[29] The goodwill generated by the law continued throughout the year. In December 1924 a group of workers from El Salvador Mining Company, in Antequera, wrote Oruro's prefect to confirm their support for Cristóbal Terrazas as their representative under the workplace accident law. A different group of workers previously had written to express their disagreement with Terrazas's representation. The 130 workers who supported Terrazas's nomination promised, "If you, Sr. Prefect, act on our appeal, we are all ready to go to Poopó and vote to request another term of service for our President, Dr. Bautista Saavedra, because he is the one who has made these good works and issued laws in favor of the great working masses, and in payment, we are bound to work for his Excellency."[30] Working-class political independence obviously needed further development.

Another law adopted during Saavedra's presidency provided no immediate benefit to industrial workers but set an important precedent by promoting the ideal of an eight-hour workday. On November 20, 1924, Saavedra signed legislation that declared the eight-hour workday standard for the "employees of commercial enterprises and other industries."[31] The law's implications were actually quite limited, for the word *empleado,* or "employee," applied only to white-collar workers. Despite the semantic nuance, blue-collar workers frequently referred to the law in their disputes with employers. The government sought to clarify the point on January 8, 1925, with another law specifying that the eight-hour workday applied only to "a mine's employees, and office personnel that receive a monthly salary in the railroad companies."[32] The law—an important step toward a national standard—resulted from the activism of the League of Commercial and Industrial Employees of La Paz, founded in 1919.[33] Oruro saw the organization of its own League of Commercial and Industrial Employees in October 1924.[34] As the law suggests, despite the government's liberal economic orientation, authorities began to feel greater confidence in their right to regulate private business.

President Saavedra also sought to ensure that older workers had a minimum retirement savings. On January 25, 1924, the government established the Obligatory Workers' Savings Program. The program aimed to funnel 5 percent of a worker's wage into a government-run account.[35] Surprisingly, the initiative generated conflict in some enterprises; the Bolivian Railway Company, for instance, already had a retirement fund with a corresponding deduction from worker salaries. With the implementation of the government's program, the Railway Federation demanded that the company abolish its fund so that workers would not have to pay into two different accounts with two different paycheck deductions. On September 12, 1924, the Railway Federation threatened a strike over the issue.[36] In addition, the funds generated by the Obligatory Workers' Savings Program sometimes suffered diversion into other projects. Thus, on December 14 and 16, 1927, President Hernando Siles issued laws allowing the Council for the Development of Worker Housing to employ some of the retirement funds.[37]

President Saavedra eventually institutionalized oversight of workplace conditions and the enforcement of labor legislation with the creation of a special agency; on March 1, 1925, he issued an executive decree establishing the National Department of Labor. A year later Congress and President Hernando Siles elevated the decree to the status of law. The department would have offices in La Paz, Oruro, and Uncía, plus two traveling inspectors and a medical assessor. These officials possessed substantial powers of inspection and enforcement. The government charged the agency to "gather statistics about the cost of living and the situation of the working classes, especially in the mining centers, and statistics about work-related accidents." Inspectors were to have unrestricted access to "carry out the inspection of mines, factories, and other industrial establishments," with a view toward ensuring that the companies complied "with the legal prescriptions and regulations concerning labor, safety, hygiene, and the prevention of accidents"; violators could face "fines of up to five hundred bolivianos." The government hoped that, in addition to enforcing the law, the National Department of Labor might help formulate future legislation. The law empowered the department to "compile the existing legislation about working conditions and to formulate reform projects for the Ministry of Industry in everything that concerns the branch of social legislation." The government also charged the department to resolve disputes between workers and their employers over issues of salary and other contractual points. The National Department of Labor had a special charge to "investigate and to resolve all sorts of issues relating to workplace accidents, including those . . . in the mines." The police were to collaborate in these investigations, and the law declared the police "the direct collaborators and the active organs of the National Department of Labor." If a disagreement arose over a workplace accident or illness, officials were to investigate "the manner in which the accident occurred, the nature of the occupational illness, the amount of salary or any other point." The interested parties had eight days to make their arguments. Once the department made a decision, "the company or the employer" could annul a decision about "the level of indemnity that had been imposed" only by an appeal to the Supreme Court.[38] Previously, investigating workplace accidents and other labor conditions had fallen to *corregidores,* subprefects, and prefects. The new agency elevated labor legislation to a specialized concern of the national executive.

One year after the National Department of Labor's creation, President Hernando Siles felt the need to clarify the police's relationship with the new agency. He saw that the police needed a more detailed guide to the "norms of investigation." On March 20, 1926, in an executive order mandating a swift response to workplace accidents, Siles wrote: "As soon as the police receive news of an accident that causes temporary incapacity, they will designate an agent to interview the injured individual, listening to his version of the incident and verifying the information submitted by the employer, especially concerning salary and the length of employment; [the agent] will also investigate if medical and pharmaceutical aid was given and, if necessary, see that the [injured] individual is hospitalized in the paying section." If the accident caused permanent incapacity, the police needed to conduct a more thorough investigation: "The agent should visit the place of the accident to investigate the manner in which it occurred, taking the testimony of witnesses and if necessary naming special investigators whose work might clarify the circumstances that surround the incident." The police, however, could delegate these tasks to a canton's *corregidor*—a continuation of the old system. In the case of accidental death, the police were to "take note of the cost of the funeral and to inquire as to the relatives of the victim and the persons who might have been under his protection." For an occupational illness, the police would simply collect information from an employer and turn it over to the National Department of Labor. If an employer refused to provide information, the police could apply a fine. If an employer refused "to give medical assistance to the injured individual or to pay the costs of the funeral," the police could arrest him.[39] Despite the codified norms, local officials exercised enormous autonomy in implementing the law.

Some Republican Party legislation acknowledged the strength organized labor had achieved by the second half of the 1920s, and the status of the May Day holiday illustrates this recognition. On April 29, 1926, President Siles issued a straightforward, one-article decree: "It is the duty of the Government to celebrate Labor Day in honor of the Nation's working classes." Siles recognized a working-class and artisan victory in making May Day a de facto national holiday; he was simply filing the paperwork to make it official.[40]

Despite all these developments, including some new labor laws and some new restrictions on business, workers still found much that needed improvement. Among other things, even with the reforms, the workers suffered from a disconnection between law and practice.

SOLID LAWS, CAPRICIOUS ENFORCEMENT

Even though the Republican Party courted organized labor, workers continued to suffer from the pervasive gap between written legislation and active enforcement. For example, although the government first adopted laws demanding that large mining companies provide free medical attention to workers in 1913, and later legislation reiterated the requirement, some employers continued to scrimp on medical services. The constant turnover among government officials contributed to the failures of enforcement, too, for new officials often lacked familiarity with the pertinent labor legislation. When government officials did launch a comprehensive investigation of worker complaints, the administrative process often dragged along and arrived at only ambiguous resolutions. These failures to enforce existing laws helped the labor movement continue to expand its membership during this period of relative industrial peace.

On July 1, 1924, Oruro prefect Aniceto Arce chided the Morococala Mining Company administration for "reiterated complaints about the lack of a doctor to attend to work-related accidents or other cases of illness in the mining interest Santa Isabel," which the company operated. The omission violated laws mandating that companies with more than 150 workers had to employ a doctor. The prefect sought an immediate explanation for the company's failure to fulfill "the indicated law."[41] Arce also admonished the Negro Pabellón Mining Company for the same reason. That enterprise responded with a letter explaining that smaller companies in isolated encampments faced difficulties in implementing the law. The company's owner, Isabel de Duncan, informed the prefect of the situation on July 18, 1924: "Until recently we had a Doctor to attend to our workers in Negro Pabellón, but said doctor stopped working a couple of days ago without giving a reason, and today we are looking for one who could take over said service." She continued, "As we have only begun preparing our mine for exploitation—constructing houses for the workers, buildings for the employees and Management, etc.—we are not yet in a condition to have a permanent doctor, and it is for this reason that we have been using a doctor that comes occasionally." De Duncan assured the prefect that the company would ultimately obey the law and asked for lenience: "As soon as we complete the houses, the administration, etc., we will hire a permanent doctor in Negro Pabellón, but in the meantime we believe a bit of tolerance is reasonable given that no doctor would want to come and live without the comforts of his station."[42] By mid-August the situation in Negro Pabellón was still unresolved, and on August 18, 1924, its police chief, Donato Careagua, informed Oruro's prefect that he had fined the company Bs 250.[43]

Lax enforcement, however, was only part of the problem. Despite a growing corpus of labor legislation, workers often found themselves in situations not covered by the law or even previously contemplated by the labor movement. In early December 1924 the Patiño company ordered the worker Félix Balderrama to move from Uncía to a company subsidiary in another town, the Kami Mining Company. Balderrama refused and enlisted the support of the Workers' Labor Federation of Uncía to fight the transfer (the Workers' Labor Federation of Uncía was a new organization, different from the Central Labor Federation of Uncía, which the government had repressed a year and a half earlier). Oruro's prefect, Aniceto Arce, intervened, but only to ensure that Balderrama would receive "the same salary" in the new location. Balderrama initially declined the arrangement, stating that "it was not in his interests, having made his home in Uncía," where his family lived.[44] Two days later Balderrama bent to economic necessity and accepted the transfer.[45]

Further slippage between ideal and practice in Oruro emerged from the unequal quality and knowledge of the prefects assigned to the department. Many prefects knew nothing of earlier decrees regulating the mining industry. Some did not have a positive history with the labor movement. Lieutenant Colonel José Ayoroa became Oruro's prefect on January 30, 1925, and served in that position for over a year.[46] Ayoroa was the military officer who had commanded at the Uncía Massacre on June 4, 1923. On March 17, 1925, Prefect José Ayoroa wrote both the Penny and Duncan and Japo mining companies to inform them that a number of the companies' workers had requested that "the Prefecture intervene and employ its good graces" with the companies in question "to secure a contribution for the maintenance of a school." In 1913 the government had issued regulations requiring all mining enterprises employing more than fifty individuals to maintain a school. Ayoroa never mentioned this twelve-year-old regulation, however, and instead appealed to management's benevolent paternalism: "In view of the goodwill contained in the mentioned petition, this Prefecture would view kindly the creation of a school, which would greatly benefit the working classes and perhaps the companies which you manage, given that these kinds of works signify a progressive step each time that they represent an increase in intellectual culture."[47]

On other issues Ayoroa proved more knowledgeable. On the same day that he dispatched the letters about education, he sent a second letter to the Japo Mining Company, an enterprise owned by Simón I. Patiño, to remind the company of the nation's employment laws. The Japo Mining Company had recently fired two workers—Valentín Guerros and Pedro Calle Primero—without following extant legislation. This was apparently a common company practice, for Ayoroa complained about the frequency: "Continually workers are fired from jobs with this Company without clear justification, and without giving them warning of their firing with fifteen days anticipation or paying them the equivalent in cash." Ayoroa asked that in the future the enterprise "avoid complaints of this type that undoubtedly rebound and damage the prestige of the Company's standing."[48]

Lieutenant Colonel José Ayoroa's memory was sharp, however, and his knowledge of the law impeccable when it came to legislation regulating the workers' right to strike. With the ethos of a military man, Oruro's prefect sought strict adherence to the presidential decree of 1920 mandating eight days' notice before any strike. In March 1925 the Railway Federation of Oruro and Potosí threatened a strike to influence its negotiations with the Bolivian Railway Company. Ayoroa sought to impose the authority—down to the hour—of the regulations. On March 18 he wrote the federation's president to establish the particulars: "Having received your letter today at 5 p.m., the general strike that you propose should begin next Thursday, the twenty-sixth of this month, at 5 p.m., as established by the second article of the Supreme Decree, dated September 29, 1920, which established a term of eight days, so this is how it would legally be calculated."[49] With Ayoroa in the prefecture, a union's liberty to declare a work stoppage met severe limitations.

A dispute from the mining town of Vinto, just outside the city of Oruro, illustrates some of the complexities of enforcing new government regulations. In May 1925, soon after President Bautista Saavedra created the National Department of Labor but before that agency could begin functioning, a group of workers submitted a formal complaint against the Vinto Tin Company, a subsidiary of the Mining Company of Oruro.[50] The government addressed the complaint by the old system, in which *corregidores*, subprefects, and prefects resolved workplace disputes, but the case nevertheless illustrates some of the issues with which the new National Department of Labor would soon be dealing.

Victoriano Ponce, Dámaso Zabalaga, and Santiago Flores leveled a broad range of accusations against the Vinto Tin Company, though not all of them would hold up when investigated. The three claimed to "represent all the workers . . . in Vinto," who, they added, had named them their delegates, "if just verbally." The workers first complained that the company forced them to work a thirteen-hour day "by force of clubs and whips." This contravened their interpretation of a November 21, 1924, law stipulating that employers "should impose on commercial and industrial employees the daily work of only a maximum eight hours" or, failing that, pay an overtime wage. As was mentioned before, however, the government had no intention that this law apply to manual laborers. Ponce, Zabalaga, and Flores labeled themselves *jornaleros,* or wage laborers, whereas the law covered only *empleados,* or salaried employees. Despite the government's intent, the workers sought a broader reading of the statute.[51]

The three men also denounced the Vinto Tin Company because, they said, it forced workers to labor at least one Sunday every two weeks and threatened to deduct a day's pay if they refused: "On the Sunday that we are forced to work, they drive us from our individual homes in the camp with whips." A worker might hide or plead sick, but to no avail: "In the first case, he loses the fine or discounted wage, or [in the second case] he is thrown into the river with all of his things, without a right to medicine or treatment by the Company." Only when a worker put in a thirteen-hour Sunday did the company supposedly return the discounted sum.[52]

Ponce, Zabalaga, and Flores also had a litany of grievances related to the company store, which they labeled "completely lacking." They alleged that the weights employed in the store were "inexact" and that workers were "cheated of two ounces of each pound." They complained that, in general, prices in the store were "impossibly high." They especially complained of the underweight bread. Each loaf of bread weighed only two ounces—well under the legal limit. In fact, the police had previously fined the company for selling underweight bread. The workers noted that, "in case of inspection," the company kept "a special loaf of legal weight." The men also objected to the store's stinginess with credit. The company would not extend credit to workers for items that cost more than sixty

cents. They claimed that the store manager, a Peruvian, brutalized anyone asking for credit: "[He] kicks and punches us when we show up at the
company store looking to buy on credit."[53]

The document also denounced substandard living conditions. The
daily wage supposedly varied from Bs 1.80 to Bs 2.30, sums considered
exceptionally low. The company was accused of not providing medical
care or a pharmacy. Housing reportedly consisted of a bare room with no
roof, "where the majority of workers find themselves exposed to the elements." The three men added, "Said rooms even lack doors—houses with
doors are rare." Workers also supposedly suffered a lack of water: "Potable
water does not exist, and there is only a well with salt water from which
we have to serve ourselves so as not to die." Ponce, Zabalaga, and Flores
concluded by observing, "In general they treat us like animals."[54]

The workers supposedly took these issues to the Mining Company of
Oruro, the parent company. There, they claimed, the manager who heard
their grievances "became angry," pushing them from the room without
hearing their "just complaints." Now, the workers were appealing to the
prefect: "Because of these crimes we come to ask that they be prevented,
and that you give us guarantees not just as workers but because of the
men we are, and as such we should be granted considerations as humans,
respecting us, and respecting our rights, before we take justice into our
own hands and perhaps commit a crime in justly reclaiming what we deserve or what belongs to us." The three hoped that any decision would
help prevent the company from committing "more crimes with the poor
working class and would succor the national proletariat, preventing foreign elements from mistreating" workers in their "own homes."[55]

The arguments struck home with an unlikely benefactor—Lieutenant
Colonel José Ayoroa, Oruro's prefect at the time. On May 13, 1925, Ayoroa
fined the Vinto Tin Company Bs 250 for the supposed infractions. A month
later, on June 15, the company's manager, Jorge Wiessing, responded to the
fine. "I found it strange that the said fine had been imposed without more
proof than the naked word of the accusers, as they have not presented a
single proof of the rash assertions made in their petition," Wiessing wrote.
He assured the prefect that all the accusations were "absolutely false" and

requested an investigation. Ayoroa assented and ordered the Cercado Province subprefect and a public prosecutor to look into the matter.[56]

Even before the investigation began, solidarity among the accusing workers began to break down. On June 17 Victoriano Ponce, one of the original complainants, wrote to say that he had never given permission to use his name on the original petition and that the document "was false in all its accusations." Ponce added that Dámaso Zabalaga and his brother had composed the complaint and "sought to provoke a strike."[57] The government inspection a week later was even more illuminating than this sudden retraction.

The investigation confirmed some accusations, clarified others, and showed some to be exaggerations or fabrications. The subprefect and the public prosecutor visited the Vinto Tin Company on June 24 and interviewed four workers. The first, Máximo Castro, swore that the workers labored from "sunup to sundown, with a one-hour break," but could not give an exact account of the hours because, he said, "there is no public clock here." Castro confirmed that the company made a small deduction from the workers' paychecks every two weeks, but he clarified that this was a preemptive measure to ensure that workers did not miss the Monday after payday. If a worker missed, the company kept the money. Castro also testified that most believed the company store's goods to be underweight. He judged his own salary "deficient," because it was insufficient to "satisfy one's dietary needs." On other points, he noted that the company employed 120 workers but did not have a permanent doctor or a pharmacy. Castro claimed that when a worker fell ill, the company gave only a "generic medicine" in "limited quantities." A second witness, Tomás Ayza, testified that one of the managers often threatened the workers "with a whip" and sometimes used it. Ayza noted that his daily wage of Bs 2.70 was not enough to feed his family. He also clarified the company's problems with potable water. The camp's well provided water that was "somewhat salty," and the company charged workers for fresh water from a tap in the mill. The final two witnesses held a better opinion of the company— they also earned more than the first two men. Antonio Llanque, who earned Bs 3.20 a week and was "content with the salary," testified that no one was ever thrown into the river and that the company provided a doctor in case of severe illness. Llanque had seen him twice. The highest-paid worker interviewed, Demetrio Lujan, earned Bs 4.00 and judged it sufficient for his dietary needs. He also noted that the company supplied a doctor in case of illness. This particular case did not contain a final ruling.[58] When the National Department of Labor took over investigations, cases often ended with a similar ambiguity. The seeming indecision and erratic enforcement of Republican Party labor laws irritated workers. Activists would capitalize on the simmering discontent to further radicalize the political ideology of the urban popular classes.

CHAPTER 7

An Ideology of Their Own

IN APRIL 1927 some one hundred and fifty labor representatives gathered in Oruro's municipal theater for the Third Workers' Congress. For the first time a national gathering of the labor movement included twenty delegates from the rural, indigenous population. "The International," the anthem of the global socialist movement, played during the congress's inaugural session, and the schoolteacher Víctor Vargas Vilaseca read a message of greeting from Tristan Marof, an intellectual who did much to introduce Marxist thought to the labor movement. The meeting continued to advance the idea of a national federation and examined the difficult conditions confronting the country's rural population.[1] "The liberation of the Indian will be his own accomplishment, just as the redemption of the workers will be their own accomplishment; as such, all labor organizations should work for the formation of federations and unions among the Indians," the congress declared.[2] At the meeting's conclusion the delegates resolved to gather again in Potosí on June 5, 1928, a date chosen to commemorate the Uncía Massacre.[3] Given its makeup and pronouncements, this meeting indicated a substantial leftward shift in organized labor's ideology. By the 1930s the framework of a movement that would threaten the oligarchy's dominance was clearly established.

TRISTAN MAROF AND THE
THIRD WORKERS' CONGRESS

The Third Workers' Congress, held in 1927, symbolized organized labor's expanding ambitions. The meeting displayed a growing ideological sophistication that contrasted with the period's relative industrial peace; Tristan Marof, an intellectual from Sucre who traveled extensively in Europe, exemplified this increasing theoretical sophistication and played a pivotal role in promoting Marxist thought in Bolivia. "Tristan Marof" was the penname and political pseudonym of Gustavo A. Navarro. Navarro was born in 1898 to a poor family in Sucre and grew up scarred by the aristocratic pretensions in the colonial capital. He started his political life as a militant in Bautista Saavedra's Republican Party. After the Republican coup of July 1920, he enjoyed a twenty-four-hour appointment as director of the National High School in La Paz; jealous political rivals quickly drove him from the post. Eventually, President Saavedra appointed the young man consul in Geneva, Switzerland. In Europe, Marxist and socialist thought exerted a profound influence on the expatriate intellectual.[4] A press in Belgium produced his first political work, *La justicia del Inca,* in 1926.[5] With the publication of this short book, Navarro adopted his Tristan Marof pseudonym and catapulted himself to a position of ideological leadership within Bolivia's labor movement.

Marof looked to an idealized Andean past for inspiration. He, like a number of other thinkers in Europe and the Americas at the time, had become convinced that the Inca Empire had practiced a primitive yet effective form of communism.[6] "During the Inca dominion over the nation that is called Bolivia, it undoubtedly enjoyed greater benefits than those provided today by a republican regime," Marof concluded. He denounced the politics of the 1920s and the class structure they held in place:

It does not matter if an electoral victory belongs to the Liberal, Progressive, Radical, Blue, or Conservative Party[;] the personalities are the same, and their programs are—with small variations—identical, their methods identical. All share a tacit agreement to exploit the indigenous class and to maintain their privileges. Their only objective: private property and political power in their hands. The rest must labor to maintain the politics of bourgeois ambition—simple hate, imbecilic pretensions—and work the land without owning it. In other words, a happy life for 20 percent of the population at the cost and sacrifice of the rest.

What the young socialist proposed was a return to the supposed communist ideals of the Inca past, but with "the advantages of modern advances —efficient machines that economize time—leaving the spirit free for other speculations."[7]

Marof drew political lessons from the 1917 Russian Revolution. He acknowledged Bolivia's limited industrial development, particularly the uneven advance of industrial capitalism in the country. Despite the nation's poverty, however, he still called for an immediate socialist revolution. "The formidable fighting spirit of the new continent cannot tranquilly await, with arms crossed, its material evolution," he argued. "Spirit and utility should begin the socialist era without believing that capitalist development is first necessary. Capitalist development in the new states will simply turn them over with their hands and feet bound to the Yankees," he concluded. This was Marof's own reformulation of Leon Trotsky's idea of "permanent revolution." The Russian revolutionary argued that the dominant classes in underdeveloped nations could not deliver on all the promises of liberal democracy and that revolutionaries should seek to leap over the capitalist stage of economic development directly into socialism. But this was only a partial reformulation, for Trotsky warned against the isolation of socialism in a handful of impoverished nations. Socialism in only one country could not succeed.[8] Marof was less careful: "I declare that the American revolution should not wait for a capitalist flowering. . . . It should capture its own national capital and harmoniously begin its own development." Marof employed a rather flexible definition of capital, writing, "The capital of America is the mines, the oil wells, the thousands of workers, the intelligentsia in service to the State."[9] All Marof's proposals depended on the nationalization of Bolivia's mining industry.

Marof played an important role in popularizing the slogan "Land to the people, mines to the state." Both parts were significant. With the expropriation of large landholdings and their redistribution to the rural poor, revolutionaries might reverse one of South America's historic injustices, but agrarian reform alone would not provide a financial base for further change. "Taxing agriculture makes no sense as articles of consumption should not be exported," Marof argued.[10] Given the country's poverty, Marof saw only one source of revenue for a socialist Bolivia, "the exploitation of the mines by the State." With the profits of a nationalized mining industry, the country might pay its international debt and revitalize the railroads. (National ownership of the railways was a special point of honor; Marof called them "these Bolivian railroads, built with Bolivian money and the sacrificial sale of national territory!") Once the country controlled the mining industry, Marof suggested, the state could implement a planned, self-sufficient economy. "We must open new horizons according to a central plan that studies the economy of the country," he proposed, "and we must build factories to make necessities in such a manner that we are liberated from Europe and the United States."[11] Marof's was an ambitious program, and it appealed to a working class struggling to consolidate its strength. His ideas inspired many labor activists as they prepared to meet in Oruro for the Third Workers' Congress.

Two previous congresses had failed to produce a national organization. The Railway Federation, which represented the Antofagasta-Bolivia Railroad/Bolivian Railway Company's workers, organized the meeting that became known as the First Workers' Congress in Oruro in late 1920. The meeting produced nothing concrete, and when the Workers' Center for Social Studies in La Paz called for a congress in 1925, it erroneously christened its own gathering the first.[12] The center's letter of invitation, dated June 20, 1925, read, "Until today, the worker and proletarian societies and federations have been without solid guidance, without a unity of action or a system of organization regulated by a body capable of keeping them in frank and mutual contact in our needs and in our struggles for working-class demands; as such, it is indispensable and cannot be postponed that we orient our ideals and our actions in the future."[13] The letter showed a basic familiarity with Marxist literature and was probably written by a law student and tailor from La Paz: Carlos Mendoza Mamani.[14] The invitation employed the words of the *Communist Manifesto*: "If today the exploited have nothing to lose but their chains and have in exchange a world to win, we will resolve to struggle at the start of the century to break these chains that have bound us until today and seek the conquest of this world." The activists continued, "We will make real that old refrain of Karl Marx, never fulfilled but greatly hoped for by all and for all: 'Workers of all countries, unite.'"[15] This meeting—the Second Workers' Congress—opened in La Paz on August 26, 1925, and attracted mainly organizations from that department. The congress resolved to found a national confederation, promote legislation defending women and children in the workplace, support rural literacy programs, stimulate the creation of working-class universities and schools, proclaim "The International" as the official anthem of the working class, and plan for another congress in 1926.[16] Little adopted at the congress actually occurred.

The Third Workers' Congress, held in Oruro in 1927, brought together a broader collection of organizations than the ones assembled at the meeting in La Paz. Federations, societies, and activists from the departments of La Paz, Oruro, Cochabamba, Potosí, and Chuquisaca participated; the congress even attracted observers from Peru. Leadership at the meeting fell to Rómulo Chumacero, a tailor from Sucre with a history of activism in Oruro and elsewhere. He had also served as president of the Second Workers' Congress. The gathering in Oruro sought to build on points discussed at earlier meetings, especially the formation of a national labor federation. But the Third Workers' Congress was not without its complications and difficulties—in particular, accusations and rumors that some labor leaders had accepted money from the government. One particularly damning accusation was that Antonio Carvajal, a representative of the Workers' Labor Federation of Oruro, had embezzled some Bs 7,000 given to the congress by President Siles's government. An open struggle also developed between activists inclined toward anarcho-syndicalism and those who considered themselves socialist, Marxist, or communist.[17] This ideological struggle would plague the labor movement through the end of the 1920s and into the next decade. Those identifying themselves as socialists held the upper hand at the Third Workers' Congress, but their grip was slipping.

The third meeting spent a significant amount of time discussing the state of the rural population, the so-called Indian question. The topic carried special weight since twenty representatives from indigenous communities and haciendas were attending the congress.[18] Labor activists hoped to organize the rural population along lines mirroring those used for urban artisans and workers. "This will be the only means by which the Indian ceases to be the pariah he is today," they wrote.[19] The congress also used the exploitation of the Indian population to launch attacks on the Catholic Church and its clergy, seeking the expansion of civil marriage "so that the benefits of civil marriage, which the law extends to all whites, might be extended to the Indian," thus placing them "on an equal footing in national law."[20] The congress also discussed plans to expand education in the countryside, leaving open the possibility of worker tutelage and political guidance: "Not forgetting the subject of Indian Education, the Government was asked to decree special measures so that the Indians might establish schools in any part of the Republic; without impeding that, the Confederation of its own volition, in the provinces and in the cantons, might instruct the natives with a leftist orientation."[21] Finally, the congress called for the payment of indemnities to hacienda tenants facing eviction and for the expropriation of land "for the benefit of families and rural communities."[22] The call for land reform was particularly provocative and important.

The gathering continued the ongoing struggle to create a national labor federation. The Second Workers' Congress had resolved to organize a national confederation of labor, but it never happened. The Third Workers' Congress succeeded in organizing the basic infrastructure of a nationwide body, known as both the National Workers' Confederation and the Bolivian Labor Confederation.[23] This body never functioned effectively at a national level, but after the congress the Workers' Labor Federation of

Oruro began to identify itself as part of the national organization, re-naming itself the Departmental Council of Oruro of the Bolivian Labor Confederation. The renamed organization claimed to represent industrial councils in mining camps across southern La Paz, Oruro, and northern Potosí: Catavi, Llallagua, Siglo XX, Cancañiri, Avicaya, Sepulturas, Viloco, Caracoles, Machacamarca, Antequera, Negro Pabellón, Morococala, Paui-rumani, Colquiri, Caxata, Itos, and Santo Cristo. It also represented unions in Uncía, Huanuni, Poopó, and Caracollo. In Oruro the body consisted of various associations of railway workers, mechanics, graphic artists, bakers, construction workers, carpenters, cobblers, electricians, taxi drivers, butchers, hotel employees, and truck drivers. The Departmental Council of Oruro also claimed three cultural bodies.[24]

Finally, the Third Workers' Congress issued a number of declarations that illustrated the continued leftward drift of working-class leaders. In their final pronouncement, "Declaration of Principles," the delegates as-serted that "the primary proletarian struggle is to destroy the whole of the bourgeois economic system." Despite this revolutionary rhetoric, how-ever, the labor movement still kept its political plans within the existing framework of government and society. The declaration proposed to con-tinue known tactics: "to pressure the bosses and even the State to secure our rights by employing boycotts, strikes, actions in the streets, and dem-onstrations."[25] Although they were becoming radicalized, activists did not yet advocate an overthrow of government as they would in future decades. Instead, they continued to push for a societal transformation with pro-gressive legislative reform.

President Hernando Siles immediately moved to suffocate any momen-tum gained at the Third Workers' Congress. Denouncing a supposed "com-munist" plot to overthrow the government, Siles exiled Tristan Marof and a number of other political and labor leaders.[26] Events in the countryside —a major rebellion centered in the Chayanta region of northern Potosí— deepened the government's paranoia, especially when an investigation of the rebellion revealed linkages between the Third Workers' Congress and the rural revolt. While prosecutors exaggerated the cooperation between urban "communists" and angry peasant rebels, lines of communication and a certain mutual sympathy clearly existed.

A new organization seeking to defend the rural population's interests appeared in the late 1920s: the Pro-Indian League of Oruro. The body was a manifestation of worker and artisan concern for the peasantry's well-being. The league's president, José F. Avila, had once served as president of the Mutual Aid Society of Artisans.[27] Avila also played a critical role in establishing the Workers' Labor Federation of Oruro in 1916, serving as that organization's first president.[28] At the end of the 1920s the Pro-Indian League appeared prominently in letters sent to government officials on behalf of peasants throughout the department. The league was perhaps seeking to fill a role traditionally—and poorly—played by urban lawyers, that of intermediary between rural residents and the government. The epithet generally used to describe these lawyers, *tinterillos*, translates as "ink men." Government officials, the oligarchs who confronted them in court, and even those sympathetic to the peasantry all criticized these lawyers. Tristan Marof would write of the *tinterillos* in the 1930s:

> The schemes of the Altiplano's lawyers are several to convince their clients and charge them fees. Once, a poor Indian went to the office of one of these predatory men. He explained his case to the lawyer . . . and asked how he might receive justice. The lawyer quickly put the following question to the Indian, indicating two books: one voluminous and the other small. "With this big book," he said, "one wins every case; the defense costs 500 pesos. While with this small book, there is no such assurance of success; it costs 200. With which do you prefer that I defend you?" The Indian did not hesitate; he preferred the big one, but at that point the lawyer demanded his payment ahead of time.[29]

Some lawyers working for peasant clients deserved the criticism, but others did not. The Pro-Indian League of Oruro seemed honest and claimed political impartiality. In one 1927 document the league wrote of itself, "It has nothing to do with the upcoming election, nor with any political party. Its statutes prohibit its members from directly intervening in politics, and subjects them to strict sanctions."[30]

The 1927 Chayanta Rebellion, the largest rural uprising in Bolivia since the Federalist War some three decades earlier, saw a flirtation between peasant leaders and urban, working-class organizers. The Chayanta revolt first exploded in the agricultural valleys of northern Potosí that border the department of Chuquisaca, where hacienda owners had been expanding their landholdings since the nineteenth century. The violence quickly spread to the neighboring departments of Chuquisaca and Oruro.[31] The rebellion allowed a number of northern Potosí communities to settle some long-standing personal vendettas. In one community rebels killed a local hacienda owner and consumed part of his heart in a form of ritual cannibalism. They then sacrificed his remains to a local mountain deity. In Chuquisaca the communities also lashed out at Indians and mestizos who had cooperated with landowners in their expropriation schemes, again threatening ritual sacrifice and cannibalism.[32] Yet the rebels drew on more than traditional Andean beliefs in attacking their enemies. Many leaders maintained contacts with urban socialists, and several had served as delegates to the Third Workers' Congress.[33] Additionally, some communities used mock court proceedings to prosecute hacienda owners—an unusual affirmation of the court's legitimacy in the chaotic swirl of rebellion.[34]

Earlier contacts between the rebels and urban labor activists had assured many in the rebellion that they had allies elsewhere in Bolivia. Urban socialist thinkers—the rising leadership of the working class—had links to the insurgents in Chayanta. The scholars Olivia Harris and Xavier Albó see an early, fleeting peasant-worker alliance in the Chayanta Rebellion; they view the work of Tristan Marof as a unifying force.[35] This view is not universally accepted, however. Both Erick Langer and Silvia Rivera Cusicanqui discount accusations of "communist" influence, which they label oligarchic or government propaganda.[36] Silvia Rivera prefers to keep the focus on the peasant insurgents, and Erick Langer argues that urban socialists sought to direct the insurgency but failed.[37] The historian Forrest Hylton has yet another interpretation. "Socialists *did not* enjoy broad support in the Bolivian countryside in 1927. . . . Indians *did* take the initiative, organizing themselves on the basis of their ayllus," he contends. But a tenuous understanding did hold between urban activists and some peasant leaders on the eve of rebellion.[38]

In fact, concrete connections developed between Indian leaders in Potosí and Chuquisaca and urban socialist thinkers both before and during the Third Workers' Congress. The government eventually accused Tristan Marof, Rómulo Chumacero, and Alberto Murillo Calvimonte, a socialist lawyer from Potosí, of being the liaisons with the Indian insurgents.[39] Indian leaders from Chuquisaca and Potosí who attended the congress in Oruro in 1927 did have a preestablished relationship with these urban activists. Despite the dialogue and the declarations of the Third Workers' Congress, however, once the rebellion began, urban workers played no part in it.

Even with the frightening magnitude of the rebellion, the government response showed significant restraint. In October 1927 President Hernando Siles granted an amnesty to all 184 individuals jailed for the insurrection. The government also verbally indicted the corruption and greed of a few landlords, local officials, and priests as the true causes of the rebellion. In a way, the rebellious communities achieved their goals; historians agree that the 1927 revolt put an end to community land loss in the valleys of northern Potosí.[40] There is no way to measure how sympathy among the urban popular class for peasant complaints might have influenced the government to employ a certain level of diplomacy.

At the close of the Third Workers' Congress the delegates resolved to hold their next gathering in Potosí on June 5, 1928. An extended state of siege forced the meeting's cancellation.[41] On October 25, 1928, the Workers' Labor Federation of Potosí wrote its counterpart in La Paz to cancel the project: "The country's situation, the persecution of its working elements, and the bold-faced interference of party politics in our affairs have made it impossible to carry out the Fourth Congress." The Potosí activists continued, "It surely does not escape the thinking of your Regional Council that the realization of the Fourth Congress might provoke grave and fatal consequences for the life, action, and movement of anarcho-syndicalists, because none of its resolutions would be beneficial once the congress was overseen by government forces and would precipitate arrest orders against independent working elements that seek to secure the victory of their highest ideals above and beyond personal interests."[42] The emphasis on "anarcho-syndicalists" indicated a continued ideological struggle inside the labor movement. The anarcho-syndicalists were temporarily ascendant, with the government hounding the most prominent socialist and Marxist leaders. The anarcho-syndicalists wanted to avoid a similar persecution.

In 1929 some in Potosí sought to make up for the previous year's cancellation, though the growing ideological split within the labor movement continued to complicate activists' work. The new meeting's invitation mentioned a couple of pressing topics confronting the labor movement: the rising tension in the Chaco between Bolivia and Paraguay and the need to inject energy into a paralyzed national confederation. Only a handful of organizations attended the gathering, which began on January 13, 1929: elements of the Workers' Labor Federation in Sucre and La Paz and a faction from Potosí's federation. Federations in Oruro and Cochabamba ignored the meeting. One conference report described the external opposition workers faced and the debilitating internal fractures. "When the capitalists perceived the struggle that they confronted, they restricted all the workers' liberty of action without permitting them a minimal liberty of thought. Every attempt at reorganization was followed by a categorical but temporary failure." The report continued:

> The study of modern doctrines without the required systematic approach required by these questions brought about the alienation of some sectors that, without measuring the outrageous consequences, insisted with tenacious persistence upon separating themselves from already organized institutions to craft a prejudicial anarchism inside the workers' ranks. The apathy of others provoked the momentary death of some of the departmental entities. Such a load of factors—both economic and political—were the cause of the consequences that we have felt since the state of siege to which each one of us has recently been subjected.[43]

Despite doubts about the gathering's power to modify resolutions adopted by the Third Workers' Congress, the conference sought to tinker with the structure of the Bolivian Labor Confederation and to establish contacts with socialist labor associations in other countries. Anarcho-syndicalists, however, did not attend the Potosí meeting. As for the growing tension between Bolivia and Paraguay, the gathering foresaw peace through labor organization: "appreciating that the base of international peace rests upon the principal of affection and solidarity between the workers of all countries, and that all wars are inspired by the imperialist interests of capitalism, and as such, ruinous for the true interests and the future of the proletariat, . . . the Bolivian Labor Confederation will continue maintaining fraternity and proletarian unity."[44] The activists sought to preempt any factional criticism in their final memorandum: "It is easy to criticize, to protest, and to refuse to recognize an effective labor, when, with an absolute betrayal of class spirit for childish personal complaints, one seeks to break the harmonious bonds of the family of workers."[45]

The attempt at preemption failed, however, for other factions within the labor movement immediately denounced the Potosí conference. Anarcho-syndicalists were particularly angry and sought to bury the socialist-led meeting. The Workers' Labor Federation of La Paz, a portion of which did not attend the Potosí conference, excoriated the meeting with particular vigor. On March 4, 1929, the federation observed, "The Workers' Conference of Potosí, not having the character of a Congress, cannot destroy the fundamental principles adopted in the Third Congress of Oruro." It also noted "that the Conference of Potosí was carried out without the proper quorum." The federation therefore resolved "to disown the Workers' Conference of Potosí as illegal and to declare in recess the National Workers' Labor Confederation until the Fourth Congress."[46]

The struggle between anarcho-syndicalists and socialists intensified in the run-up to the Fourth Workers' Congress, held in 1930.[47] The anarcho-syndicalist leadership ascendant in the Workers' Labor Federation in several departments believed that the workers had played a critical role in the military coup that threw President Siles from power in May and June 1930, a belief that led to a misplaced faith in the progressive character of the new government.[48] Indeed, liberal-democratic illusions continued to bedevil the labor movement in unexpected ways. Just fourteen days after Siles's defeat, Cochabamba's departmental council of the Bolivian Labor Confederation (i.e., the Workers' Labor Federation of Cochabamba) wrote, "The labor federations of Bolivia were in agreement with the military entities of the Camacho Regiment, etc. and . . . this contingent launched the revolution having as a reserve the workers' regiments."[49]

Anarcho-syndicalist leaders seeking to organize the Fourth Worker's Congress hoped to repudiate earlier gatherings.[50] The Local Labor Federation of La Paz (an anarcho-syndicalist offshoot of the Workers' Labor Federation) issued the call for a new meeting to be held on July 20, 1930, and attended by "all groupings that sympathize with the anarcho-syndicalist labor carried out by this Federation in favor of the socioeconomic demands of the Bolivian proletariat." The federation emphasized the superiority of anarcho-syndicalist thought and tactics: "We wish to impart to the distinct federations a definitive orientation guided by the principles of anarcho-syndicalism, because this economic ideology is the system of organization that truly seeks the emancipation of the workers, securing the improvement of the moral, social, and intellectual conditions of the worker while the bourgeois and capitalist exploiter still exist." The La Paz federation, misreading the overthrow of President Siles, insisted that it was an auspicious time for a national meeting, mentioning "the relative liberty" labor then enjoyed, which it described as "one of the consequences of the recent revolution to whose triumph" workers had contributed with "blood" and "moral support."[51]

The Fourth Workers' Congress opened in Oruro on August 5, 1930. Anarcho-syndicalist activists dominated the meeting.[52] In fact, the split between socialists and anarcho-syndicalists grew to such a point that the latter sought to call the meeting the country's first, to rename the national body, and to establish different international contacts than those already created.[53] Socialists and Marxists walked out of the meeting. Oruro's newspaper, La Patria, observed that anarcho-syndicalist delegates accused the socialists of "having contacts with professional agitators from Moscow and Montevideo" who ostensibly bribed them so that they could "live a bourgeois lifestyle in exchange for dragging the Bolivian proletariat toward the dictatorship of the proletariat, seeking to reestablish the despotism of the bourgeoisie." The newspaper explained that Marxism "seeks to gain power through the workers, that is, to take it from the capitalists and the bourgeoisie, forming a completely proletarian government." Anarcho-syndicalism, it added, "refuses to recognize all government and proclaims anarchy."[54] The split ensured the congress's failure, and a divided labor movement found itself under assault when the Chaco War erupted in 1932. Labor activists would not rebuild their unity until 1936.[55]

The split within the labor movement at the end of the 1920s might seem to close the period on a downbeat, yet when comparing the battle between socialists and anarcho-syndicalists to the working-class illusions in Bautista Saavedra and the Republican Party in 1920, one is struck by the swift ideological evolution of the urban popular classes. From an excited belief in the benevolence of the oligarchy, Bolivia had developed, in less than ten years, two ideological tendencies that—at least in their rhetoric —foreswore all faith in oligarchic parties and called for the overthrow of the capitalist order.

WOMEN WORKERS, WOMEN ACTIVISTS

During the final years of the 1920s the labor movement sought to strengthen itself by promoting the interests of groups sometimes overlooked during the early florescence of organization. Representatives of Bolivia's Indian communities and haciendas had participated in the Third Workers' Congress. Working women, too, sought and received active support from the labor movement during the decade's final years. Women frequently worked for the mining companies in specialized roles or depended indirectly on the industry for their livelihoods. Friction was perhaps inevitable. Resentment of the mining companies and of corrupt government officials thus crossed gender lines; a universal bitterness fortified the political and social strength of the urban popular classes.

Women formed a substantial percentage of Bolivia's mining workforce during the early twentieth century. Female laborers specialized in sorting raw ore according to its quality—a task known as the *palla*. The women who performed this task were called *palliris* and worked in open-air plazas outside mineshafts. As companies modernized, they sometimes moved the sorting indoors and partially mechanized the process. In his 1914 departmental report the prefect Eduardo Diez de Medina counted 116 women working for the Avicaya Mining Company of Poopó; female laborers formed nearly 20 percent of the company's workforce.[56] Three years later the Cercado Province subprefect reported that the Mining Company of Oruro employed a number of women and children sorting ore. He also noted the use of technology to—in theory—lighten the task's physical burden: "In the mine's plaza many women and some children are employed in the task of sorting; but for these individuals the work has been much simplified thanks to a mechanical procedure for the selection of metals that could be called an automatic sorter, suppressing the hammer. With this, the harsh labor of women and children has been alleviated." In other, smaller mines around Oruro—the Itos, Atocha, and La Colorada mines—the subprefect reported, "The women of the mine's plaza carry out the sorting with the antiquated system of the hammer."[57] In 1918 Poopó's subprefect, Ángel Vásquez, calculated that the region's mines employed 249 men and 86 women; additionally, the town's mill employed another 118 individuals both "men and women."[58] Oruro's San José mine reported a workforce of 250 men and 74 women in 1922.[59] More exact numbers are not available, for government officials rarely differentiated between male and female laborers in their surveys—women were just assumed to be a part of those numbers and an integral part of the industry.

Despite their importance, however, female workers appeared only occasionally in worker petitions during this period. Government attention was also sporadic and superficial. Women stood at the bottom of the wage scale, and no union petition sought to modify the hierarchy. When women were included in government regulations, the laws smacked of control or limitation rather than protection and uplift. During the government's first systematic attempt to improve working conditions in the mines in 1913, Minister of Justice and Industry José S. Quinteros lamented "the entry of women into the deep labors of the subsoil." The minister believed that companies sometimes employed "the weaker sex" in the mine's interior as a "means to take advantage of the low wages earned by women." Quinteros also believed that in these "unhealthy subterranean places" prostitution flourished, "extinguishing the morality of the lower class." This "promiscuity" supposedly led to further "criminal acts and unfortunate developments." Quinteros therefore sought to bar women from work inside the mines, but their occupation as *palliris* continued.[60]

Mining touched the lives of almost all women in Oruro, however, even those not directly employed by the industry. Family ties yoked mothers, daughters, and wives to the mines. Beyond that, women engaged in commerce often confronted the companies' authoritarian tendencies, especially in smaller mining camps, where management wielded disproportionate power. The companies' attempts to regulate markets in the shadows of their installations sparked conflict and resentment. On June 24, 1918, Alberto Guesny, of the Consolidated Totoral Tin Society, wrote Poopó's subprefect to complain of female merchants selling alcohol during payday. Every two weeks, he reported, "traveling vendors . . . come bringing domestic commercial articles that are well received by the workers—a commerce that this company does not prevent in the least, because it is a benefit to the management." But Guesny identified four women as chronic irritants: "The merchants Brigida Calisaya, Victoria Soto, Leandra Salazar, and Teofila Vargas, residents of Poopó, introduce liquor, getting a great number of workers drunk, which produces disorder and damages the development of this Company's labors." Guesny's concerns were not novel, though, for the Consolidated Totoral Tin Society had a history of prohibitionist tendencies. Indeed, Guesny already faced a lawsuit for having confiscated all the camp's alcohol, including that in workers' homes. The manager asked that the subprefect instruct the police to ensure that the women stopped coming to Totoral to sell on payday, since it was "impossible to search for the bottles of liquor hidden among their clothes and commercial goods."[61] Such an approach could easily backfire, though; when managers alienated female merchants, they created bonds of sympathy between those employed by the companies and others simply irritated by the swaggering imposition of money and influence.

Officials who abused women further undermined the urban popular classes' sympathy for government. Low pay and incompetence corroded the police throughout Oruro and northern Potosí; women sometimes suffered as a result. On May 27, 1907, for example, Huanuni's police arrested a women named Fabiana. A witness later reported that the woman was drunk, and as the police dragged her to the station, she was "yelling and complaining of her unjust detention." The police chief, Ladislao Vásquez, ordered her tied up, gagged, and thrown into a cell. According to the witness, Fabiana "gave a few loud groans that soon stopped." Not long after the police "found the woman dead in her cell." The witness, Trinidad Rojas, another woman incarcerated at the time of the incident, denounced the death to Oruro prefect Víctor Sanjinez, who ordered the arrest of the accused police chief, but such instances of abuse continually reappeared throughout the early decades of the twentieth century.[62]

Female merchants could accumulate significant personal wealth, and women who made and sold *chicha* (an alcoholic drink of fermented corn) became common targets of corrupt officials seeking money and alcohol. In June 1926 Valentín Garnica, a *chichera* (a woman who makes or sells *chicha*) in the railroad and mill town of Machacamarca, wrote Oruro's prefect to lodge a complaint against Machacamarca's *corregidor*, Nicolás Morales. Garnica alleged that on the night of June 13, Morales barged into her home, "in a state of drunkenness, so that one could not understand a word he spoke." "He sought to oblige me to serve him *chicha*, which I refused to do; this was enough motive for him to order my arrest." Garnica refused to go, and Morales tried to drag her away "by force." The *chichera* reported, "When I told him that I would present myself in his office the following day, he set upon me with blows from his fist and a whip leaving me nearly unconscious, giving me numerous contusions and a wound on my head." Garnica called Morales the "terror of Machacamarca." She reported that he exacted bribes from the town's *chicheras* to ignore the liquor laws, as, she claimed, had happened on the night in question: "He offered not to fine us, but as I did not wish to accept this, he committed abuses with my person in the form that has already been described."[63] Financial success thus sometimes had a darker side for female merchants.

Poverty was no protection, however. Less financially secure women, too, suffered from officials indulging their power. Single mothers or mothers seeking to raise children in a husband's absence could find themselves exposed. On April 18, 1931, Úrsula M. de Aramayo filed a complaint with the Cercado Province subprefect against Machacamarca's *corregidor*. De Aramayo reported that she lived in Machacamarca: "I occupy myself in caring for my young children and with my domestic duties." Her husband lived and worked in the city of Oruro. She wrote that for a couple of months, she had been having "small inconveniences with the concubine of the current *Corregidor* Honorato Arias"; in her complaint, she wrote, "I was insulted by the mentioned woman, whose name I do not know, who in addition to continually insulting me, threatened me with a small knife that is always on her person." After the incident, the *corregidor* burst into de Aramayo's home to threaten her and to warn her to avoid future clashes with his domestic partner. De Aramayo's need to support her family put her in danger of further attack.

> As I have said, in the town where I live, I do not have the support of my husband, and I take care of my young children alone; additionally, my principal business consists in going to the train station every night in the dark to sell a few items, and to arrive at the station I have to pass before the door of *Corregidor* Arias, where his concubine also lives, and at that hour of the night they might attack me; more so now that he is a government authority, he tries to instill terror in the inoffensive residents of this Canton.[64]

Women such as Úrsula M. de Aramayo sought the paternal protection of benevolent officials to remedy the attacks of the corrupt. With the emergence of female labor and business associations at the end of the 1920s, however, some women sought new avenues of self-defense.

A variety of organizations led by women and representing women's interests appeared in Oruro beginning in 1928.[65] They had close links with the labor movement, so that their development substantially strengthened organized labor. The women's organizations also tackled topics male activists sometimes glossed over or ignored, specifically ethnicity. Working-class organizations rarely wrote about the ethnicity of the urban popular classes—a clear contrast with the obsessions of oligarchic intellectuals. Instead, class consistently emerged as the principal frame of reference. In contrast, Oruro's first association of female workers and merchants developed in response to an attack on a key marker of urban popular-class ethnicity: the dress of mestiza women.

On July 9, 1928, Oruro's municipal government passed a resolution seeking to ban clothing associated with the mestizo and Indian populations. It specifically sought to ban the *pollera*, the multilayered skirts worn by the women of the urban popular classes. The municipality ordered Oruro's residents to "dress in the clothing of modern, civilized nations," although it permitted "popular and national garments [to] be worn in the countryside and towns."[66] In response, working-class and market women formed Oruro's first specifically female organization of the urban popular classes: the Feminine Committee for the Defense of the Working Woman. Organized on October 2, 1928, the association emerged proclaiming "the necessity to care for the conservation of certain rights and prerogatives that are integral to [women's] condition as persons." The Feminine Committee for the Defense of the Working Woman included married, widowed, and single women and had a membership of at least seventy.[67] The leadership of the new body crafted a persuasive nationalist argument in defense of the female dress of the urban popular classes. In an October 3 letter the committee asked Prefect Adolfo Navarro for permission to hold a public rally so as to pressure the municipal council to reverse itself. The activists emphasized their "pure, patriotic sentiment and genuine nationalism" and portrayed the council as somewhat disloyal: "With the disappearance of the typical dress of the *pollera*, they would surely hide the last vestiges that are left to us of our national character and would also make disappear the traditions that weave the history of the people."[68] A year after the incident Oruro's new prefect, General Raimundo González Flor, acknowledged the law's defeat. "This poorly understood ordinance was vehemently condemned by the popular classes, who not only labeled it unconstitutional but refused to comply with it," he wrote. While González held a favorable opinion of the law's objectives, he felt it conflicted with the inertia of Bolivian culture. The prefect continued, "While the mentioned ordinance is praiseworthy, as it sought to improve the culture of the people, the measure was too brusque in its imposition and clashed with deeply ingrained customs." González highlighted the committee's resistance and opposition rally. He reported, "The Council, in view of the resistance it encountered among the working class, had to indefinitely postpone the measure's implementation."[69] Ethnic markers condemned by the Eurocentric oligarchy became, in the argumentation of the Feminine Committee for the Defense of the Working Woman, essential symbols of Bolivian nationalism.

The development of one female association opened the door for others. In April 1929 women who made or sold *chicha* formed an organization to defend their collective interests. In its first letter to Oruro's prefect, the Chicha Industrial Union emphasized that the preparation of this particular alcoholic beverage was, for the union's members, not only "a question of business" but also "a question of life."[70] As did the earlier Feminine Committee for the Defense of the Working Woman, the Chicha Industrial Union enjoyed ties to the labor movement; the lists of advisers for both bodies included Antonio Carvajal, who had attended the Third Workers' Congress as a representative of the Workers' Labor Federation of Oruro and once served as president of that body; in 1928 Carvajal became president of the Workers' National Union in Oruro, a party closely linked with the presidency of Hernando Siles.[71]

One final female organization that appeared during this period was the Feminine Union of Various Occupations. This body participated in Oruro's May Day parade of 1930, which had been organized by the Workers' Labor Federation. The women marched in the parade's second position, right after the federation's central committee.[72] Female activists, as this shows, had quickly won a respected place for themselves within the labor movement.

The country's working class and artisans needed the extra strength provided by female mobilization at the end of the 1920s. With the onset of the Great Depression, tin mining entered a period of unprecedented contraction. As the authority of liberal economic orthodoxy collapsed, the labor movement and its intellectual allies provided some of the few viable alternatives. Throughout the crisis, the solidarity of working-class families—male and female—provided a consistent reinforcement to the labor movement.

THE CRISIS BEGINS

Although tin's value had been declining for a number of years, the price did not enter total free fall until the second half of 1929. Between June 1929 and June 1930 tin's value fell by 44 percent. The government lacked the financial resources and budgetary flexibility to respond effectively to the crisis. Even before tin's collapse, moreover, President Hernando Siles's administration had felt an anticipatory economic pinch. Debt obligations and previous deficit spending began to restrict government options as early as 1926. Oligarchic politicians ineffectually sought remedies when the economic storm hit with full force, but their options were limited. The country's budget in 1929 showed burdensome commitments to unproductive expenditures: 37 percent went to service the foreign debt, and 20 percent went to the military.[73] Even if the oligarchic parties could invent a plan to deal with the crisis, the government lacked the money to implement it.

As the crisis deepened, ideological infighting plagued the labor movement. In Oruro the disagreements among socialists, Marxists, and anarcho-syndicalists intensified during the first half of 1930 in the run-up to the Fourth Workers' Congress. The Bolivian Labor Confederation in Oruro reorganized itself in March 1930 with a new anarcho-syndicalist leadership. Gabriel Moisés became the general secretary, and Luis Gallardo, the secretary of exterior relations. Moisés was born in a northern Potosí mining town, spent part of his childhood in Chile, and eventually came to work in a La Paz textile mill. In 1929 he moved to Oruro to inject new energy into that city's labor movement. Luis Gallardo was a carpenter and a member of Oruro's Woodworkers' Union, a bastion of anarcho-syndicalism in the city.[74] On March 27, 1930, the confederation's new leadership issued a circular to the department's various laboring associations calling for greater activism: "Conscious of our duty in these difficult and trying moments for the country's proletariat, and especially for that of this mining region, we call for the union of all of the workers of all of the societies, so that united in this way we might alleviate, in some small measure, the horrendous evils that threaten humble proletarian homes."[75] Just two weeks later the confederation was involved in a dispute with one of Oruro's principal mining companies.

The Mining Company of Oruro sought to frustrate the Bolivian Labor Confederation's activism among its workers.[76] Oruro prefect Raimundo González Flor, a general in the Bolivian military, mediated negotiations between the company and the union, but the slow pace of the talks frustrated Gabriel Moisés and Luis Gallardo. On April 15, 1930, they wrote González, complaining, "The conciliatory gestures carried out by this Federation, with the intercession of the Authorities—even of the President of the Republic—have not produced any result other than making evident, once again, the intransigence of foreign exploiters." Because of the impasse, the confederation resolved to adopt a more radical stance: "Taking into account the ineffectual intervention of the Authorities in the conflict produced between the workers and the mine owners because of the tin crisis; Be it resolved: That the Working Class will resolve its differences directly with the Capitalists." The resolution contained a threatening edge, yet Moisés and Gallardo still thanked the prefect for his "benevolent mediation of this issue." González eventually negotiated a peaceful settlement.[77] The Mining Company of Oruro accepted a plebiscite in which its workers voted to approve representation by the Bolivian Labor Confederation.[78]

Gabriel Moisés and Luis Gallardo still enjoyed a comfortable relationship with Prefect Raimundo González Flor at the end of April 1930. In the days right before May Day, Moisés and Gallardo wrote the prefect to assure him that the Bolivian Labor Confederation's march and rally "would be carried out with the best of order respecting the authorities and without altering public order." The confederation's anarcho-syndicalist leaders promised to "take responsibility for any infraction that the marchers might commit." As for the speeches, they promised to "observe the greatest moderation and avoid phrases offensive to the public powers of the State."[79] But this comfortable relationship with the prefecture did not last.

By the end of May the confederation had begun to irritate Oruro's prefecture. The union wrote Prefect Raimundo González Flor on May 26, 1930, to clarify a recent dispute between the labor organization and the government: "A false interpretation of an inoffensive paragraph published in the recently confiscated edition of *El Proletario* [the union's newspaper] and, more than anything else, fanciful suspicions and childish fears of Proletarian Organizing, have induced you to order the arrest of our comrades Gabriel Moisés and Luis Gallardo, Secretary General and Secretary of External Relations, respectively, of the Bolivian Labor Confederation," the union wrote. The confederation employed strong language with the prefect, though such forceful rhetoric was unusual for union correspondence with the government. The confederation wrote, "The Delegates of the different Labor Unions to the Central Council composing this letter, desirous to avoid complications that might alter the peaceful spirit of the country's workers, and especially those of this district, come to you, Sr. Prefect, to demand the liberty of our comrades." The union did close its letter with more diplomatic language, though, writing of the prefect's "deep understanding and just spirit, and . . . wisdom": "You will know how to avoid difficulties that would aggravate the delicate situation the country is experiencing[;] we appeal to you as your servants." Twelve different artisan and working-class bodies signed the petition, and the prefect eventually released Moisés and Gallardo.[80]

The spat between the Bolivian Labor Confederation and Oruro's prefecture indicates the deteriorating legitimacy of President Hernando Siles's administration. In April 1930, as the government floundered in the face of the Great Depression, Siles announced his intention to cancel the scheduled presidential election. The decision was unpopular. On May 28 Siles resigned and handed power to an interim council, albeit one that he and his political allies controlled. The council called for a new constitution. On June 12 students across the country began protesting the political status quo. On June 16 a poorly organized band of revolutionaries led by Roberto Hinojosa crossed into Bolivia from Argentina, seizing the town of Villazón, but the military pushed them back across the border within a few days. On June 22 the military also attempted to repress striking students in La Paz, killing several; the incident became known as "Tragic Sunday." Three days later a much wider revolt broke out in several other cities, and a number of military units joined the insurrection. By June 27 military officers supporting another Republican Party politician—Daniel Salamanca—had control of the country. The former president, Hernando Siles, and his allies sought asylum in a number of foreign embassies in La Paz. General Carlos Blanco Galindo headed a caretaker governing council until new elections could be held. Daniel Salamanca—one of the Republican Party's original founders—was sworn in as president on March 5, 1931.[81]

The seizure of Villazón by Roberto Hinojosa's revolutionaries was the most radical, if ultimately ineffectual, element of the broad-based movement against President Siles. The invasion cast a dark cloud over the labor movement, for oligarchic politicians and military officers believed that working-class activists shared some of the would-be revolutionaries' threatening political proclivities. Hinojosa, for example, had served as president of Cochabamba's Federation of Students in 1920 and adhered to an eclectic mixture of leftist and populist political programs.[82] After he and forty followers seized government offices in Villazón on June 16, 1930, they issued a manifesto to "the Bolivian Nation on the first day of the revolution" and a seventy-point "Program of Principles."[83] The manifesto declared that the Quechua and Aymara people would build "a future society without masters and without tyrants" and declared theirs to be "a social revolution." The young revolutionaries employed a number of slogans associated with the labor movement: "Land and liberty! Is the standard of the Bolivian revolution that will fly over the confiscated haciendas with their redistribution"; "The mines to the state! And more clearly: the mines to the Bolivian workers!"[84] Hinojosa's program called for, among other things, the nationalization of the mines and the railroads, the abolition of large landholdings, mandatory unionization, an eight-hour workday, and strident economic nationalism.[85] Despite the influence of communist thinkers such as Tristan Marof, Hinojosa swore off a Marxist affiliation. "We do not want to be a colony of Bolshevism, because Moscow is not the proper center to orient our revolution ideologically and politically," he wrote.[86] With the defeat of Hinojosa's invasion and the ejection of President Siles, government fell to far more conservative forces.

Oruro's labor movement sought to assure the military caretaker government that it had nothing to do with Roberto Hinojosa. The anarcho-syndicalist Fourth Workers' Congress, held in August 1930, repudiated the attack on Villazón.[87] On September 10, 1930, the Bolivian Labor Confederation in Oruro sent the prefect a letter assuring him of its sympathies: "The Workers' Federation and organized labor are foreign to all 'communist' movements and repudiate the actions of the bandit Roberto Hinojosa." The union continued, "Organized labor does not follow Communist or Anarchist doctrines," adding, "The Workers' Federation and organized labor are prepared to enforce respect for private property and the imperative mandate of the Constitution." With respect to a public prosecutor in Oruro who was engaged in a campaign to indict the local labor movement as subversive and communist, the confederation called his accusations "nothing more than intrigues" and characterized the prosecutor as "a declared enemy of the working class, pursuing and oppressing without justifiable cause."[88] Such protestations of sympathy failed to assure, however, and around the time of this letter, the government forced the Bolivian Labor Confederation in Oruro into a period of dormancy.

Oruro's labor movement was undergoing a period of political transition in the wake of President Hernando Siles's overthrow. Previously the Bolivian Labor Confederation and the Workers' Labor Federation of Oruro had operated as one, using organizational names interchangeably. In September 1930, however, the two bodies seemed to be operating independently, as different bodies with different leaders. The Workers' Labor Federation thus avoided the government repression that fell on the Bolivian Confederation of Labor.

On September 4, 1930, the Workers' Labor Federation of Oruro wrote the government in La Paz recommending a series of immediate reforms to alleviate the Great Depression's devastating impact on the working class. On September 3 the federation had organized a special body—the Labor Union of the Unemployed—to consider issues related to the crisis. In a mass assembly the new union proposed three immediate reforms and a potential longer-term solution. The workers asserted that their only goal was to "procure the immediate remedy of the grave problem of the unemployed workers' desperate situation." For immediate remedies, the labor activists proposed that the government establish a system of soup kitchens, that rents be deferred, and that the authorities suspend the annual road tax and fees for identification cards. The union also recognized that these three proposals were "not a radical solution to the unemployment problem" and thus "resolved to propose the following points as a definitive solution": the "distribution of land near to commercial centers" and "subsidies for the respective installation and acquisition of the means of cultivation."[89] The proposed agricultural solution to an industrial crisis suggested that many unemployed workers had some experience in agriculture but did not have access to their own land. Also, many doubted the immediate recovery of industrial production or did not want to return to the dependence and instability of industrial employment.

In October and November 1930 workers and artisans sought to revive the Bolivian Labor Confederation in Oruro. When the confederation re-emerged, anarcho-syndicalist leaders were no longer ascendant. On October 20 union members wrote Oruro's prefect, Colonel Miguel Alaiza, to request permission to meet and reorganize the body. The men seeking to restart the union attempted to disown the confederation's support for a number of strikes following President Hernando Siles's overthrow. "We repudiate these acts, and as such, we offer to collaborate in the maintenance of public order whenever it might be necessary," they wrote.[90] By late November the government allowed the confederation to resume its activities. The body met and elected new leaders on November 28, 1930. Neither Gabriel Moisés nor Luis Gallardo—the two anarcho-syndicalist leaders heading the confederation during the first half of the year—appeared in leadership positions in the reorganized body. In their first communiqué to Oruro's new prefect, Colonel Armando Bretel, the confederation noted, "The new leadership council has the intention to labor for the moral, material, and economic improvement of the working class, adhering to the proscriptions established by the law; it will confront with Justice and prudence the differences that develop between capital and labor."[91] The missive's seeming obedience might indicate either political moderation or just a pragmatic recognition of the government's impatience with disruptive dissent. A number of the confederation's leaders inclined toward socialism but chose to funnel their political advocacy into a new political party rather than the labor confederation. The Bolivian Labor Confederation thus adopted a pose of political neutrality.

The new party emerged in the same month as the confederation's reorganization. The Workers' Party attracted activists with a long history of labor organizing in Oruro and northern Potosí. Gumercindo Rivera, the tailor who had served as vice president for the Central Labor Federation of Uncía in 1923, was the new party's president. One of the party's secretaries, too, had connections to the old Central Labor Federation of Uncía: Primitivo Albarracín. Albarracín and Rivera had both been confined to the provincial town of Corque for several months in 1923. The Workers' Party also shared membership with the reorganized Bolivian Labor Confederation; party members Severo Delgadillo and Eduardo Castellón Alvéstegui were confederation leaders. The new party ran a slate of candidates in Oruro's municipal elections of December 1930 but scored no significant victories.[92]

The Workers' Party of Oruro was still active in the early months of Daniel Salamanca's presidency, before the Chaco War killed all political dissent. The Workers' Party wrote Oruro's prefect, Francisco Fajardo, on June 8, 1931, to criticize a traditional government subsidy of the Catholic Church. The economic crisis fueled the party's indignation: "With the right that is ours as Bolivian citizens and contributors directly and indirectly to the National coffers and, as such, to the Departmental and Municipal treasuries, we ask: 'In exchange for what services are these payments given?'" The socialists noted, "The Prefecture in your charge cannot ignore the state of hunger and misery with which the unemployed working element— which is 75 percent of it—is struggling." The Workers' Party observed that so far, the country had experienced relative calm, but the situation might not last: "If until now there have been no tragedies to lament, it is because it is harvest season, and those who have little are in the valleys or on the farms earning food to calm their hunger, but the situation cannot last, all resources run out, especially at the pace things are going. Necessity will make people act in a manner that is difficult to predict, and the only guilty party will be the Government and those authorities who have not worked seriously to improve the situation." The party concluded by observing, "We cannot conceive of how the Government and the authorities, having so many unemployed and, complaining of a lack of resources, are still giving away thousands to elements that produce no benefits whatsoever."[93] Popular rumblings similar to those of the Workers' Party of Oruro would eventually lead President Daniel Salamanca to launch a war with Paraguay in a desperate attempt to hide his government's inability to manage the economic crisis. The ensuing debacle of the Chaco War (1932–1935) initially led to a repression of working-class activism, but eventually the war's fallout led to the decay of oligarchic political control, opening a new and expansive horizon for the urban popular classes.

Epilogue

THE CHACO WAR AND ITS AFTERMATH

As THE dominant classes struggled to maintain their political monopoly in the 1930s and 1940s, government and industry ratcheted up the pressure on the country's popular classes. The Chaco War stands out as the most brutal of these exactions. Just months after the ouster of President Hernando Siles in 1930, but following years of ambitious scheming, Daniel Salamanca assumed the presidency. Unable to resolve the economic crisis, the Salamanca administration plunged into the war as a vainglorious distraction. When the government ordered a national mobilization on July 21, 1932, it became clear that the popular classes—both urban and rural— would bear the brunt of the fighting. The military dispatched impressment squads to all corners of the republic to round up resistant peasants and workers. In three years of fighting against Paraguay more than 56,000 Bolivians died. On November 27, 1934, the military deposed President Salamanca because of his disastrous mismanagement of the war effort; Vice President José Luis Tejada Sorzano assumed the reins of government. With the consent of the military, the Tejada Sorzano administration negotiated an armistice with the Paraguayan government that went into effect on June 14, 1935. Following the war political anarchy ensued; the working class saw the instability as an opportunity to push for higher wages long delayed by combat in the Chaco. The military, led by a group of young officers seeking to put a stop to the chaos, overthrew Tejada Sorzano on May 17, 1936. This was the effective end of nearly sixty years of oligarchic governance; the Liberal and Republican parties soon went the way of the long-deposed Conservative Party and faded from the political scene. The reform-minded military administrations of first David Toro and then Germán Busch began to experiment with new political and social models.[1]

These two generals termed their eclectic nationalist and populist policies "military socialism." The civilian politicians and military men who cycled through government in the 1930s and 1940s espoused a number of left-of-center economic and political policies seeking a regimented capitalist development of the country. These "socialists" called for limitations on the political power of the largest mining concerns and sought to persuade foreign capital to reinvest profits in the continued economic growth of the republic. Eventually, these ideas coalesced in the formation of a quasi-populist middle-class political party named the Nationalist Revolutionary Movement (Movimiento Nacionalista Revolucionario, or MNR) in 1940–1941.[2]

The oligarchs made a brief comeback between 1940 and 1943 during the conservative military government of General Enrique Peñaranada. A slaughter of striking workers that far eclipsed the Uncía Massacre occurred during these years. In late 1942, in the northern Potosí town of Catavi, 9,300 workers employed by Simón I. Patiño's firm agitated for a Christmas bonus and the enforcement of labor laws long ignored by the company. On December 21 the military twice opened fire on the town's working-class residents. The first incident between miners and the army left thirty-five dead. When thousands of women and children gathered to rally against the killings, the soldiers again opened fire, slaying hundreds of peaceful protesters. Popular revulsion at the Catavi Massacre eventually led to the fall of the conservative military administration. In 1943 the reformers again captured the presidential palace when the army officer Gualberto Villarroel overthrew Peñaranada with the cooperation of the MNR.[3]

During the Villarroel presidency, the country's mine workers organized a more combative union. In June 1944 thirty labor delegates met in Huanuni, Oruro, to form the Syndicalist Federation of Bolivian Mine Workers—the union that represents the country's miners to this day. The ferment of post–Chaco War politics also began to resonate in the countryside during the Villarroel administration. In May 1945 the MNR-military government organized the First National Indian Congress, an important political milestone for Bolivia's rural majority. By 1946 an eclectic left-right alliance had developed to confront the Villarroel and MNR administration. Calling itself an antifascist front, this motley assortment of political parties and interest groups combined to overthrow the reformist military-civilian government. The popular-front movement combined the Stalinist Leftist Revolutionary Party; university students; elements of an older national labor federation, the Syndicalist Confederation of Bolivian Workers, of which the mine workers were no longer a part; and the remnants of the traditional oligarchic parties, the Liberals and Republicans. Eventually, this coalition launched a revolt in the city of La Paz on July 14, 1946—a revolt the military declined to repress. A mob dragged Villarroel from the presidential palace, lynched him, and hung his body from a lamppost in the city's principal plaza.[4]

The participation of the Leftist Revolutionary Party in the coalition government from 1946 to 1952 completely discredited it in the eyes of the working class. The rival Revolutionary Workers' Party—a Trotskyist organization—quickly occupied a dominant ideological position on the far left of the country's political spectrum. This party was first organized in Argentina in December 1934 by political exiles expelled during the Chaco War. The radical intellectual Tristan Marof was a founding member of the party, but he eventually left it in 1938.[5] The Trotskyism of the Revolutionary Workers' Party had an enormous impact on the young but powerful Syndicalist Federation of Bolivian Mine Workers.[6] After Gualberto Villarroel's government fell in July 1946, this federation met in the mining town of Pulacayo, Potosí, to hold a meeting it dubbed the "Extraordinary Miners' Congress" and define its response to the new popular-front government. Guillermo Lora, the leading theorist of the Revolutionary

Workers' Party, occupied a position of ideological ascendancy at the meeting.[7]

Guillermo Lora Escóbar was a native of Uncía and a law student in La Paz. The miners of Llallagua elected him a voting delegate to the Extraordinary Miners' Congress, but the working class of the mines did not extend him a universally warm welcome. Several representatives of the Syndicalist Federation of Bolivian Mine Workers objected to his attendance, since he was not a mine worker himself. Lora nevertheless played an important role at the November 1946 congress, for he and other members of the Revolutionary Workers' Party proposed to union delegates the *Thesis of Pulacayo*—a summary of the Trotskyist idea of "permanent revolution" and its application to the Bolivian context. Although Marxism guided the Syndicalist Federation of Bolivian Mine Workers, workers opposed the two-stage approach to socialist revolution pushed by the Stalinist government in Moscow and represented in Bolivia by the politics of the Leftist Revolutionary Party. The *Thesis of Pulacayo* cast its gaze back over 120 years of Bolivian republican history and concluded that, because of their dependence on foreign capital and foreign imperialism, the dominant classes had failed to carry out the most basic of liberal-democratic and nationalist objectives. Only the working class could carry out the democratic and socialist transformation of the republic, and this had to be done in one decisive stroke.[8]

The *Thesis of Pulacayo* identified Bolivia as a capitalist nation, but—because of the country's limited economic development—a strange amalgam of precapitalist and capitalist labor relations continued to reign. "The most primitive of economic forms and the latest word in technology and capitalist civilization exist together," the document read. The country was a "backward capitalist nation," and lagging economic development retarded political and social reform. "The Bolivian peculiarity arises because there is no bourgeoisie on the political scene capable of liquidating the *latifundio* [the semifeudal hacienda] and other precapitalist economic forms, of unifying the nation, and of liberating it from the imperialist yoke. . . . these bourgeois-democratic objectives must be carried out immediately," the *Thesis* argued. In South America, the document stated, the dominant classes were so compromised in their dependence on foreign capital that "the proletariat of a backward nation is obliged to combine the struggle for bourgeois-democratic objectives with the struggle for socialist change."[9]

According to the *Thesis of Pulacayo*, this radical socialist restructuring of the nation would require that the working class overthrow the government. The document asserted that the government stood in fundamental opposition to the interests and well-being of the popular classes. "The feudal-bourgeois state exists as an organ of violence to maintain the privileges of the landowner and the capitalist," it read; "only traitors and imbeciles can continue to argue that the state is capable of elevating itself above the various social classes and paternally decide what is best for each group."[10] (This sentiment was not simply theoretical; at one point during the Extraordinary Miners' Congress, labor delegates sympathetic to the popular-front government then in power in La Paz had to flee for their lives through the windows of the theater in which the miners were gathered.)[11] The miners' program called for the complete political independence of the working class and derided the popular-front governments of the 1930s and 1940s: "The FSTMB [Syndicalist Federation of Bolivian Mine Workers] will never form a part of bourgeois governments, for this would signify a frank betrayal of the exploited and forget that our line is the revolutionary line of class struggle." In placing the proletariat at the head of the future revolution, however, the federation overstated the ideological independence of the working class in Bolivian history. "The Bolivian proletariat has remained almost virgin in its political aspect, because it has no tradition of parliamentarianism and class collaboration," the document erroneously asserted.[12] Nonetheless, although the union delegates at the 1946 Extraordinary Miners' Congress underestimated the influence of bourgeois and petite bourgeois political thought on the working class in the past, they formally renounced the leadership of other social classes in the future.

While the Syndicalist Federation of Bolivian Mine Workers claimed a position of revolutionary leadership for the working class of the mines, it recognized the need for cooperation: "The proletarian revolution in

Bolivia means not the exclusion of other exploited groups in the nation," the *Thesis* asserted, "but a revolutionary alliance of the proletariat with the peasants, the artisans, and other sectors of the urban petite bourgeoisie." The federation classed the nation's peasant majority with other "petit bourgeois" groups that might ally with the working class in overthrowing government and the capitalist economy. Yet in a typical formulation of Trotskyist thought, it expressed a strong pessimism as to the independent revolutionary potential of the peasantry and other non-working-class segments of the popular classes. The *Thesis de Pulacayo* declared that "the class independence of the petite bourgeoisie is a myth." The document argued that in times of domestic tranquility, the petite bourgeoisie followed the political lead of the dominant classes: "Petty merchants and small property owners, technicians, bureaucrats, artisans, and the peasantry have not until now been able to develop a politics of class independence, and they will not be able to do so in the future." In times of social ferment, however, the working class had to lead the unhappy and exploited segments of the popular classes in revolt if a new socialist order was to be established. "The leader of the revolution will be the proletariat," the *Thesis* asserted. To that end the federation proposed a systematic program to recruit the numerous and decisive peasantry: "The workers must organize peasant unions and work together with Indian communities. For this, it is necessary that the miners support the struggle of the peasants against the *latifundio* and second their revolutionary activities."[13] A few years later activists would attempt to do just that. Following the 1952 National Revolution, a newly reorganized national labor federation, the Bolivian Workers' Central, began a concerted effort to organize the rural population of the country into effective peasant unions.[14]

Just six years after adopting the *Thesis of Pulacayo,* mine workers had a chance to implement the theory. The National Revolution started in La Paz, where the vertical geography of the city reflected (inversely) the country's social structure. The wealthy and powerful occupied the river bottom, monopolizing the most temperate sector of this precipitous Andean valley carved by the Chuquiapu River, a tributary of the expansive Amazon. The poor and politically marginalized carved their precarious homes from the ascending valley walls—the higher altitude meant cold and biting winds. On April 9, 1952, this vertically segmented city erupted in revolution. That morning the frustrated middle-class militants of the Nationalist Revolutionary Movement (MNR) and a group of sympathetic police officers seized several important government buildings in downtown La Paz. The insurgents sought to inspire a quick and bloodless coup to defeat a military council led by General Hugo Ballivián, itself the product of a coup carried out the year before that had scuttled the MNR's 1951 electoral victory. Although the April 1952 rebellion began like many other political coups in Bolivian history—the product of party factionalism and military rivalry—its final result surprised everyone. General Antonio Seleme pledged his police officers to the MNR's cause; in exchange, he sought the presidency. The conspirators envisioned a sudden victory, yet the overwhelming majority of the military remained loyal to General Ballivián. In the end, the popular classes of La Paz and the miners decided this contest of power.

Throughout the day on April 9 and into the night, the population of La Paz rose in rebellion against military units moving through the city to strangle the coup. Despite the popular support, General Seleme and his followers sought refuge in the Chilean Embassy. The MNR leaders, also pessimistic about the rebellion's chances for success, sought an accord with the military council. The popular classes of La Paz continued to fight. On April 10 military units attempting to sweep the capital's streets encountered barricades and a population in arms. In the afternoon mine workers from Milluni attacked the rear of army units encircling La Paz. The military council also received word that miners in Oruro had already destroyed three reinforcing army regiments. The Bolivian military evaporated.[15]

The National Revolution of 1952 is the most important event in twentieth-century Bolivian history. It is also the only social revolution in Latin America carried out by workers for workers. Without the mobilization of the urban popular classes, most especially the miners, the revolution never would have occurred. Without the rebellion of the Syndicalist Federation of Bolivian Mine Workers, historians would remember the events of 1952 as just another attempted coup. Only six years after the

Extraordinary Miners' Congress in Pulacayo, the membership of the Syndicalist Federation of Bolivian Mine Workers seized the opportunity to become the principal arbiters of national politics. In 1952 an alliance of the miners and the popular classes of La Paz overthrew the last vestiges of oligarchic power in the country. The *Thesis of Pulacayo* had correctly predicted that only the popular classes led by the working class of the mines had the will to carry out fundamental liberal-democratic reforms long ignored by the dominant classes. After the National Revolution of 1952, the illiterate peasant majority of the nation (both men and women) finally won the right to vote. In 1953, moreover, peasants across the country —organized by new rural unions—pushed through a sweeping revolution in rural land-tenure patterns. Peasant unions seized hacienda after hacienda. The semifeudal rural oligarchy virtually disappeared. Finally, the Syndicalist Federation of Bolivian Mine Workers forced the government to expropriate the nation's principal mines, expelling the bosses. Unfortunately, the working class did not follow all the precepts laid down in 1946. The miners destroyed the military as they swore to do in the *Thesis of Pulacayo,* but they refused to take the reins of the republic following their triumph. Between 1952 and 1964 the middle-class MNR and a rebuilt army successfully mobilized the demographic weight of the peasantry to suffocate the permanent revolution—already partially betrayed by a vacillating and scheming union leadership.

The history of the urban popular classes during the first three decades of the twentieth century suggested that they alone had the ideological tools and organizational strength to substantially alter the outline of Bolivian society; the eventual physiognomy of the 1952 National Revolution confirmed that. While the country's labor unions did not yet have the power to stop the oligarchy's disastrous management of national affairs in the 1930s, the groundwork existed for the working class to clear away the rubble of economic liberalism after the collapse. Rather than wonder at the late arrival of unionism and radical ideologies such as socialism, Marxism, and anarcho-syndicalism to Bolivia, one is instead struck by the rapid ascent and consolidation of those modern elements once they arrived.

NOTES

Prologue

1. For some interpretations of the workers' role in the National Revolution of 1952, see Barcelli S., *Medio siglo de luchas sindicales*; Zavaleta Mercado, *Bolivia*; Justo (Quebracho), *Bolivia*; Lora, *Historia del movimiento obrero boliviano*; Delgado Gonzales, *100 años de lucha*; Rahal, *Sangre y estaño*; and Grindle and Domingo, eds., *Proclaiming Revolution*.

2. Oficina Nacional de Inmigración, *Censo general*, 2:17–18.

3. Klein, *Bolivia*, 228.

4. Bolivia, *Censo general*, 2:17.

5. Nash, *Practicing Ethnography*, 20.

6. For the twentieth-century mining history of Bolivia, see Albarracín Millán, *El poder minero*; Albarracín Millán, *Bolivia*; Mitre, *Los patriarcas de la plata*; Mitre, *Bajo un cielo de estaño*; Querejazu, *Llallagua*; Rodríguez Ostria, *El socavón y el sindicato*; Lehm A. and Rivera C., *Los artesanos libertarios*; and Nash, *We Eat the Mines*.

CHAPTER 1: Laboring in the Boss's Shadow

1. Geddes, *Patiño, rey de estaño*, 45, 48, 52, 63–67. A 1901 newspaper report in Oruro suggested that Artigue was recruiting another mercenary band in Potosí, but nothing ever came of this second attempt. The newspaper was sympathetic to Patiño and ridiculed Artigue: "Artigue . . . alleging to claim eight hectares with the title 'La Negra,' whose location must be on the moon, because in Uncía there is not a hand span of open land" ("Otra vez Uncía. Cuadrillas que organizan en Potosí," *El Vapor* [Oruro, Bolivia], Sept. 22, 1901; translations are my own unless otherwise specified).

2. Arzáns de Orsúa y Vela, *Historia de la Villa Imperial*, 1:34–36; Capoche, *Relación general de la Villa Imperial*, 77–78. For other discussions of Potosí's foundation, see Bakewell, *Miners of the Red Mountain*; Hanke, *Imperial City of Potosí*; and Mangan, *Trading Roles*, 21–23.

3. Bakewell, *Miners of the Red Mountain*, 49–51.

4. The word *wayra* is often spelled in colonial documents as *huayra* or *guayra*.

5. De Cieza de León, *La crónica del Perú*, 335–36.

6. Bakewell, *Miners of the Red Mountain*, 17.

7. De Cieza de León, *La crónica del Perú*, 336.

8. Bakewell, *Miners of the Red Mountain*, 36.

9. De Cieza de León, *La crónica del Perú*, 336.

10. Bakewell, *Miners of the Red Mountain*, 49–51.

11. Capoche, *Relación general de la Villa Imperial*, 108–9.

12. For a technical discussion of the mercury amalgamation technique written in the Spanish colonial period, see Alonso Barba, *Arte de los metales*.

13. Bakewell, *Miners of the Red Mountain*, 18–19.

14. De Toledo, *Ordenanzas del Virrey Toledo*, vol. 8, *Gobernantes del Perú*, 143–44, 146.

15. Bakewell, *Miners of the Red Mountain*, 56–59, 67, 77, 79–80; Zulawski, "*They Eat from Their Labor,*" 48. For works on the mita system of Potosí, see Abecia Baldivieso, *Mitayos de Potosí*; and Cole, *The Potosí Mita*.

16. Bakewell, *Miners of the Red Mountain*, 26, 28–29.

17. Pauwels, "Oruro 1607," 96.

18. Zulawski, "*They Eat from Their Labor,*" 94; Escobari de Querejazu, *Caciques, yanaconas y extravagantes*, 285–86. For insights on the colonial mining economy of Oruro, see also Cornblit, *Power and Violence in the Colonial City*.

19. Zulawski, "*They Eat from Their Labor,*" 125, 129, 202–3.

20. Bakewell, *Miners of the Red Mountain*, 122–23, 181; Tandeter, *Coacción y mercado*, 110–11.

21. Arzáns de Orsúa y Vela, *Historia de la Villa Imperial*, 3:201.

22. Ibid., 3:201–2.

23. Ibid., 3:201, 203–5.

24. Tandeter, *Coacción y mercado*, 13–14, 18–21.

25. Ibid., 281.

26. Lofstrom, *Dámaso de Uriburu*, 7–8, 31–32.

27. Platt, "Producción," 397, 400–401.

28. Ibid., 396, 410, 418, 420.

29. "Expediente de los capchas de esta ciudad . . . ," AHP PDE 1094 (1837), qtd. in Platt, "Producción," 412–14.

30. Ibid.

31. Platt, "Producción," 411; Mitre, *Los patriarcas de la plata*, 58–61, 90.

32. Mitre, *Los patriarcas de la plata*, 65–66, 68–69; Klein, *Bolivia*, 131, 135–41.

33. *Exposición que los artesanos de Sucre dirijen al Supremo Gobierno*.

34. Mitre, *Los patriarcas de la plata*, 18, 32, 34, 37, 92–93, 98–99; Klein, *Bolivia*, 143.

35. For more on this topic, see Antezana Salvatierra, *Estructura agraria en el siglo XIX*; Grieshaber, "Survival of Indian Communities"; Klein, *Haciendas and Ayllus*; Langer, *Economic Change and Rural Resistance*; Platt, *Estado boliviano y ayllu andino*; Platt, *La persistencia de los ayllus*; and Rivera Cusicanqui, "Oppressed but Not Defeated."

36. Klein, *Bolivia*, 123; Mitre, *Los patriarcas de la plata*, 148–49; Rodríguez Ostria, *El socavón y el sindicato*, 35–36, 38–43.

37. Dalence, *Bosquejo Estadístico de Bolivia*, 212. For the idea of "everyday resistance," see Scott, *Weapons of the Weak*.

38. *El Comercio* (Colquechaca), February 22, 1891, qtd. in Rodríguez Ostria, *El socavón y el sindicato*, 52.

39. Rodríguez Ostria, *El socavón y el sindicato*, 24, 36–37, 45–46.

40. Mitre, *Los patriarcas de la plata*, 148–49.

41. Bellessort, *La Jeune Amérique*, qtd. in Rodríguez Ostria, *El socavón y el sindicato*, 28–29.

42. Mitre, *Los patriarcas de la plata*, 26–27, 99–102.

43. Condarco Morales, *Zárate, el "Temible" Willka*, 83–84, 107–21, 142, 157, 311.

44. Ibid., 91–93, 178–84, 379, 391–92.

45. Qtd. in Téllez Fernández, *Rasgos biográficos del Dr. Dn. Macario Pinilla*, 83–84.

46. Condarco, *Zárate, el "Temible" Willka*, 91–93, 178–84, 379, 391–92.

47. Ibid., 218, 234–36.

48. Lora, *Historia del movimiento obrero boliviano*, 1:251–52.

49. Soria Galvarro, *Como adquirió el Sr. Alonso la mina San José*, 29.

50. E. Benavides to Severo Fernández Alonso, "Relación del Jefe del Batallón 'Alonso,'" Sucre, March 9, 1918, in Soria Galvarro, *Últimos dias del Gobierno-Alonso*, 200–213.

51. Ibid.

52. Ibid.

53. Condarco, *Zárate, el "Temible" Willka*, 157, 311.

54. For the besieged prefect's recollections of this conflict, see Soria, *Últimos dias del Gobierno-Alonso*.

55. Identifying the commander of the rural insurgents is difficult, for several of Pablo Zárate Willka's allies and lieutenants also used the title or name "Willka" (Larson, *Trials of Nation Making*; and Gotkowitz, *A Revolution for Our Rights*, 302).

56. Benavides to Fernández Alonso, "Relación del Jefe del Batallón 'Alonso,'" in Soria, *Últimos dias del Gobierno-Alonso*, 200–213; Condarco, *Zárate, el "Temible" Willka*, 306–15.

57. Benavides to Fernández Alonso, "Relación del Jefe del Batallón 'Alonso,'" in Soria, *Últimos dias del Gobierno-Alonso*, 200–213; Condarco, *Zárate, el "Temible" Willka*, 320–21, 327, 342.

58. Klein, *Parties and Political Change*, 38.

59. Editorial, "Actualidad," *Ideales*, August 26, 1900.

60. Klein, *Parties and Political Change*, 37–38.

61. Ibid., 37–39.

62. Ibid., 161, 163.

63. Mitre, *Bajo un cielo de estaño*, 104–6.

64. M. Ascarrunz, "Informe prefectural, 1909," "Ministerio de Gobierno. desde 12 de julio 1909 hasta 28 de agosto 1911," vol. 157, APDO.

65. Constantino Morales to the Minister of State in the Office of Government and Development, Oruro, July 1, 1911, "Ministerio de Gobierno. desde 12 de julio 1909 hasta 28 de agosto 1911," vol. 157, APDO.

66. M. Ascarrunz, "Informe prefectural, 1909," "Ministerio de Gobierno. desde 12 de julio 1909 hasta 28 de agosto 1911," vol. 157, APDO.

67. Oficina Nacional de Inmigración, *Censo general,* 2:45–47, and 2:116–19.

68. The 1900 census used community membership and the payment of tribute as its benchmark for "Indian" ethnicity. Later censuses (e.g., the 1950 census) used different markers, such as language; see Gotkowitz, A *Revolution for Our Rights,* 13; and Grieshaber, "Fluctuaciones en la definición del indio."

69. Oficina Nacional de Inmigración, *Censo general,* 2:19, 32, 35, and 2:93, 98–101.

70. Oficina Nacional de Inmigración, "I. Departamento de Oruro," in ibid., 1:16–17.

71. Mitre, *Bajo un cielo de estaño,* 220–21; Trotsky, *The Permanent Revolution,* 62–63.

72. Bergquist, *Labor in Latin America,* vii.

73. Óscar de Santa Cruz to San José Mines Administrator, Oruro, November 25, 1899, "Varias Autoridades, 1899–1900," APDO.

74. Óscar de Santa Cruz to Minister of Finance, Oruro, November 18, 1899, "Hacienda, 1899–1901," APDO.

75. "Sobre emisión de fichas en los establecimientos mineros," *El Vapor,* November 24, 1901.

76. "Acta: Meetin [*sic*] 16 de Agosto," Oruro, August 24, 1920, "Copiador Asuntos Administrativos, Comensando en 22 de Mayo 1920. Terminado en 2 de Junio de 1926," vol. 286, APDO.

77. Colquechaca-Aullagas Company, *Novena memorial del directorio,* 1–2.

78. Ibid., 7.

79. Ibid., 8–10, 12.

80. Arturo Quesada Alonso to Andacaba Company President, Cuchu Ingenio, July 16, 1907, *Administración de la Compañía Andacaba,* Correspondencia, 1907–1911, Giménez Collection, BANB-ANB.

81. Julio M. Trigo to Andacaba Company President, Cuchu Ingenio, September 17, 1907, *Administración de la Compañía Andacaba,* Correspondencia, 1907–1911, Giménez Collection, BANB-ANB.

82. Zacarías Ponce to Germán Zelada, Colquechaca, October 12, 1907, *Compañía Consolidada. Libro de Cuentas* (1907–1913), Giménez Collection, BANB-ANB.

83. Contract between Matías Paredes and Zacarías Ponce, *Compañía Consolidada. Libro de Cuentas* (1907–1913), Giménez Collection, BANB-ANB.

84. Prefect to Paria Canton *Corregidor,* Oruro, June 17, 1909, "Varios, 1909," vol. 155, APDO.

85. Morales to Minister of Finance, Oruro, March 28, 1911, "Telegramas desde marzo 17/1910 hasta noviembre 10/1911," vol. 163, APDO.

86. Morales to Huanuni Police Chief, Oruro, July 21, 1911, "'Telegramas desde marzo 17/1910 hasta noviembre 10/1911," vol. 163, APDO.

87. Castaños to Prefect, Huanuni, July 24, 1911, qtd. in Castaños to Prefect, Huanuni, July 24, 1911, "Telegramas desde marzo 17/1910 hasta noviembre 10/1911," vol. 163, APDO.

88. Castaños to Prefect, Huanuni, July 24, 1911, qtd. in Morales to Minister of Government, Oruro, July 25, 1911, "'Telegramas desde marzo 17/1910 hasta noviembre 10/1911," vol. 163, APDO.

89. Castaños to Prefect, Huanuni, July 24, 1911, "Telegramas desde marzo 17/1910 hasta noviembre 10/1911," vol. 163, APDO.

90. Morales to President, Oruro, October 18, 1911, "'Telegramas desde marzo 17/1910 hasta noviembre 10/1911," vol. 163, APDO.

CHAPTER 2: Artisan Initiative

1. Santiago Franichevich and Francisco Armaza to Prefect, Oruro, April 27, 1915, "Archivo de Oficios, 1915, Varios, 1," vol. 220, APDO.

2. E. Diez de Medina to Mutual Aid Society of Artisans President, Oruro, April 29, 1915, "Archivo de Copias, 1915, Varios," vol. 222, APDO.

3. Klein, *Parties and Political Change*, 58.

4. Sociedad Industriosa de Artesanos, "Reglamento Manuscrito," Oruro, August 22, 1876, Archivo Presidencial de la Sociedad de Socorros Mutuos de Artesanos, qtd. in Delgado, *100 años de lucha obrera*, 31–32.

5. For an example from Mexican history, see French, *A Peaceful and Working People*.

6. Sociedad Industriosa de Artesanos, "Reglamento Manuscrito," Oruro, August 22, 1876, Archivo Presidencial de la Sociedad de Socorros Mutuos de Artesanos, qtd. in Delgado, *100 años de lucha obrera*, 32, 34.

7. Delgado, *100 años de lucha obrera*, 31; Sociedad de Socorros Mutuos de Artesanos, *Boletín* 10, 3.

8. Sociedad de Socorros Mutuos de Artesanos, *Boletín 10*, 8–10.

9. Teachers of the Municipal School for Boys in the Quillacas Canton to Prefect, July 20, 1897, "Año de 1899, Agencias y Resguardos, 1897–1899," APDO.

10. Prefect to the General Directorate of Primary Instruction, Oruro, May 13, 1897, "Año de 1899, Agencias y Resguardos, 1897–1899," APDO.

11. Andrés Muñoz to University Rector, Oruro, July 18, 1905, "1905," vol. 128, APDO.

12. Víctor E. Sanjinés to Minister of State, Oruro, August 3, 1907, "Ministerios de Gobierno, Desde 13 marzo 1906 hasta 11 de julio de 1909," vol. 142, APDO.

13. Constantino Morales to Minister of State, Oruro, July 1, 1911, "Ministerio de Gobierno. desde 12 de julio 1909 hasta 28 de agosto 1911," vol. 157, APDO.

14. Víctor E. Sanjinés to Minister of State, Oruro, July 31, 1906, "Ministerios de Gobierno, Desde 13 marzo 1906 hasta 11 de julio de 1909," vol. 142, APDO.

15. Víctor E. Sanjinés to Minister of State, Oruro, August 3, 1907, "Ministerios de Gobierno, Desde 13 marzo 1906 hasta 11 de julio de 1909," vol. 142, APDO.

16. Constantino Morales to Minister of State, Oruro, July 6, 1910, "Ministerio de Gobierno. desde 12 de julio 1909 hasta 28 de agosto 1911," vol. 157, APDO.

17. Constantino Morales, "Exposisión para la reinstalación del año escolar en esta Universidad de San Agustín," January 3, 1911, "Varios, 1910–1911," vol. 164, APDO.

18. Moisés Ascarrunz, "Informe que Presenta ante el Supremo Gobierno el Prefecto y Comandante General del Departamento de Oruro, Doctor Moisés Ascarrunz," Oruro, July 20, 1908, "Ministerios de Gobierno, Desde 13 marzo 1906 hasta 11 de julio de 1909," vol. 142, APDO.

19. "Informe del Prefecto y Comandante General del Departamento de Oruro, 1915," 191, "Ministerio de Instrucción y Agricultura, Comensado en 14 de Octubre de 1913, Termina en . . . ," vol. 191, APDO.

20. Prefect to Minister of Public Education and Development, Oruro, July 12, 1902, "Justicia 1899 a 1905," APDO.

21. Guillermo Sanjinés to Minister of Education, Oruro, August 22, 1902, "Justicia 1899 a 1905," APDO.

22. Víctor E. Sanjinés to Mutual Aid Society of Artisans President, Oruro, December 4, 1906, "Varios, 1906–1908," vol. 140, APDO.

23. Sanjinés to Mutual Aid Society of Artisans President, Oruro, June 30, 1906, "Varios, 1905–1906," vol. 129, APDO.

24. Víctor E. Sanjinés to Mutual Aid Society of Artisans President, Oruro, July 5, 1907, "Varios, 1906–1908," vol. 140, APDO.

25. V. E. Sanjinés to Mutual Aid Society of Artisans President, Oruro, December 4, 1907, "Varios, 1906–1908," vol. 140, APDO.

26. M. Ascarrunz to the Minister of State, Oruro, May 21, 1908, "Justicia y Instrucción, 1905–1906," vol. 132, APDO.

27. Moisés Ascarrunz, "Informe que Presenta ante el Supremo Gobierno el Prefecto y Comandante General del Departamento de Oruro, Doctor Moisés Ascarrunz," Oruro, July 20, 1908, "Ministerios de Gobierno, Desde 13 marzo 1906 hasta 11 de julio de 1909," vol. 142, APDO.

28. Ascarrunz to Demóstenes Peláez, Oruro, May 21, 1908, "Copiador de Telegramas desde Mayo 8/1908 hasta Marzo 8/1909," vol. 153, APDO.

29. Constantino Morales to Mutual Aid Society of Artisans President, Oruro, December 30, 1910, "Varios, 1910–1911," vol. 164, APDO.

30. Morales, Oruro, March 11, 1911, "Telegramas desde marzo 17/1910 hasta noviembre 10/1911," vol. 163, APDO.

31. Constantino Morales to Mutual Aid Society of Artisans President, Oruro, July 14, 1911, "Varios, 1910–1911," vol. 164, APDO.

32. C. Morales to Mutual Aid Society of Artisans President, Oruro, July 18, 1911, "Varios, 1910–1911," vol. 164, APDO.

33. C. Morales to Mutual Aid Society of Artisans President, Oruro, July 18, 1912, "Varios, 1911–1912," vol. 166, APDO.

34. C. Morales to Mutual Aid Society of Artisans President, Oruro, May 10, 1913, "Varios 1912–1913," vol. 178, APDO.

35. Constantino Morales to Minister of Education, Oruro, May 17, 1913, "Ministerio Instrucción Pública desde abril 22/1905 hasta octubre 6/1913," vol. 144, APDO.

36. Constantino Morales to Nícanor Leclere, Oruro, December 30, 1911, "Varios, 1911–1912," vol. 166, APDO.

37. Constantino Morales to Minister of State, Oruro, June 20, 1913, "Ministerios de Gobierno desde 7 de septiembre de 1911 hasta 10 de octubre de 1913," vol. 172, APDO. (The term "indigenous class" was used by the prefect, not by the leadership of the Workers' Union of Artisans.)

38. Zalles to Prefect, La Paz, April 30, 1913, qtd. in C. Morales to First Batallion Commander, Oruro, April 30, 1913, "Varios 1912–1913," vol. 178, APDO.

39. Constantino Morales to Minister of State, Oruro, July 23, 1913, "Ministerio Instrucción Pública desde abril 22/1905 hasta octubre 6/1913," vol. 144, APDO.

40. "Informe del Prefecto y Comandante General del Departamento de Oruro, 1915," "Ministerio de Instrucción y Agricultura, Comensado en 14 de Octubre de 1913, Termina en . . . ," vol. 191, APDO.

41. L. Salinas Vega to Prefect, La Paz, November 7, 1916, qtd. in M. Lemaitre to Mutual Aid Society of Artisans President, Oruro, November 14, 1916, "Espedido a Varios, 1916," vol. 229, APDO.

42. President of the Sociedad "Obreros de San José" Esequiel Aguilar to the Prefect, Oruro, February 1, 1918, "Recibidos: Judicial, Corregimientos, Ferrocarriles y otros, Varios, 1918, Prefectura-Oruro," vol. 252, APDO.

43. M. Lemaitre to Subprefect, Oruro, June 29, 1916, "Espedido: Circulares, Ferocariles, Prefecturas, Tesoros, 1916," vol. 233, APDO.

44. Delgado, *100 años de lucha obrera*, 55.

45. Rigoberto E. Toro, President of the May 25 Mutual Aid Society of Artisans, Potosí, August 1, 1912, qtd. in ibid., 57–58.

46. Adolfo Dulón and Abel de Alencar to Prefect, Oruro, February 4, 1915, "Archivo de Oficios, 1915, Varios, 1," vol. 220, APDO.

47. E. Diez de Medina to Adolfo Dulón, Oruro, February 5, 1915, "Archivo de Copias, 1915, Varios," vol. 222, APDO.

48. Defense of Labor to Prefect, Potosí, April 28, 1915, P.D. 3831 (Varios) 1915, enero 4–diciembre 24, CNM-AH.

49. Carlos M. de Villegas to Minister of State, Oruro, June 24, 1905, "1904–1906, Copiador de Ministerios de Gobierno, Desde Octubre 26/1904 hast Marzo 10/1906," vol. 122, APDO.

50. Víctor E. Sanjinés to Minister of State, Oruro, August 3, 1907, "Ministerios de Gobierno, Desde 13 marzo 1906 hasta 11 de julio de 1909," vol. 142, APDO.

51. Eloy de Castillo to Subprefect Oruro, February 8, 1906, "Telegramas, 1905–1908," vol. 135, APDO.

52. Constantino Morales to Minister of State, Oruro, July 1, 1911, "Ministerio de Gobierno. desde 12 de julio 1909 hasta 28 de agosto 1911," vol. 157, APDO.

53. Constantino Morales, "Exposisión para la reinstalación del año escolar en esta Universidad de San Agustín," Oruro, January 3, 1911, "Varios, 1910–1911," vol. 164, APDO.

54. Santa Rosa Mine to Prefect, Oruro, July 26, 1897, "Año de 1899, Agencias y Resguardos, 1897–1899," APDO.

55. Constantino Morales to Guillermo Gray, Oruro, July 8, 1911, "Varios, 1910–1911," vol. 164, APDO; Penny and Duncan to Prefect, Oruro, July 8, 1911, qtd. in Constantino Morales to Morococala Police Chief, Oruro, July 10, 1911, "Varios, 1910–1911," vol. 164, APDO.

56. "Policia de Condeauqui," Oruro, October 8, 1916, "Copiador de órdenes de Ferrocarril, Comensado en 14 de Octubre de 1913, Termina en . . . ," vol. 190, APDO.

57. Penny and Duncan Mining Company of Morococala to Prefect, Morococala, December 22, 1916, "Recibido de Varios, 1916," vol. 228, APDO.

58. Víctor E. Sanjinés to Minister of State, Oruro, August 3, 1907, "Ministerios de Gobierno, Desde 13 marzo 1906 hasta 11 de julio de 1909," vol. 142, APDO.

59. Huanuni Police Chief to Prefect, qtd. in Donato Encinas to Minister of State, Oruro, January 30, 1911, "Ministerio de Gobierno. desde 12 de julio 1909 hasta 28 de agosto 1911," vol. 157, APDO.

60. Constantino Morales to Poopó Province Subprefect, Oruro, February 5, 1912, "Prefectos y Subprefectos, 1910–1913," vol. 167, APDO.

61. General Directorate of the Security Police of the Republic to Prefect, La Paz, February 11, 1914, "Archivo de Oficios, 1914, Varios, 3," APDO.

62. M. Ascarrunz to Huanuni Police Chief, Oruro, September 8, 1908, "Varios, 1908," vol. 150, APDO.

63. Minister of War and Colonization to Prefect, La Paz, March 18, 1911, qtd. in C. Morales, March 22, 1911, "Circulares desde sbre 17, 1908 hasta sebre. de 1913," vol. 165, APDO.

64. Alberto Diez de Medina to the Ministry of War, Oruro, September 24, 1913, "Telegramas desde noviembre 10/1911 hasta octubre 16/1913," vol. 168, APDO.

65. Prefect to Luis J. Iraola, Oruro, November 30, 1909, "Varios, 1909," vol. 155, APDO.

66. José F. Avila to Prefect, Oruro, August 3, 1916, "Recibido de Varios, 1916," vol. 228, APDO; José F. Avila to Prefect, Oruro, August 12, 1916, "Recibido de Varios, 1916," vol. 228, APDO.

67. Alberto Diez de Medina to Minister of State, "Sustitución del Intendente de la Policia de Huanuni," Oruro, August 11, 1914, "Archivo de Copias, 1914, Ministerios," vol. 208, APDO.

68. Alejandro Pacheco Pereira to Prefect, Huanuni, October 30, 1914, "Archivo de Oficios, 1914, Varios, 3," APDO.

69. M. Ascarrunz to Mininster of State, Oruro, September 23, 1908, "Hacienda, 1906–1913," vol. 143, APDO.

70. José S. Quinteros to Prefect, "Circular N° 32," La Paz, July 14, 1913, qtd. in C. Morales to Subprefect, Oruro, July 21, 1913, "Circulares desde sbre 17, 1908 hasta sebre. de 1913," vol. 165, APDO.

71. Ibid.

72. President Ismael Montes, National Congress, and Ministry of Government and Development, La Paz, November 23, 1915, "Archivo de Oficios, 1915, Ministerios, 2," vol. 217, APDO.

73. M. Lemaitre to Subprefect, Oruro, June 29, 1916, "Espedido: Circulares, Ferocariles, Prefecturas, Tesoros, 1916," vol. 233, APDO.

74. For early twentieth-century Bolivian public health policy, see Zulawski, *Unequal Cures*.

75. Director of Public Assistance to Prefect, Oruro, May 4, 1916, "Recibido de Varios, 1916," vol. 228, APDO.

76. Morococala Police to Subprefect, Morococala, October 23, 1917, "Varios: Ramos, Prefecturas, Policias, Correjimientos y otros, 1917, Prefectura-Oruro," vol. 241, APDO.

77. J. Alvéstigui to Prefect, Oruro, June 11, 1921, "Tesoros, Subprefecturas, 1921, Prefectura, Oruro," vol. 279, APDO.

CHAPTER 3: Crisis and Organization

1. José F. Avila to Prefect, Oruro, August 3, 1916, "Recibido de Varios, 1916," vol. 228, APDO.

2. Klein, *Parties and Political Change*, 45–48.

3. Ministry of Government and Development to Prefect, La Paz, August 8, 1914, "Archivo de Oficios, 1914, Ministerios, 1," vol. 207, APDO.

4. Klein, *Parties and Political Change*, 48; Eduardo Diez de Medina, "Informe Departamental 1914," "Ministerio de Instrucción y Agricultura, Comensado en 14 de Octubre de 1913, Termina en . . . ," vol. 191, APDO.

5. Ministry of Government and Development to Prefect, La Paz, August 8, 1914, "Archivo de Oficios, 1914, Ministerios, 1," vol. 207, APDO.

6. Klein, *Parties and Political Change*, 43, 45–48, 67–68, 127–28.

7. Ibid., 48–50.

8. Ibid., 50–51. For an in-depth discussion of the Bolivian political process during the nineteenth century and the first half of the twentieth, see Irurozqui Victoriano, *"A Bala, Piedra y Palo."*

9. Melitón Lemaitre to Arturo Molina Campero, Oruro, December 13, 1915, "Archivo de Copias, 1915, Ministerios," vol. 221, APDO.

10. Klein, *Parties and Political Change,* 53.

11. A. Molina Campero to Prefect, La Paz, April 13, 1917, "Ministerios: Gobierno y Fomento, Hacienda, 1917, Prefectura-Oruro," vol. 242, APDO.

12. Pampilio Antezana to Prefect, Huanuni, May 6, 1917, 241, "Varios: Ramos, Prefecturas, Policias, Correjimientos y otros, 1917, Prefectura-Oruro," vol. 241, APDO.

13. Klein, *Parties and Political Change,* 53.

14. Ministry of Government and Development to Prefect, La Paz, August 8, 1914, "Archivo de Oficios, 1914, Ministerios, 1," vol. 207, APDO.

15. Klein, *Parties and Political Change,* 52.

16. Mitre, *Bajo un cielo de estaño,* 140–41.

17. Police Chief Miguel Arzet to Prefect, Negro Pabellón, June 18, 1914, "Archivo de Oficios, 1914, Varios, 3," APDO.

18. P.D. 3825, "Informe Provincia Bustillos, 1915 mayo 28–30," CNM-AH.

19. Police Chief Jorge Ardiles M. to Prefect, Huanuni, November 22, 1917, "Varios: Ramos, Prefecturas, Policias, Correjimientos y otros, 1917, Prefectura-Oruro," vol. 241, APDO.

20. *Corregidor* Marcial Vergara to Prefect, Paria, May 15, 1917, "Varios: Ramos, Prefecturas, Policias, Correjimientos y otros, 1917, Prefectura-Oruro," vol. 241, APDO.

21. Marcial Vergara Rivas to Subprefect, Oruro, September 28, 1920, "Bloque No 2 documentos y otros gestion 1911–1949," ASPC-PDO.

22. For the radical politics of Chile's nitrate camps, see, among others, Devés, *Los que van a morir;* Pinto-Vallejos, *Trabajos y rebeldías;* and Pizarro, *La huelga obrera.*

23. Ascarrunz to Minister of Government, Oruro, May 24, 1908, "Copiador de Telegramas desde Mayo 8/1908 hasta Marzo 8/1909," vol. 153, APDO.

24. Eduardo Diez de Medina, "Informe Departamental 1914," "Ministerio de Instrucción y Agricultura, Comensado en 14 de Octubre de 1913, Termina en . . . ," vol. 191, APDO.

25. Police to Prefect, Oruro, November 18, 1914, "Archivo de Oficios, 1914, Varios, 3," APDO.

26. E. Diez de Medina to Minister of Government, "Repatriados de Chile," Oruro, August 26, 1914, "Archivo de Copias, 1914, Ministerios," vol. 208, APDO.

27. Zalles to Prefect, qtd. in E. Diez de Medina to Minister of State, "Repatriados de Chile," Oruro, August 26, 1914, "Archivo de Copias, 1914, Ministerios," vol. 208, APDO.

28. E. Diez de Medina to Minister of State, "Repatriados de Chile," Oruro, August 26, 1914, "Archivo de Copias, 1914, Ministerios," vol. 208, APDO.

29. E. Diez de Medina to Minister of State, "Olla del Pobre," Oruro, September 25, 1914, "Archivo de Copias, 1914, Ministerios," vol. 208, APDO.

30. E. Diez de Medina to Juan María Zalles, "Informe sobre el viaje a Carangas," Oruro, November 20, 1914, "Archivo de Copias, 1914, Ministerios," vol. 208, APDO.

31. Eduardo Diez de Medina, "Informe Departamental 1914," "Ministerio de Instrucción y Agricultura, Comensado en 14 de Octubre de 1913, Termina en . . . ," vol. 191, APDO.

32. Ministry of Government and Development to Prefect, La Paz, August 26, 1914, "Archivo de Oficios, 1914, Ministerios, 1," vol. 207, APDO.

33. Eduardo Diez de Medina to Inspector of Traffic, Oruro, November 18, 1915, "Archivo de Copias, 1915, Tesoro Nacional y Departamental, Ferrocarriles, Bandos y Circulares," vol. 216, APDO.

34. Fidel Carranza qtd. in A. Molina Campero to Prefect, La Paz, November 25, 1915, "Archivo de Oficios, 1915, Ministerios, 2," vol. 217, APDO.

35. M. Lemaitre to Arturo Molina Campero, Oruro, November 29, 1915, "Archivo de Copias, 1915, Ministerios," vol. 221, APDO.

36. D. Ascarrunz to Policia Chief, "Venta de pasajes otorgados por el Gobierno," Oruro, March 14, 1919, "Copiador de Tesoros y policias y Subprefecturas de 21 de Mayo de 1918, asta 27 de Marzo de 1919," vol. 247, APDO.

37. A. del Carpio S. to the Minister of Government and Justice, "Asunto: Enganche de obreros bolivianos," Antofagasta, November 3, 1923, qtd. in Minister of Government and Justice to Prefect, La Paz, December 13, 1923, "Ministerios, P.O., 1923," vol. 299, APDO.

38. A. Arce to Eduardo Avaroa, Oruro, December 22, 1923, "Copiador de Varios Oficios de 24 de Marzo de 1923 hasta el 14 de abril de 1924," vol. 303, APDO.

39. Constantino Morales to Minister of State, Oruro, March 31, 1912, "Ministerios de Gobierno desde 7 de septiembre de 1911 hasta 10 de octubre de 1913," vol. 172, APDO.

40. Alberto Salinas Aldunate, Max Siles, and Napoleón Rivero (Chief of Investigations), Oruro, September 17, 1918, "Copiador de Varios Oficios. De 8 de Mayo 1918 hasta 15 de Enero de 1919," vol. 248, APDO.

41. M. Lemaitre to Arturo Loaiza, Oruro, March 27, 1916, "Espedido a Varios, 1916," vol. 229, APDO.

42. M. Lemaitre to Manuel Vicente Ballivian, Oruro, May 11, 1916, "Espedido a Varios, 1916," vol. 229, APDO.

43. Constantino Morales to Guillermo Gray, July 8, 1911, "Varios, 1910–1911," vol. 164, APDO.

44. M. Lemaitre to Ismael Vasquez, Oruro, April 24, 1916, "Correspondencia Expedido: Ministerios, Gobierno y Fomento, Justicia e Industria, Hacienda, Guerra y Colonizacion, Relaciones E.E. y Culta, Instruccion y Agricultura," vol. 230, APDO.

45. M. Lemaitre to Mining Chamber of Commerce President, Oruro, September 21, 1916, "Espedido a Varios, 1916," vol. 229, ADPO.

46. José F. Avila to Prefect, Oruro, August 12, 1916, "Recibido de Varios, 1916," vol. 228, APDO.

47. José F. Avila to Prefect, Oruro, August 23, 1916, "Recibido de Varios, 1916," vol. 228, APDO.

48. Julio Saavedra and N. Leclere to Representatives, Oruro, October 7, 1916, qtd. in Congress of Representatives to Prefect, La Paz, October 19, 1916, "Recibido de Varios, 1916," vol. 228, APDO.

49. Congress of Representatives to Prefect, La Paz, October 19, 1916, "Recibido de Varios, 1916," vol. 228, APDO.

50. M. Lemaitre to Guild Society of Carpenters President, "Recibo y Felicitación," Oruro, February 3, 1917, "1917," vol. 244, APDO; M. Lemaitre to Apolinar Zambrana M., Oruro, February 10, 1917, "1917," vol. 244, APDO.

51. M. Lemaitre to Ezequial Aguilar, "Acuso de Recibo," Oruro, June 19, 1917, "1917," vol. 244, APDO.

52. Silvestre Flores to Prefect, Pazña, January 4, 1916, "Recibido de Varios, 1916," vol. 228, APDO.

53. N. Murgia to Prefect, Oruro, February 24, 1917, "Subprefecturas, 1917, Prefectura-Oruro," vol. 243, APDO.

54. Juan Béjar to Prefect, Oruro, March 19, 1920, "Varios, 1920, Prefectura, Oruro," vol. 273, APDO.

55. Juan Béjar and Gregorio Castro to Prefect, Oruro, March 19, 1920, "Varios, 1920, Prefectura, Oruro," vol. 273, APDO.

56. Juan Béjar and Gregorio Castro Celis to Prefect, "Varios, 1920, Prefectura, Oruro," vol. 273, APDO.

57. César M. Ochávez to Workers' Democratic Institution President, La Paz, May 17, 1920, qtd. in César M. Ochávez to Prefect, La Paz, May 17, 1920, "Ministerios, Hacienda, Industria, Guerra, 1920, Prefectura, Oruro," vol. 271, APDO.

CHAPTER 4: Strikes and Contracts

1. Klein, *Parties and Political Change,* 63.

2. Prefect to the Secretary General, Oruro, August 17, 1920, "Copiador de Varios Oficios de 16 de 1919 hasta el 15 de Septiembre de 1920," vol. 263, APDO.

3. "Acta," Oruro, August 14, 1920, "Copiador Asuntos Administrativos, Comensando en 22 de Mayo 1920. Terminado en 2 de Junio de 1926," vol. 286, APDO.

4. Mitre, *Bajo un cielo de estaño,* 140–41, 221.

5. Republican Party's Workers and Youth Presidents to Prefect, Oruro, December 14, 1920, "Varios, 1920, Prefectura, Oruro," vol. 273, APDO; Klein, *Parties and Political Change,* 57.

6. Klein, *Parties and Political Change,* 51, 57–58.

7. D. Ascarrunz to Minister of State, Oruro, May 11, 1920, "Copiador de Ministerios de 11 de Mayo de 1920 hasta el 27 de Agosto de 1921," vol. 270, APDO.

8. Klein, *Parties and Political Change,* 58, 63.

9. Ibid., 64–66.

10. Lora, *Historia del movimiento obrero boliviano,* 2:355.

11. "Prefecturas de Oruro: desde el año de 1882 hasta el año de . . . ," APDO; Klein, *Parties and Political Change,* 411.

12. Juan L. Rojas, Guillermo Bozo, Segundino Flores, Darus Vargas, Saturnino Aranibar, Luis Delfin Heredia, Juan Bustos, and Teofilo Vargas to Prefect, Pazña, "Varios, 1920, Prefectura, Oruro," vol. 273, APDO.

13. Anonymous to Prefect, Oruro, December 14, 1920, "Varios, 1920, Prefectura, Oruro," vol. 273, APDO.

14. Choque Canqui, *Historia de una lucha desigual,* 64–68; Dunkerley, *Rebellion in the Veins,* 24; Klein, *Parties and Political Change,* 69.

15. J. Wiessing to Prefect, Oruro, March 14, 1922, "Varios, Prefectura, Oruro, 1922," vol. 292, APDO (Wiessing was a native of Holland and served as that country's consul in Oruro); A. Arce to Minister of State, Oruro, November 21, 1923, "Copiador de Ministerios de 24 de Marzo de 1923. Hasta 29 de Julio de 1924," vol. 302, APDO.

16. Crespo to Subprefect, Huanuni, September 5, 1919, qtd. in Liberato Tovar to Prefect, Oruro, September 5, 1919, "Tesoros, Subprefecturas, 1919, Prefectura, Oruro," vol. 261, APDO.

17. Huanuni Police Chief to Prefecto, Oruro, September 8, 1919, "Policias, Regimentos, Estado Mayor, 1919, Prefectura, Oruro," vol. 262, APDO.

18. V. B. Sandoval and V. M. Zubieta to Oruro Police Chief, Oruro, October 16, 1919, "Policias, Regimentos, Estado Mayor, 1919, Prefectura, Oruro," vol. 262, APDO.

19. Lora, *Historia del movimiento obrero boliviano,* 2:369.

20. V. B. Sandoval and V. M. Zubieta to Oruro Police Chief, Oruro, October 16, 1919, "Policias, Regimentos, Estado Mayor, 1919, Prefectura, Oruro," vol. 262, APDO.

21. Ibid.

22. Ibid.

23. D. Ascarrunz to Huanuni Police Chief, Oruro, October 9, 1919, "Copiador de Varios Oficios de 15 de Enero de 1919. hasta el 12 de Diciembre de 1919," vol. 265, APDO.

24. V. B. Sandoval and V. M. Zubieta to Oruro Police Chief, Oruro, October 16, 1919, "Policias, Regimentos, Estado Mayor, 1919, Prefectura, Oruro," vol. 262, APDO.

25. D. Ascarrunz to Minister of State, Oruro, October 17, 1919, "Copiador de Ministerios de 30 de Abril de 1919 hasta el 11 de Mayo de 1920," vol. 266, APDO.

26. Ministry of Government and Justice to Prefect, La Paz, October 24, 1919, "Ministerios: Gobierno, Justicia, Instruccion, 1919, Prefectura-Oruro," vol. 259, APDO.

27. D. Ascarrunz to Huanuni Police Chief, Oruro, January 6, 1920, "Copiador de Varios Oficios de 16 de 1919 hasta el 15 de Septiembre de 1920," vol. 263, APDO.

28. Prefect to Secretary General, Oruro, August 14, 1920, "Copiador de Varios Oficios de 16 de 1919 hasta el 15 de Septiembre de 1920," vol. 263, APDO.

29. "Meetin [*sic*] 16 de Agosto," "Acta," Oruro, August 24, 1920, "Copiador Asuntos Administrativos, Comensando en 22 de Mayo 1920. Terminado en 2 de Junio de 192," vol. 268, APDO. Antonio Frías, Rómulo Chumacero, Alejandro Asteti, and Demetrio Tórrez represented the workers of the Mining Company of Oruro; Elías Cárdenas, José R. Ponce, Néstor P. Rodríguez, Félix Béjarano, and Juan Mérida represented the workers of the San José Mining Company; and Víctor Ortiz represented the workers of the Santo Cristo Mining and Agricultural Company. Because of damage to the document, the names of the delegates representing the workers of the Tetilla Company could not be recovered.

30. Lora, *Historia del movimiento obrero boliviano*, 2:122–31, 178.

31. "Meetin [*sic*] 16 de Agosto," "Acta," Oruro, August 24, 1920, "Copiador Asuntos Administrativos, Comensando en 22 de Mayo 1920. Terminado en 2 de Junio de 192," vol. 268, APDO.

32. Ibid.

33. Ibid.

34. Ibid.

35. Ibid.

36. Ibid.

37. Prefect to Secretary General, Oruro, August 17, 1920, "Copiador de Varios Oficios de 16 de 1919 hasta el 15 de Septiembre de 1920," vol. 263, APDO.

38. Lt. Col. José Ml. Gonzales to Prefect, Oruro, August 21, 1920, qtd. in Prefect to Government Junta, Oruro, August 23, 1920, "Copiador de Varios Oficios de 16 de 1919 hasta el 15 de Septiembre de 1920," vol. 263, APDO.

39. To Prefect, Uncía, August 13, 1920, "Varios, 1920, Prefectura, Oruro," vol. 273, APDO.

40. Chilliguani Post to Simpat, Machacamarca, qtd. in Simón I. Patiño to Prefect, Oruro, August 14, 1920, "Varios, 1920, Prefectura, Oruro," vol. 273, APDO.

41. Lt. Col. José Ml. Gonzales to Prefect, Oruro, August 21, 1920, qtd. in Prefect to Government Junta, Oruro, August 23, 1920, "Copiador de Varios Oficios de 16 de 1919 hasta el 15 de Septiembre de 1920," vol. 263, APDO.

42. The unrest in northern Potosí in August 1920 and the Uncía Massacre of July 1923 left a similar number of workers dead. The later incident became a celebrated, symbolic moment for the working class, while the deaths in 1920 were almost forgotten.

43. Prefect to the Secretary General of the Government Council, Oruro, August 24, 1920, "Copiador de Varios Oficios de 16 de 1919 hasta el 15 de Septiembre de 1920," vol. 263, APDO.

44. Ibid.

45. Prefect to Francisco Blieck, Oruro, August 19, 1920, "Copiador de Varios Oficios de 16 de 1919 hasta el 15 de Septiembre de 1920," vol. 263, APDO.

46. Antonio Frias et al. to Prefect, Oruro, August 23, 1920, qtd. in Prefect to Mining Company of Oruro Manager, Oruro, August 23, 1920, "Copiador de Varios Oficios de 16 de 1919 hasta el 15 de Septiembre de 1920," vol. 263, APDO.

47. Santo Cristo Mining Company to Prefect, Santo Cristo, February 23, 1921, "Varios, 1921, Prefectura, Oruro," vol. 281, APDO.

48. J. Alvéstigui to Prefect, Oruro, September 2, 1921, "Tesoros, Subprefecturas, 1921, Prefectura, Oruro," vol. 279, APDO.

49. Herbert Klein (Parties and Political Change, 73) records that a group calling itself the Workers's Socialist Party was founded in La Paz on September 22, 1920.

50. "A la clase obrera de Oruro," Oruro, December 1, 1919, qtd. in Lora, Historia del movimiento obrero boliviano, 3:137.

51. Fernando Frontanilla to Prefect, Poopó, December 15, 1919, "Fiscalias, T.N. de Cuentas, Aduana, Corte S., Municipalidades y Otros, 1919, Prefectura, Oruro," vol. 258, APDO.

52. Donato Téllez to Prefect, Oruro, November 13, 1920, "Varios, 1920, Prefectura, Oruro," vol. 273, APDO.

53. Ricardo Perales, qtd. in Lora, Historia del movimiento obrero boliviano, 2:355.

54. Lora, Historia del movimiento obrero boliviano, 2:402–4, 409.

55. "Memoria del Sr. Pdte. del Directorio Central de la Liga . . . ," La Paz, 1920, qtd. in ibid., 2:409.

56. Lora, Historia del movimiento obrero boliviano, 2:416.

57. L. Solórzano, Uyuni, qtd. in ibid., 2:410.

58. "Memoria del Sr. Pdte. del Directorio Central de la Liga . . . ," La Paz, 1920, qtd. in Lora, Historia del movimiento obrero boliviano, 2:410.

59. General Tejada to President, Oruro, January 28, 1921, "Copiador de Telegramas de 20 de Julio de 1920, Hasta 28 de Septiembre de 1921," vol. 278, APDO.

60. Lora, Historia del movimiento obrero boliviano, 2:416.

61. Ricardo Soruco Ipiña, qtd. in ibid., 2:417.

62. Tejada to Prefect, Oruro, "Copiador de Telegramas de 20 de Julio de 1920, Hasta 28 de Septiembre de 1921," vol. 278, APDO.

63. Donato Téllez and R. Perales to Prefect, Oruro, January 28, 1921, qtd. in ibid.

64. General Tejada to President, Oruro, "Copiador de Telegramas de 20 de Julio de 1920, Hasta 28 de Septiembre de 1921," vol. 278, APDO.

65. Óscar de Santa Cruz to Prefect, La Paz, January 29, 1921, "Fiscalias, T.N. de Cuentas, Aduana, Corte S., Municipalidades y otros, 1921, Prefectura, Oruro," vol. 282, APDO.

66. General Tejada to President, Oruro, January 28, 1921, "Copiador de Telegramas de 20 de Julio de 1920, Hasta 28 de Septiembre de 1921," vol. 278, APDO.

67. Enrique Mallea Balboa to Prefect, Oruro, July 22, 1921, "Fiscalias, T.N. de Cuentas, Aduana, Corte S., Municipalidades y otros, 1921, Prefectura, Oruro," vol. 282, APDO.

68. Ibid.

69. Both Herbert Klein and Guillermo Lora record the "First National Congress of Workers" as having occurred in 1921 (Klein, *Parties and Political Change*, 75; Lora, *Historia del movimiento obrero boliviano*, 3:11). During this meeting, which probably occurred in December 1920, the politician Ricardo Soruco spoke to the Railway Federation (Lora, *Historia del movimiento obrero boliviano*, 2:416). A document held by activists in northern Potosí and used by the Central Labor Federation of Uncía during its battle with the region's mining companies in May and June 1923 also refered to a meeting hosted by the Railway Federation in December 1920. The federation specifically mentioned a national agreement signed on December 18, 1920. The Machacamarca-Uncía Railway Federation had provided the Central Labor Federation of Uncía with a copy of these accords (Rivera, *La masacre de Uncía*, 118).

70. Klein, *Parties and Political Change*, 75–76.

71. Tejada Fariñez to Railway Federation President, Oruro, April 26, 1922, "Copiador Varios Oficios de 31 de Marzo de 1922. Hasta el 26 de Marzo de 1923," vol. 288, APDO.

72. Administrator to Bolivia Railway, qtd. in Tejada Fariñez to Railway Federation President, Oruro, April 28, 1922, "Copiador Varios Oficios de 31 de Marzo de 1922. Hasta el 26 de Marzo de 1923," vol. 288, APDO.

73. Oruro, August 9, 1921, "Copiador Asuntos Administrativos, Comensando en 22 de Mayo 1920. Terminado en 2 de Junio de 1926," vol. 286, APDO.

74. Klein, *Parties and Political Change*, 73–74.

75. Donato Téllez to Prefect, Oruro, May 4, 1923, "Varios, 1923, P.O.," vol. 301, APDO.

CHAPTER 5: The Uncía Massacre, 1923

1. Rivera, *La masacre de Uncía*, 18–19.

2. Miguel Ramos to Prefect, Huanuni, February 20, 1923, "Copia Legalizada," "Tesoros, Subprefecturas, Policias, 1923, P.O.," vol. 298, APDO.

3. H. Iraola and Pablo Salas to Prefect, Huanuni, December 6, 1923, "Varios, 1923, P.O.," vol. 301, APDO.

4. Rivera, *La masacre de Uncía*, 12–18.

5. Ibid., 11–12.

6. Qtd. in ibid., 19–20.

7. Ibid., 20–21.

8. Rivera, *La masacre de Uncía*, 22.

9. Guillermo Gamarra and Ernesto Fernández to Subprefect, Uncía, May 3, 1923, qtd. in ibid., 22–23.

10. Guillermo Gamarra and Ernesto Fernández to Manager of . . . , Uncía, May 3, 1923, qtd. in Rivera, *La masacre de Uncía*, 24–25.

11. Francisco Blieck to Central Labor Federation of Uncía President, Uncía, May 8, 1923, qtd. in Rivera, *La masacre de Uncía*, 25–26.

12. Guillermo Gamarra and Ernesto Fernández to La Salvadora Company Manager, Uncía, May 11, 1923, qtd. in Rivera L., *La masacre de Uncía*, 26–27.

13. Rivera, *La masacre de Uncía*, 27–30.

14. Ibid., 30.

15. Juan Miranda et al. to Gumercindo Rivera L. et al., Catavi (Llallagua), May 7, 1923, qtd. in ibid., 34–35.

16. Ibid., 34–37.

17. Gumercindo Rivera L. et al., to Juan Miranda et al., Uncía, May 8, 1923, qtd. in Rivera, *La masacre de Uncía*, 39–41.

18. Rivera, *La masacre de Uncía*, 77–78.

19. Ibid., 61–63.

20. Ibid., 63–64.

21. Ibid., 64.

22. Manuel Herrera and M. Rojas to Central Labor Federation of Uncía Vice-President, Catavi, May 14, 1923, qtd. in ibid., 64–65.

23. Rivera, *La masacre de Uncía*, 65–71.

24. Ibid., 71–72.

25. Guillermo Gamarra and Ernesto Fernández to Gumercindo Rivera L. et al., Uncía, May 15, 1923, qtd. in ibid., 72.

26. Rivera, *La masacre de Uncía*, 79.

27. "Pliego de Peticiones que la 'Federación Obrera Central Uncía' presenta ante el Excmo. Presidente de la República, Doctor Bautista Saavedra," Uncía, May 14, 1923, qtd. in ibid., 85–87.

28. Rivera, *La masacre de Uncía*, 80, 84–85.

29. Ibid., 87–88, 90.

30. Francisco Iraizós to G. Rivera L. et al., La Paz, May 22, 1923, qtd. in ibid., 94–95.

31. G. Rivera L. et al. to Minister of Government and Justice, La Paz, May 22, 1923, qtd. in Rivera, *La masacre de Uncía*, 95–96.

32. Rivera, *La masacre de Uncía*, 96–98, 106.

33. Ibid., 88–89.

34. Gamarra and Fernández, "Circular multiple," Uncía, May 19, 1923, qtd. in ibid., 89.

35. Gamarra and Fernández to Gumercindo Rivera, Uncía, May 21, 1923, qtd. in Rivera, *La masacre de Uncía*, 100.

36. Rivera, *La masacre de Uncía*, 91–94.

37. "Conferencia celebrada entre el Señor P. D. Pacheco de Oruro y el Señor F. Blieck de Uncia.—De hrs. 15.28 a 15.50 del 17 Mayo 1923," "Telegramas, Mayo 1 a Mayo 31 de 1923," ACSP-UTO.

38. "Conferencia telegrafica celebrada entre el Sr. P. D. Pacheco de Oruro y el

Sr. F. Blieck de Uncia. De hrs. 17.20 a 17.40 del 18/5/1923," "Telegramas, Mayo 1 a Mayo 31 de 1923," ACSP-UTO.

39. "Conferencia celebrada entre el Señor P. D. Pacheco de Oruro y el Señor F. Blieck de Uncia. De horas 21.33 a 22.10 del 20 Mayo de 1923," "Telegramas, Mayo 1 a Mayo 31 de 1923," ACSP-UTO.

40. "Conferencia celebrada entre el Señor P. D. Pacheco de Oruro y el Señor F. Blieck de Uncia. De hrs. 10.20 a 10.58 del 21 Mayo de 1923," "Telegramas, Mayo 1 a Mayo 31 de 1923," ACSP-UTO.

41. Guillermo Gamarra and Ernesto Fernández to Workers' Labor Federation President, Uncía, May 22, 1923, qtd. in Rivera, *La masacre de Uncía*, 101–3.

42. Guillermo Gamarra and Ernesto Fernández to Railway Federation President, Uncía, May 22, 1923, qtd. in Rivera, *La masacre de Uncía*, 103–5.

43. "Conferencia celebrada entre el Señor P. D. Pacheco de Oruro y el Señor F. Blieck de Uncia. De hrs. 9.40 a 10.05 del 22 mayo de 1923," "Telegramas, Mayo 1 a Mayo 31 de 1923," ACSP-UTO.

44. "Conferencia celebrada entre el Señor E. Diaz de Oruro y el Señor F. Blieck de Uncia. De hrs. 11.-3 a 11.25 del 22 Mayo 1923," "Telegramas, Mayo 1 a Mayo 31 de 1923," ACSP-UTO.

45. "Conferencia celebrada entre los srs. Scott y López de Llallagua y el Sr. E. Díaz de Oruro. De hrs. 14.10 a 15.-5 del 22 de Mayo 1923," "Telegramas, Mayo 1 a Mayo 31 de 1923," ACSP-UTO.

46. "Conferencia celebrada entre el Sr. P. D. Pacheco de Oruro y el señor F. Blieck de Uncía. De hrs. 16.20 a 17.-5 del 22 Mayo de 1923," "Telegramas, Mayo 1 a Mayo 31 de 1923," ACSP-UTO.

47. Rivera, *La masacre de Uncía*, 106–7.

48. Gumercindo Rivera to José Paravicini, Pedro N. López, and Ricardo Soruco, Oruro, May 23, 1923, qtd. in ibid., 108.

49. Soruco to Gumercindo Rivera, La Paz, qtd. in Rivera, *La masacre de Uncía*, 108–9.

50. Rivera, *La masacre de Uncía*, 112–13.

51. "Conferencia celebrada entre el Sr. Pacheco de Oruro y el Señor Blieck de Uncia.—De horas 9.20 a 10.33 del 24 Mayo de 1923," "Telegramas, Mayo 1 a Mayo 31 de 1923," ACSP-UTO.

52. Ibid.

53. Ibid.

54. "Conferencia celebrada entre el señor P. D. Pacheco de Oruro y el señor F. Blieck de Uncia. De hrs. 17.20 a 18.10 del 24 Mayo. 1923," "Telegramas, Mayo 1 a Mayo 31 de 1923," ACSP-UTO.

55. "Conferencia celebrada entre el Sr. P. D. Pacheco de Oruro y el Sr. F. Blieck de Uncia.—De Hrs. 17.15 a 18.20 del 25 de Mayo de 1923," "Telegramas, Mayo 1 a Mayo 31 de 1923," ACSP-UTO.

56. Rivera, *La masacre de Uncía*, 53–54.

57. "Conferenia celebrada entre el Sr. P.D. Pacheco de Oruro y el Señor F. Blieck de Uncia. De hrs. 9.14 a 11.22 del 26 de Mayo. 1923," "Telegramas, Mayo 1 a Mayo 31 de 1923," ACSP-UTO.

58. Rivera, *La masacre de Uncía*, 114–15; "Conferencia celebrada entre el señor P. D. Pacheco de Oruro y el señor Naeter de Uncia. De hrs. 22.50. a 23.10 del 30 de Mayo de 1923," "Telegramas, Mayo 1 a Mayo 31 de 1923," ACSP-UTO.

59. "Conferencia celebrada entre el señor P. D. Pacheco de Oruro y el señor Naeter de Uncia. De hrs. 22.50. a 23.10 del 30 de Mayo de 1923," "Telegramas, Mayo 1 a Mayo 31 de 1923," ACSP-UTO.

60. Rivera, *La masacre de Uncía*, 116.

61. G. Rivera and Primitivo Albarracín to Workers' Labor Federation and Railway Federation, Uncía, May 30, 1923, qtd. in ibid., 116.

62. Rivera, *La masacre de Uncía*, 116–17.

63. "Conferencia celebrada entre el Sr. P. D. Pacheco de Oruro con los señores Naeter y Dr. Iporre de Uncia. De hrs. 17.30 a 17.55 del 31/5/23," "Telegramas, Mayo 1 a Mayo 31 de 1923," ACSP-UTO.

64. Rivera, *La masacre de Uncía*, 117–18.

65. Guillermo Gamarra et al., "Poder Especial que otorga el Cuerpo Directivo de la Federación Obrera Central Uncía, al compañero Melquiades Maldonado, miembro activo de dicha agrupación," Uncía, May 31, 1923, qtd. in ibid., 117–18.

66. Rivera, *La masacre de Uncía*, 122–23, 125.

67. President Bautista Saavedra, "Decreto," La Paz, June 1, 1923, "Copiador de Circulares. Comensando en 28 de Marzo 1919. Terminados en 12 de Marzo 1927," vol. 245, APDO.

68. Lora, *Historia del movimiento obrero boliviano*, 2:386.

69. Rivera, *La masacre de Uncía*, 130–32.

70. Lora, *Historia del movimiento obrero boliviano*, 2:388–89; Rivera, *La masacre de Uncía*, 132–34.

71. Rivera, *La masacre de Uncía*, 135–38.

72. Major Ayoroa to President, Uncía, June 6, 1923, qtd. in ibid., 148–52.

73. Rivera, *La masacre de Uncía*, 138–43.

74. "Telegrama transmitido a h. 10.—pm del 4 de Junio de 1923," Catavi de Uncia, Simpat Oruro, ACSP-UTO.

75. Rivera, *La masacre de Uncía*, 144.

76. Major Ayoroa to President, Uncía, June 6, 1923, qtd. in ibid., 148–52.

77. Rivera, *La masacre de Uncía*, 146.

78. Ibid., 143, 147.

79. Major Ayoroa to President, Uncía, June 6, 1923, qtd. in ibid., 148–52.

80. Díaz, "Telegrama transmitido a h. 21 del 6 de Junio de 1923," Llallagua, Simpat Oruro, ACSP-UTO.

81. Pacheco, Díaz, and Blieck, "Telegrama transmitido a h. 1.30 del 6 de Junio de 1923," Uncia, Simpat Oruro, ACSP-UTO.

82. Lora, *Historia del movimiento obrero boliviano*, 2:392–93.

83. A. Arce to Minister of State, Oruro, September 25, 1923, "Copiador de Ministerios de 24 de Marzo de 1923. Hasta 29 de Julio de 1924," vol. 302, APDO.

84. Rivera, *La masacre de Uncía*, 157–58.

85. B. Saavedra to Gumercindo Rivera et al., La Paz, December 28, 1923, qtd. in ibid., 158–59.

86. B. Saavedra to Subprefect, La Paz, December 28, 1923, qtd. in Rivera, *La masacre de Uncía*, 159.

87. A. Arce to House of Simón I. Patiño Manager, Oruro, January 8, 1924, "Copiador de Varios Oficios de 24 de Marzo de 1923 hasta el 14 de abril de 1924," vol. 303, APDO.

88. "Telegrama transmitido a h. 16.55 del 11 de Junio de 1923," Uncía, Simpat Oruro, ACSP-UTO.

89. "Conferencia con Uncía. De horas 10.35 del 5 de Julio 1923," "Telegramas, Mayo 1 a Mayo 31 de 1923," ACSP-UTO.

90. Ibid.

91. "Conferencia con Uncía de horas 14.10 del 9 de Julio 1923," "Telegramas, Mayo 1 a Mayo 31 de 1923," ACSP-UTO.

92. "Conferencia con Uncia, de horas 11.10 del 26 julio de 1923," "Telegramas, Mayo 1 a Mayo 31 de 1923," ACSP-UTO.

93. Geddes, *Patiño, rey de estaño*, 180–83.

94. Guillermo Gamarra, "Carta al director de 'La República,'" La Paz, June 7, 1926, qtd. in Lora, *Historia del movimiento obrero boliviano*, 2:400.

CHAPTER 6: The Vicissitudes of Republican Rule

1. A. Arce to Antofagasta-Bolivia Railroad Manager of Traffic, Oruro, April 7, 1924, "Copiador de Varios Oficios de 24 de Marzo de 1923 hasta el 14 de abril de 1924," vol. 303, APDO.

2. Mitre, *Bajo un cielo de estaño*, 114, 116, 124–25, 135, 138.

3. Klein, *Parties and Political Change*, 82–87.

4. Ibid., 65, 71.

5. Tejada Fariñez to Machacamarca-Uncía Railway Federation President, Oruro, May 18, 1922, "Copiador Varios Oficios de 31 de Marzo de 1922. Hasta el 26 de Marzo de 1923," vol. 288, APDO.

6. Wálter Gutiérrez Monje and Ésther Murillo to Prefect, Oruro, March 11, 1923, "Colegios. Consulados. Ferrocarriles. P.O. 1923," vol. 300, APDO.

7. Ofelia G. de Aguirre to Prefect, Oruro, March 16, 1923, "Colegios. Consulados. Ferrocarriles. P.O. 1923," vol. 300, APDO.

8. Enrique Quintela H. to Prefect, Oruro, March 16, 1923, "Colegios. Consulados. Ferrocarriles. P.O. 1923," vol. 300, APDO.

9. For a study of working-class voting patterns in Bolivia's mining camps (mainly focused on the period after 1931), see Whitehead, "Miners as Voters."

10. J. Vera P. to Prefect, Poopó, July 20, 1923, "Oficios, Segundo Semestre, 1924, Prefectura de Oruro," vol. 312, APDO.

11. A. Arce to Workers' Labor Federation President, Oruro, December 1, 1923, "Copiador de Varios Oficios de 24 de Marzo de 1923 hasta el 14 de abril de 1924," vol. 303, APDO.

12. H. Iraola and Pablo Salas to Prefect, Huanuni, December 6, 1923, "Varios, 1923, P.O.," vol. 301, APDO.

13. A. Arce to H. Iraola, Oruro, January 30, 1924, "Copiador de Varios Oficios de 24 de Marzo de 1923 hasta el 14 de abril de 1924," vol. 303, APDO.

14. Iraola and José Pérez to Prefect, Oruro, January 29, 1924, "Varios Oficios, Primer Semestre, 1924, Prefectura de Oruro," vol. 314, APDO.

15. G. Mier y León to Prefect, Oruro, July 21, 1924, "Varios Oficios, Segundo Semestre, 1924, Prefectura de Oruro," vol. 309, APDO.

16. A. Arce to Workers' Labor Federation President, Oruro, June 13, 1924, "Copiador de Varios Oficios de 14 de Abril de 1924 hasta 1º de Mayo de 1925," vol. 308, APDO.

17. Casto Eyzaguirre to Prefect, Poopó, July 19, 1924, "Oficios, Segundo Semestre, 1924, Prefectura de Oruro," vol. 312, ADPO.

18. Casto Eyzaguirre to El Salvador Mining Company in Antequera, Poopó, July 19, 1924, "Oficios, Segundo Semestre, 1924, Prefectura de Oruro," vol. 312, APDO.

19. Casto Eyzaguirre to Prefect, Poopó, July 22, 1924, "Oficios, Segundo Semestre, 1924, Prefectura de Oruro," vol. 312, APDO.

20. Subprefect to Prefect, Oruro, September 10, 1924, "Oficios, Segundo Semestre, 1924, Prefectura de Oruro," vol. 312, APDO.

21. A. Zevallos to Mine Administrator, Oruro, September 2, 1924, qtd. in ibid.

22. Subprefect to Prefect, Oruro, September 10, 1924, "Oficios, Segundo Semestre, 1924, Prefectura de Oruro," vol. 312, APDO.

23. President Bautista Saavedra, La Paz, November 13, 1923, qtd. in Ministry of Government and Justice to Prefect, Circular No. 42, La Paz, November 13, 1923, "Ministerios, P.O., 1923," vol. 299, APDO.

24. Prefect to Municipal Council President, Oruro, April 27, 1921, "Copiador de Varios Oficios Consules de 17 de Septiembre de 1920 hasta el 3 de Mayo de 1921," vol. 268, APDO.

25. Railway Federation to Prefect, Oruro, April 25, 1921, "Correos, Telegrafos, Bancos, Ferrocacciles, 1921, Prefectura, Oruro," vol. 284, APDO.

26. H. Achá Panoso to Prefect, Poopó, November 27, 1923, "Tesoros, Subprefecturas, Policias, 1923, P.O.," vol. 298, APDO.

27. B. Saavedra to Prefect, La Paz, February 20, 1924, qtd. in A. Arce to Police Chief, February 23, 1924, "Copiador de Tesoros y Policias y Subprefecturas Co-

mensando del 22 de Agosto de 1923, y terminado en 24 de Febrero de 1926," vol. 304, APDO.

28. Railway Union Mutual Aid Society (Sports and Recreation) to Prefect, Machacamarca, April 17, 1928, "Oficios Varios, Abril, Mayo, Junio, 1928," vol. 369, APDO.

29. Juan B. Zuleta to Prefect, Huanuni, January 29, 1924, "Oficios, Primer Semestre, 1924, Prefectura de Oruro," vol. 311, APDO.

30. El Salvador Mining Company Workers to Prefect, Antequera, December 30, 1924, "Varios Oficios, Segundo Semestre, 1924, Prefectura de Oruro," vol. 309, APDO.

31. Lora, *Historia del movimiento obrero boliviano,* 3:361.

32. Qtd. in ibid.

33. Lora, *Historia del movimiento obrero boliviano,* 3:364.

34. A. Arce to League of Commercial and Industrial Employees President, Oruro, October 11, 1924, "Copiador de Varios Oficios de 14 de Abril de 1924 hasta 1º de Mayo de 1925," vol. 308, APDO.

35. Lora, *Historia del movimiento obrero boliviano,* 3:383.

36. Villareal and Moisés Béjar of the Railway Federation F.C.B. and F.C.A.B., Oruro, September 12, 1924, "Varios Oficios, Segundo Semestre, 1924, Prefectura de Oruro," vol. 309, APDO.

37. Lora, *Historia del movimiento obrero boliviano,* 3:383.

38. President Hernando Siles and the National Congress, "Decreto," La Paz, March 22, 1926, "Copiador de Circulares. Comensando en 28 de Marzo 1919. Terminados en 12 de Marzo 1927," vol. 245, APDO.

39. President Hernando Siles, "Decreto," La Paz, March 20, 1926, "Copiador de Circulares. Comensando en 28 de Marzo 1919. Terminados en 12 de Marzo 1927," vol. 245, APDO.

40. President Hernando Siles, "Decreto," La Paz, April 29, 1926, "Copiador de Circulares. Comensando en 28 de Marzo 1919. Terminados en 12 de Marzo 1927," vol. 245, APDO.

41. A. Arce to Guillermo Grey, Oruro, July 1, 1924, "Copiador de Varios Oficios de 14 de Abril de 1924 hasta 1º de Mayo de 1925," vol. 308, APDO.

42. Isabel de Duncan to Prefect, Oruro, July 28, 1924, "Varios Oficios, Segundo Semestre, 1924, Prefectura de Oruro," vol. 309, APDO.

43. Police Chief Donato Careagua to Prefect, Negro Pabellón, August 18, 1924, "Oficios, Segundo Semestre, 1924, Prefectura de Oruro," vol. 312, APDO.

44. A. Arce to Workers' Labor Federation President, Oruro, December 4, 1924, "Copiador de Varios Oficios de 14 de Abril de 1924 hasta 1º de Mayo de 1925," vol. 308, APDO.

45. A. Arce to Workers' Labor Federation President, Oruro, December 6, 1924, "Copiador de Varios Oficios de 14 de Abril de 1924 hasta 1º de Mayo de 1925," vol. 308, APDO.

46. "Prefecturas de Oruro: desde el año de 1882 hasta el año de . . . ," APDO.

47. Lt. Col. Ayoroa to Penny and Duncan and Japo Mining Companies, Oruro, March 17, 1925, "Copiador de Varios Oficios de 14 de Abril de 1924 hasta 1° de Mayo de 1925," vol. 308, APDO.

48. Lt. Col. Ayoroa to Japo Mining Company, Oruro, March 17, 1925, "Copiador de Varios Oficios de 14 de Abril de 1924 hasta 1° de Mayo de 1925," vol. 308, APDO.

49. Lt. Col. Ayoroa to Railway Federation President, Oruro, March 18, 1925, "Copiador de Varios Oficios de 14 de Abril de 1924 hasta 1° de Mayo de 1925," vol. 308, ADPO.

50. Prefecture of Oruro, "Expediente Relativo A Denuncia infracciones Policía Minera, Seguido por Jornaleros 'Cia. Estañífera Vinto,' Victoriano Ponce, Dámaso Zabalaga, Sgo. Flores, con ña la misma, Ingresó en 5 de mayo 1925," "Bloque N° 12, Expedientes 1916 a 1997 años," ASPC-PDO.

51. Ibid.

52. Ibid.

53. Ibid.

54. Ibid.

55. Ibid.

56. Ibid.

57. Ibid.

58. Ibid.

CHAPTER 7: An Ideology of Their Own

1. Lora, *Historia del movimiento obrero boliviano*, 3:21–25.

2. Qtd. in ibid., 3:25.

3. Lora, *Historia del movimiento obrero boliviano*, 3:28.

4. Ibid., 3:296–98, 302–4.

5. Marof, *La justicia del Inca*.

6. One work that particularly influenced Marof was Rouma, *L'Empire des Incas*.

7. Marof, *La justicia del Inca*, 7, 18, 25.

8. Trotsky, *Permanent Revolution*, 279.

9. Marof, *La justicia del Inca*, 15.

10. At the beginning of the twentieth century Bolivia's government relied on import-export taxes. Aside from the proposal to nationalize the mining industry, Marof did not propose new taxes to expand the country's revenue base.

11. Marof, *La justicia del Inca*, 27, 54–56.

12. Lora, *Historia del movimiento obrero boliviano*, 3:11–12.

13. Qtd. in ibid., 3:12.

14. Lora, *Historia del movimiento obrero boliviano*, 3:13, 245–47.

15. Qtd. in ibid., 3:12–13; see Marx and Engels, *The Communist Manifesto*, 77.

16. Lora, *Historia del movimiento obrero boliviano*, 3:13, 15–17, 20–21.

17. Ibid., 3:21, 23, 24, 28.

18. Ibid., 3:21.

19. Qtd. in ibid., 3:25.

20. Ibid., 3:24.

21. Bolivian Confederation of Labor, Third Workers' Congress, "Conclusiones," Oruro, April 1927, qtd. in Delgado, *100 años de lucha obrera*, 81.

22. Qtd. in Lora, *Historia del movimiento obrero boliviano*, 3:24–25.

23. Lora, *Historia del movimiento obrero boliviano*, 3:28.

24. José Rueda and Néstor Rodríguez to Prefect, Oruro, January 9, 1928, "Oficios Varios, Enero, Febrero, Marzo, 1928," vol. 370, APDO.

25. Qtd. in Lora, *Historia del movimiento obrero boliviano*, 3:30.

26. Klein, *Parties and Political Change*, 97.

27. José F. Avila to Prefect, Oruro, July 3, 1916, "Recibido de Varios, 1916," vol. 228, APDO.

28. José F. Avila to Prefect, Oruro, August 12, 1916, "Recibido de Varios, 1916," vol. 228, APDO.

29. Marof, *La tragedia del altiplano*.

30. José F. Avila and J. de la A. Escóbar to Cercado Province Subprefect, Oruro, March 17, 1927, Bloque 2, ASPC-PDO.

31. For a detailed description of the 1927 Chayanta Rebellion see Langer, "Andean Rituals of Revolt"; and Hylton, "Common Ground."

32. Langer, *Economic Change*, 82–83.

33. Scholars continue to debate the extent of socialist influence on the insurrection. Erick Langer and Silvia Rivera prefer to downplay its importance, while Forrest Hylton asserts that the connections deserve further study (see Langer, *Economic Change*, 82; Langer, "Andean Rituals of Revolt"; Rivera Cusicanqui, *"Oppressed but Not Defeated"*; Rivera Cusicanqui, *Ayllus y proyectos de desarrollo*; and Hylton, "Common Ground").

34. Hylton, "Common Ground," 9.

35. Harris and Albó, *Monteras y guardatojos*, 68–69.

36. Langer, "Andean Rituals of Revolt," 227–53; Rivera Cusicanqui, *Ayllus*; Rivera Cusicanqui, "La expansión del latifundio."

37. Rivera Cusicanqui, *Ayllus*, 49, 56; Langer, "Andean Rituals of Revolt," 251.

38. Hylton, "Common Ground," 17–18.

39. Ibid., 18–19.

40. Langer, *Economic Change*, 87; Hylton, "Common Ground," 16–17, 29.

41. Lora, *Historia del movimiento obrero boliviano*, 2:28, 32.

42. Workers' Labor Federation of Potosí to Workers' Labor Federation of La Paz, Potosí, October 25, 1928, qtd. in Lora, *Historia del movimiento obrero boliviano*, 3:32.

43. Qtd. in Lora, *Historia del movimiento obrero boliviano,* 3:35.

44. Ibid., 3:36.

45. Ibid., 3:37.

46. Hugo Sevillano and Juan Paz Rojas, Workers' Labor Federation of La Paz, La Paz, March 4, 1929, qtd. in Lora, *Historia,* 3:37–38.

47. Lora, *Historia del movimiento obrero boliviano,* 3:38.

48. Ibid., 3:43.

49. Departmental Council of the Bolivian Confederation of Labor, Cochabamba, qtd. in Lora, *Historia del movimiento obrero boliviano,* 3:44–45.

50. Lora, *Historia del movimiento obrero boliviano,* 3:45.

51. Modesto Escóbar and Jacinto Centellas, Local Labor Federation of La Paz, "Circular pro-congreso," La Paz, July 20, 1930, qtd. in Lora, *Historia del movimiento obrero boliviano,* 3:46.

52. Lora, *Historia del movimiento obrero boliviano,* 3:48.

53. Ibid., 3:45, 50.

54. *La Patria* (Oruro, Bolivia), August 12, 1930, qtd. in ibid., 3:50–51.

55. Lora, *Historia del movimiento obrero boliviano,* 3:50–51.

56. Eduardo Diez de Medina, "Informe Departamental, 1914," "Ministerio de Instrucción y Agricultura, Comensado en 14 de Octubre de 1913, Termina en . . . ," vol. 191, APDO.

57. N. Murgia to Prefect, Oruro, February 24, 1917, "Subprefecturas, 1917, Prefectura-Oruro," vol. 243, APDO.

58. Angel Vásquez to Prefect, Poopó, June 15, 1918, "Recibidos: Judicial, Corregimientos, Ferrocarriles y otros, Varios, 1918, Prefectura-Oruro," vol. 252, APDO.

59. R. Valenzuela and Co. to Prefect, Mina San José, June 10, 1922, "Varios, Prefectura, Oruro, 1922," vol. 292, APDO.

60. José S. Quinteros to Prefect, "Circular N° 32," La Paz, July 14, 1913, qtd. in C. Morales to Subprefect, Oruro, July 21, 1913, "Circulares desde sbre 17, 1908 hasta sebre. de 1913," vol. 165, APDO.

61. Alberto Guesny to Poopó Province Subprefect, Totoral, June 24, 1918, "Recibidos: Judicial, Corregimientos, Ferrocarriles y otros, Varios, 1918, Prefectura-Oruro," vol. 252, APDO.

62. Víctor E. Sanjinés to Minister of State, Oruro, June 8, 1907, "Ministerios de Gobierno, Desde 13 marzo 1906 hasta 11 de julio de 1909," vol. 142, APDO.

63. Valentín Garnica to Prefect, Oruro, June 16, 1926, "Bloque No 2 documentos y otros gestion 1911–1949," ASPC-PDO.

64. Úrsula M. de Aramayo to Cercado Province Subprefect, Oruro, April 18, 1931, "Bloque No 2 documentos y otros gestion 1911–1949," ASPC-PDO.

65. For a study of the Feminine Labor Federation of La Paz, see Dibbits et al., *Polleras libertarias.*

66. González Flor, *Informe del prefecto,* 35–36.

67. Cayetana Lazarete, Tránsito Zambrana, and Juana Castro, Oruro, October 2, 1928, "Varios, Octubre, Noviembre, Diciembre, 1928," vol. 377, APDO.

68. Cayetana Lazarete and Tránsito Zambrana to Prefect, Oruro, October 3, 1928, "Varios, Octubre, Noviembre, Diciembre, 1928," vol. 377, APDO.

69. González Flor, *Informe del prefecto, 36.*

70. Inés de Aldana and Modesta C. de Flores to Prefect, Oruro, April 18, 1929, "Oficios Varios, Abril, Mayo, Junio, 1929," vol. 392, APDO. The letter to the prefect does not list the organization's total membership, but it does include the officeholders: president, Sra. Inés T. de Aldana; vice president, Srta. Modesta Gamboa; treasurer, Sra. Honorata de Saavedra; secretary, Sra. Modesta C. de Flores; consultants, Srs. A. Carvajal and D. Borda.

71. Cayetana Lazarete, Tránsito Zambrana, and Juana Castro, Oruro, October 2, 1928, "Varios, Octubre, Noviembre, Diciembre, 1928," vol. 377, APDO; Inés de Aldana and Modesta C. de Flores to Prefect, Oruro, April 18, 1929, "Oficios Varios, Abril, Mayo, Junio, 1929," vol. 392, APDO; Lora, *Historia del movimiento obrero boliviano,* 3:23; A. Arce to Workers' Labor Federation President, Oruro, December 1, 1923, "Copiador de Varios Oficios de 24 de Marzo de 1923 hasta el 14 de abril de 1924," vol. 303, APDO; Carvajal and Borda to Adolfo Navarro, Oruro, September 11, 1928, "Varios, Julio, Agosto, Septiembre, 1928," vol. 367, APDO; Klein, *Parties and Political Change,* 91–94.

72. Workers' Labor Federation "Rol de Desfile," Oruro, "Correspondencia Recibida Varios, Abril, Mayo, Junio, 1930," vol. 409, APDO.

73. Klein, *Parties and Political Change,* 103, 108, 117.

74. Lora, *Historia del movimiento obrero boliviano,* 3:86–88, 90.

75. Gabriel Moisés, Castellón A., and Luis V. Gallardo, Workers' Labor Federation, Oruro, March 27, 1930, qtd. in ibid., 3:89.

76. Lora, *Historia del movimiento obrero boliviano,* 3:88.

77. G. Moisés and Gallardo to Prefect, Oruro, April 15, 1930, "Correspondencia Recibida Varios, Abril, Mayo, Junio, 1930," vol. 409, APDO.

78. Lora, *Historia del movimiento obrero boliviano,* 3:88.

79. Gabriel Moisés and Luis Gallardo to Prefecture Secretary, Oruro, April 29, 1930, "Correspondencia Recibida Varios, Abril, Mayo, Junio, 1930," vol. 409, APDO.

80. Departmental Council of the Bolivian Confederation of Labor to Prefect, Oruro, May 26, 1930, "Correspondencia Recibida Varios, Abril, Mayo, Junio, 1930," vol. 409, APDO.

81. Klein, *Parties and Political Change,* 108–11.

82. Lora, *Historia del movimiento obrero boliviano,* 3:251.

83. Ibid., 3:250, 252, 254; Klein, *Parties and Political Change,* 109.

84. Hinojosa, *La revolución de Villazón* (La Paz: 1944), qtd. in Lora, *Historia del movimiento obrero boliviano,* 3:252–53.

85. Lora, *Historia del movimiento obrero boliviano,* 3:254.

86. Hinojosa qtd. in ibid., 3:253.

87. Lora, *Historia del movimiento obrero boliviano,* 3:259.

88. Gallardo to Prefect, Oruro, September 10, 1930, "Correspondencia Recibida, Oficios Varios, Julio, Agosto, Septiembre, 1930, Prefectura de Oruro, vol. 420, APDO.

89. José Orellana and F. Sunchilla to Prefect, Oruro, September 4, 1930, "Correspondencia Recibida, Oficios Varios, Julio, Agosto, Septiembre, 1930, Prefectura de Oruro," vol. 420, APDO.

90. Bolivian Confederation of Labor to Prefect, Oruro, October 20, 1930, "Correspondencia recibida de la Capital de Oruro de los meses de Octubre, Noviembre, y Diciembre de 1930," vol. 419, APDO.

91. José C. Peredo and Juan Chávez to Prefect, Oruro, December 1, 1930, "Correspondencia recibida de la Capital de Oruro de los meses de Octubre, Noviembre, y Diciembre de 1930," vol. 419, APDO.

92. A. Arce to Minister of State, Oruro, September 25, 1923, "Copiador de Ministerios de 24 de Marzo de 1923. Hasta 29 de Julio de 1924," vol. 302, APDO; José C. Peredo and Juan Chaves to Prefect, Oruro, December 1, 1930, "Correspondencia recibida de la Capital de Oruro de los meses de Octubre, Noviembre, y Diciembre de 1930," vol. 419, APDO; G. Rivera L. and Primitivo Albarracín to Prefect, Oruro, November 17, 1930, "Correspondencia recibida de la Capital de Oruro de los meses de Octubre, Noviembre, y Diciembre de 1930," vol. 419, APDO; G. Rivera L. and Albarracín to Prefect, Oruro, November 28, 1930, "Correspondencia recibida de la Capital de Oruro de los meses de Octubre, Noviembre, y Diciembre de 1930," vol. 419, APDO.

93. G. Rivera and Arce to Prefect, Oruro, June 8, 1931, "Correspondencia Recibida, Varios de la Capital de Oruro, Abril, Mayo, Junio, 1931, Prefectura de Oruro," vol. 432, APDO.

Epilogue

1. Klein, *Parties and Political Change,* 152, 155, 184, 187, 226–28.

2. Ibid., 234–35, 337.

3. Ibid., 355–56, 368.

4. Ibid., 375–76, 379, 381–82.

5. Ibid., 195, 295–96.

6. For a comprehensive history of Trotskyism in Bolivia, see John, "Permanent Revolution on the Altiplano."

7. Klein, *Parties and Political Change,* 384; Lora, *Historia del movimiento obrero boliviano,* 4:435.

8. Klein, *Parties and Political Change,* 384; Delgado, *100 años de lucha obrera,* 183–84; Lora, *Historia del movimiento obrero boliviano,* 4:489.

9. *Tesis de Pulacayo,* 23–24.

10. Ibid., 25.

11. Lora, *Historia del movimiento obrero boliviano*, 4:435.

12. *Tesis de Pulacayo*, 27, 36.

13. Ibid., 25–26, 28, 54.

14. For a firsthand account of these efforts in the fertile valley of Cochabamba, see Rivas Antezana, *Los hombres de la revolución*. For a comprehensive history of union activity and agrarian reform in Cohabamba, see Gordillo, *Campesinos revolucionarios en Bolivia*.

15. Justo, *Bolivia*, 166–68; Delgado, *100 años de lucha obrera*, 209.

BIBLIOGRAPHY

ARCHIVES AND ABBREVIATIONS

Oruro, Bolivia

Archivo de la Casa Simón I. Patiño, Universidad Técnica de Oruro (ACSP-UTO)
Archivo de la Prefectura del Departamento de Oruro (APDO)
Archivo de la Subprefectura de la Provincia del Cercado—La Prefectura del Departamento de Oruro (ASPC-PDO)

Sucre, Bolivia

Biblioteca y Archivo Nacional de Bolivia—Archivo Nacional de Bolivia (BANB-ANB)

Potosí, Bolivia

Casa Nacional de la Moneda—Archivo Histórico (CNM-AH)

NEWSPAPERS

El Vapor (Oruro, Bolivia)
Ideales (Oruro, Bolivia)

PUBLISHED PRIMARY AND SECONDARY SOURCES

Abecia Baldivieso, Valentín. *Mitayos de Potosí: En una economía sumergida*. Barcelona: Técnicos Editoriales Asociados, S.A., 1988.

Albarracín Millán, Juan. *Bolivia: El desentrañamiento del estaño, los republicanos en la historia de Bolivia*. La Paz: Ediciones "AKAPANA," 1993.

———. *El poder minero en la administración liberal*. La Paz: Empresa Editora "Urquiza," 1972.

Alonso Barba, Alvaro. *Arte de los metales*. Potosí: Editorial "Potosí," 1967.

Antezana Salvatierra, Alejandro Vladimir. *Estructura agraria en el siglo XIX: Legislación agraria y transformación de la realidad rural de Bolivia*. La Paz: Centro de Información para el Desarrollo (CID), 1992.

Arzáns de Orsúa y Vela, Bartolomé. *Historia de la Villa Imperial de Potosí*. Edited by Lewis Hanke and Gunnar Mendoza. 3 vols. Providence, R.I.: Brown University Press, 1965.

Bakewell, Peter. *Miners of the Red Mountain: Indian Labor in Potosí, 1545–1650*. Albuquerque: University of New Mexico Press, 1984.

Barcelli S., Agustín. *Medio siglo de luchas sindicales revolucionarias en Bolivia*. La Paz: Dirección de Informaciones de la Presidencia de la República, Editorial del Estado, 1957.

Bellessort, André. *La Jeune Amérique*. Paris: Perrin, 1894.

Bergquist, Charles W. *Labor in Latin America: Comparative Essays on Chile, Argentina, Venezuela, and Colombia*. Stanford, Calif.: Stanford University Press, 1986.

Capoche, Luis. *Relación general de la Villa Imperial de Potosí*. Edited by Lewis Hanke. Biblioteca de Autores Españoles, vol. 122. Madrid: Ediciones Atlas, 1959.

Choque Canqui, Roberto. *Historia de una lucha desigual: Los contenidos ideológicos y políticos de las rebeliones indígenas de la Pre-Revolución Nacional*. La Paz: Unidad de Investigaciones Históricas UNIH-PAKAXA, 2005.

Cole, Jeffrey. *The Potosí Mita, 1573–1700: Compulsory Indian Labor in the Andes*. Stanford, Calif.: Stanford University Press, 1985.

Colquechaca-Aullagas Company of Bolivia. *Novena memorial del directorio: Informe del administrador general*. Sucre: Imprenta "Bolívar" de M. Pizarro, 1900.

Condarco Morales, Ramiro. *Zárate, el "Temible" Willka: Historia de la rebelión indígena*. La Paz: Talleres Gráficos Bolivianos, 1966.

Cornblit, Oscar. *Power and Violence in the Colonial City: Oruro from the Mining Renaissance to the Rebellion of Tupac Amaru (1740–1782)*. New York: Cambridge University Press, 1985.

Dalence, José María. *Bosquejo estadístico de Bolivia*. La Paz: Editorial Universidad Mayor de San Andrés, 1975 [1851].

De Cieza de León, Pedro. *La crónica del Perú con tres mapas*. Madrid: Calpe, 1922.

Delgado Gonzales, Trifonio. *100 años de lucha obrera en Bolivia*. La Paz: Ediciones ISLA, 1984.

De Toledo, Francisco. *Ordenanzas del Virrey Toledo*. Edited by Roberto Levillier. Vol. 8, *Gobernantes del Perú, cartas y papeles, siglo XVI*. Colección de Publicaciones Históricas de la Biblioteca del Congreso Argentino. Madrid: Imprenta de Juan Pueyo, 1925.

Devés, Eduardo. *Los que van a morir te saludan: Historia de una masacre: Escuela Santa María Iquique, 1907*. Santiago: Nuestra América Ediciones, 1988.

Dibbits, Ineke, Elizabeth Peredo, Ruth Volgger, and Cecilia Wadsworth. *Polleras libertarias: Federación Obrera Femenina 1927*. La Paz: Tahipuma/Hisbol, 1989.

Dunkerley, James. *Rebellion in the Veins: Political Struggle in Bolivia, 1952–82*. London: Verso, 1984.

Escobari de Querejazu, Laura. *Caciques, yanaconas y extravagantes: La sociedad colo-

nial en Charcas s. XVI-XVII. La Paz: Plural Editores; Embajada de España en Bolivia, 2001.

Exposición que los artesanos de Sucre dirijen al Supremo Gobierno para la suspensión de la ley de 8 de octubre de 1872. Sucre: Imprenta de Pedro España, 1876.

French, Willam E. *A Peaceful and Working People: Manners, Morals, and Class Formation in Northern Mexico.* Albuquerque: University of New Mexico Press, 1996.

Geddes, Charles F. *Patiño, rey de estaño.* Madrid: A.G. Grupo S.A., 1984.

González Flor, Raimundo. *Informe del prefecto del Departamento de Oruro, General Raimundo González Flor, gestión administrative 1928–1929.* Oruro, Bolivia: Prefectura y Superintendencia de Hacienda y Minas, Oruro-Bolivia, 1929.

Gordillo, José M. *Campesinos revolucionarios en Bolivia: Identidad, territorio y sexualidad en el Valle Alto de Cochabamba, 1952–1964.* La Paz: Promec; Universidad de la Cordillera; Plural Editores; CEP, 2000.

Gotkowitz, Laura. *A Revolution for Our Rights: Indigenous Struggles for Land and Justice in Bolivia, 1880–1952.* Durham, N.C.: Duke University Press, 2007.

Grieshaber, Erwin P. "Fluctuaciones en la definición del indio: Comparación de los censos de 1900 y 1950." *Historia Boliviana* 5, nos. 1–2 (1985): 45–65.

———. "Survival of Indian Communities in Nineteenth-Century Bolivia: A Regional Comparison." *Journal of Latin American Studies* 12, no. 2 (Nov. 1980): 223–96.

Grindle, Merilee, and Pilar Domingo, eds. *Proclaiming Revolution: Bolivia in Comparative Perspective.* Cambridge, Mass.: Harvard University Press, David Rockefeller Center for Latin American Studies; London: Institute of Latin American Studies, 2003.

Hanke, Lewis. *The Imperial City of Potosí: An Unwritten Chapter in the History of Spanish America.* The Hague: Nijhoff, 1956.

Harris, Olivia, and Javier Albó. *Monteras y guardatojos, campesinos y mineros en el norte de Potosí en 1974.* La Paz: CIPCA, Editorial e Imprenta Alenkar, 1986.

Hylton, Forrest. "Common Ground: Indians, Urban Radicals, and the Chayanta Uprising of 1927." Master's thesis, University of Pittsburgh, 1999.

Irurozqui Victoriano, Marta. *"A Bala, Piedra y Palo": La construcción de la ciudadanía política en Bolivia, 1826–1952.* N.p.: Diputación de Sevilla, 2000.

John, Steven Sándor. "Permanent Revolution on the Altiplano: Bolivian Trotskyism, 1928–2005." Ph.D. dissertation, City University of New York, 2006.

Justo (Quebracho), Liborio. *Bolivia: La revolución derrotada, raíz, proceso y autopsia de la primera revolución proletaria de la América Latina.* Buenos Aires: Juárez Editor, 1971 [1967].

Klein, Herbert S. *Bolivia: The Evolution of a Multi-Ethnic Society.* 2d ed. New York: Oxford University Press, 1992.

———. *Haciendas and Ayllus: Rural Society in the Bolivian Andes in the Eighteenth and Nineteenth Centuries.* Stanford, Calif.: Stanford University Press, 1993.

———. *Parties and Political Change in Bolivia, 1880–1952*. Cambridge: Cambridge University Press, 1969.

Langer, Erick D. "Andean Rituals of Revolt: The Chayanta Rebellion of 1927." *Ethnohistory* 37, no. 3 (Summer 1990): 227–52.

———. *Economic Change and Rural Resistance in Southern Bolivia, 1880–1930*. Stanford, Calif.: Stanford University Press, 1989.

Larson, Brooke. *Trials of Nation Making: Liberalism, Race, and Ethnicity in the Andes, 1810–1910*. Cambridge: Cambridge University Press, 2004.

Lehm A., Zulema, and Silvia Rivera Cusicanqui. *Los artesanos libertarios y la ética del trabajo*. La Paz: Ediciones del THOA, 1988.

Lofstrom, William L. *Dámaso de Uriburu, a Mining Entrepreneur in Early Nineteenth-Century Bolivia*. Buffalo: Council of International Studies, State University of New York at Buffalo, 1973.

Lora, Guillermo. *Historia del movimiento obrero boliviano*. 4 vols. La Paz: Editorial "Los Amigos del Libro," 1967–80.

Mangan, Jane E. *Trading Roles: Gender, Ethnicity, and the Urban Economy in Colonial Potosí*. Durham, N.C.: Duke University Press, 2005.

Marof, Tristan (Gustavo A. Navarro). *La justicia del Inca*. Brussels: Librería Falk Fils, 1926.

———. *La tragedia del altiplano*. Buenos Aires: Editorial Claridad, 1934.

Marx, Karl, and Frederick Engels. *The Communist Manifesto: A Modern Edition*. London: Verso, 1998.

Mitre, Antonio. *Bajo un cielo de estano: Fulgor y ocaso del metal en Bolivia*. La Paz: Biblioteca Minera Boliviana, 1993.

———. *Los patriarcas de la plata: Estructura socioeconómica de la minería boliviana en el siglo XIX*. Lima: Instituto de Estudios Peruanos, 1981.

Nash, June C. *Practicing Ethnography in a Globalizing World: An Anthropological Odyssey*. Lanham, Md.: AltaMira Press, 2007.

———. *We Eat the Mines and the Mines Eat Us: Dependency and Exploitation in Bolivian Tin Mines*. New York: Columbia University Press, 1993 [1979].

Oficina Nacional de Inmigración, Estadística y Propaganda Geográfica. *Censo general de la población de la República de Bolivia . . . 1900*. 2 vols. La Paz: Taller Tipo-Litográfico de José M. Gamarra, 1904.

Pauwels, Gilberto. "Oruro 1607: El informe de Felipe de Godoy." *Eco andino* 7–8 (1999): 87–104.

Pinto-Vallejos, Julio. *Trabajos y rebeldías en la pampa salitrera: El ciclo del salitre y la reconfiguración de las identidades populares (1850–1900)*. Santiago: Universidad de Santiago, 1998.

Pizarro, Crisostomo. *La huelga obrera en Chile 1890–1970*. Santiago: Ediciones SUR, 1986.

Platt, Tristan. *Estado boliviano y ayllu andino: Tierra y tributo en el norte de Potosí*. Lima: Instituto de Estudios Peruanos, 1982.

———. *La persistencia de los ayllus en el norte de Potosí de la invasión europea a la República de Bolivia*. La Paz: Fundación Dialogo, 1999.

———. "Producción, tecnología y trabajo en la Rivera de Potosí durante la República temprana." In *El siglo XIX: Bolivia y América Latina*, edited by Rossana Barragún, Dora Cajías, and Seemin Qayum, 395–435. La Paz: Muela del Diablo Editores; Coordinadora de Historia, 1997.

Querejazu, Roberto. *Llallagua: Historia de una montaña*. La Paz: Los Amigos del Libro, 1978.

Rahal, Vicente. *Sangre y estaño (presencia de Bolivia)*. Santiago: Editorial Atacama, 1958.

Rivas Antezana, Sinforoso. *Los hombres de la revolución*. La Paz: Ceres; Plural Editores, 2000.

Rivera Cusicanqui, Silvia. *Ayllus y proyectos de desarrollo en el norte de Potosí*. La Paz: Ediciones Aruwiyiri, 1992.

———. "La expansión del latifundio en el altiplano boliviano: Elementos para una caracterización de una oligarquía regional." *Avances* 2 (1978): 95–118.

———. "*Oppressed but Not Defeated*": *Peasant Struggles among the Aymara and Qhechwa in Bolivia, 1900–1980*. Geneva: United Nations Research Institution for Social Development, 1987.

Rivera L., Gumercindo. *La masacre de Uncía*. Oruro, Bolivia: Universidad Técnica de Oruro, 1967.

Rodríguez Ostria, Gustavo. *El socavón y el sindicato: Ensayos históricos sobre los trabajadores mineros siglos XIX–XX*. La Paz: Instituto Latinoamericano de Investigaciones Sociales, 1991.

Rouma, Georges. *L'Empire des Incas et son communisme autocratique*. Brussels: Imprimerie Médicale et Scientifique, 1924.

Scott, James C. *Weapons of the Weak: Everyday Forms of Peasant Resistance*. New Haven, Conn.: Yale University Press, 1985.

Sociedad de Socorros Mutuos de Artesanos. *Boletín 10* (Mar. 11, 1955). Oruro, Bolivia: Editorial "Noticias," 1955.

Soria Galvarro, Rodolfo. *Como adquirió el Sr. Alonso la mina San José: Respuesta á un memorandista por Rodolfo Soria Galvarro*. Oruro, Bolivia: Tipografía-Litografía "la Economia," 1903.

———. *Últimos dias del Gobierno-Alonso: Reportage para la historia por Rodolfo Soria Galvarro, antiguo diputado nacional, ex-ministro diplomático, ex-prefecto y comandante general del Departamento de Cochabamba, etc.* Potosí, Bolivia: Imprenta Ángel Santelices, 1920.

Tandeter, Enrique. *Coacción y mercado: La minería de la plata en el Potosí colonial, 1692–1826*. Buenos Aires: Editorial Sudamericana, 1992.

Téllez Fernández, Nicanor. *Rasgos biográficos del Dr. Dn. Macario Pinilla, obra escrita sobre documentos inéditos y datos suministradas por el mismo Señor Pinilla*. La Paz: Escuela Tipográfica Salesiana, 1924.

Bibliography

Tesis de Pulacayo: Tesis política de la Central Obrera Boliviana. 1978.

Trotsky, Leon. *The Permanent Revolution and Results and Prospects.* New York: Pathfinder, 1970.

Whitehead, Laurence. "Miners as Voters: The Electoral Process in Bolivia's Mining Camps." *Journal of Latin American Studies* 13, no. 2 (Nov. 1981): 313–46.

Zavaleta Mercado, René. *Bolivia: El desarrollo de la conciencia nacional.* Montevideo, Uruguay: Editorial Diálogo S.R.L., 1967.

Zulawski, Ann. *"They Eat from Their Labor": Work and Social Change in Colonial Bolivia.* Pittsburgh, Pa.: University of Pittsburgh Press, 1995.

———. *Unequal Cures: Public Health and Political Change in Bolivia, 1900–1950.* Durham, N.C.: Duke University Press, 2007.

INDEX

Abaroa Province, 41–42
agrarian reform, 167–69, 189–90, 198,
    200. *See also* hacienda system
Aguilar, Trinidad, 97, 133
Alantaña mill, 92, 101, 149–50
Albarracín, Primitivo, 139, 191–92
alcohol, 20, 78, 95–96, 153–54, 181. See
    also *chicha*
Alonso Batallion, 23–25
Alonso Caballero, Severo Fernández, 21,
    23
Alto Perú, 12, 15
Álvarez, Patricio, 141–42
anarchism. *See* anarcho-syndicalism
anarcho-syndicalism: accusations of, 63,
    80, 132, 134; appeal of, 4–5, 111, 118,
    143, 200; and disputes with commu-
    nism, 170–71, 175–79; followers of, 92,
    186–87, 189, 191. *See also* communism
Antequera, 152, 155, 172
Antofagasta, 26, 51, 73–74, 107
Antofagasta-Bolivia Railroad/Bolivian
    Railway Company: and pension sys-
    tem, 156; worker protests against, 81,
    96, 107, 144, 161; and worker unions,
    102, 169
Aramayo, José Avelino, 19
Arce, Aniceto, 75, 139, 144, 150–51, 159–60
Argentina, 15, 23, 139, 188, 195
Arica, 69, 139
Artigue, Pedro Armando, 7–8
Arzáns de Orsúa y Vela, Bartolomé, 13–15
Ascarrunz, David, 84, 90–91
Ascarrunz, Moisés; business interests of,
    66; and emigration, 69; and the po-
    lice, 53–54; and regulation of mining,
    27–28, 56–57; and schools, 43, 45
Astorga, Simón, 84, 86

Avicaya, 85–86, 97, 172, 179
Avila, José F., 77–78, 173
Aymara, 19, 22, 24, 42, 59, 86–87, 189. *See*
    also Indians
Ayoroa, José V., 136–38, 141–42, 160–61,
    163–64

Béjar, Juan, 80–81
Benavides, Emilio, 23–25
Blieck, Francisco: as manager of La Sal-
    vadora Mining Company, 115, 124–32,
    139–42; as manager of Mining Com-
    pany of Oruro, 77, 80, 98
Bolívar High School, 40, 42–43, 149
Bolivian Labor Confederation: 171–72;
    176–77, 186–92. *See also* Workers' La-
    bor Federation of Oruro
Bolivian Railway Company. *See* Antofa-
    gasta-Bolivia Railroad/Bolivian Rail-
    way Company
Bolivian Workers' Central (COB), 198
Bolshevik Revolution. *See* Russian
    Revolution
Bolshevism. *See* communism
Bustillos Province, 6, 67, 96, 113

Calama, 72, 75
Cancañiri mine. *See* Tin Company of
    Llallagua
Canelas, Demetrio, 82–83, 92, 96–98
capitalism: conflicts sparked by, 43, 51,
    98; criticism of, 126, 168, 176–79, 196–
    98; and government, 5, 87, 138; and
    growth in Bolivia, 4, 6, 16, 18–19,
    142–43; regulation of, 64, 194; threats
    to, 110–11, 187; weakness of, 28, 34–35,
    53, 152
Capoche, Luis, 10–11

Carangas Province, 41–42, 71, 137, 139
carnival, 21, 49
Carvajal, Antonio, 150, 170, 185
Catavi: company regulation of, 116–17,
    139; government investigation of,
    119–20; mines and mills of, 4; Mas-
    sacre, 194; military occupation of,
    127; union activity in, 114–15, 124, 137,
    172. See also Tin Company of
    Llallagua
Catholic Church, 79, 171, 192
census of 1900, 2, 28, 30–31
Central Labor Federation of Uncía:
    companies' view of, 125, 127, 129–31;
    repression of, 137–40; formation of,
    110–14; and government negotia-
    tions, 119–24, 128; and the military,
    126, 132–36; and La Salvadora Mining
    Company, 115; legacy of, 142–43, 191;
    and rival unions, 116–18, 160. See also
    Uncía; Uncía Massacre
Cercado Province: subprefect and indus-
    trial regulation, 36, 79, 152, 180; sub-
    prefect and worker grievances, 60,
    82, 99, 164, 182; schools, 43
Cerro Rico, 9, 12–13
Chaco War, 4–6, 176, 179, 192–95
Challapata, 123–25, 127
Chayanta rebellion, 172–175
chicha, 14, 182, 185
Chicha Industrial Union, 185
chichera. See chicha
child labor, 56–58, 79,170, 180
Chile: Bolivian exiles to, 139; Bolivian
    migration to, 68–69, 72–73, 186; Bo-
    livian relations with, 23, 51, 199; busi-
    nesses in, 18; and business in Bolivia,
    27, 97–98, 101, 114, 120–21, 138; and
    expulsion of Bolivian workers, 62,
    70; and railroads, 26, 107; working
    conditions in 74–75; workers from 76,
    81, 102

Chumacero, Rómulo, 92, 170, 175
Chuquicamata, 72, 74–75
Chuquisaca, 15, 133, 146, 170, 174–75
COB. See Bolivian Workers' Central
    (COB)
Cochabamba (city), 2, 26, 51
Cochabamba (department): exile to, 97;
    and the Federalist War, 23–24: labor
    organizations in, 170, 176–77, 189;
    people from 8, 63, 128; and railroads
    72, 103; state of siege in, 133; workers
    from, 70, 74
Colquechaca, 23
Colquechaca-Aullagas Company, 20,
    34–35
Colquiri, 100, 172
communism: appeal of, 4, 111, 118, 143,
    200; Bolivian proponents of, 85, 92,
    166–69; and the countryside, 174–75;
    disavowal of 189; Marx, Karl, 170;
    and socialism, 80, 100–101, 105, 191–92;
    Stalinist brand of, 195; Trotskyist
    brand of, 5, 168, 196–98. See also,
    anarcho-syndicalism
company stores: government regulation
    of, 55–57, 92–93, 108; worker attacks
    on, 66, 89; worker complaints about,
    33, 75–76, 82–83, 88, 91, 99, 162–64;
    worker debts to, 58;
company unions, 116–17, 142
Condeauqui, 52, 60, 67–68
Congress, Bolivian: appeals to, 27, 78,
    128, 135; debates in, 103–4; elections
    to, 63, 84, 101, 149; exclusion from,
    26; and labor legislation, 58, 108–9,
    147, 156; members of, 93; and other
    government branches, 64
Conservative Party, 21–26, 63, 168, 194
Constitution, Bolivian: on education, 41;
    proposed changes to, 26, 188; rights
    recognized in, 32, 76, 79, 91, 128, 184,
    190

Constitutional Party. *See* Conservative
Party
Corque, 42, 53, 137, 139, 192
Carranza, Fidel, 72–73

de Cieza de León, Pedro, 10
Departmental Council of Oruro of the
Bolivian Labor Confederation. *See*
Bolivian Labor Confederation
de Santa Cruz, Óscar, 32–33, 104
de Toledo, Francisco, 11–12
Díaz, Emilio: and government authorities, 112–13, 119–20, 122, 124; and the
military, 127, 135; and the Uncía Massacre's aftermath, 138–39; union
complaints about, 114, 121, 125; union
negotiations with, 115–16
Diez de Medina, Alberto, 54–55
Diez de Medina, Eduardo, 38, 43, 47, 49,
69–72, 179

education: in artisan schools, 38–41, 44–
48, 61, 100, 170; in the countryside,
42, 171; government view of importance of, 43, 57; and mining companies, 58, 79, 127–28; 160; in Pulacayo,
30; and school construction, 71; and
student politics, 148–49; the United
States, 5; urban opportunities for, 2,
4; in vocational schools, 81. *See also*
Bolívar High School
eight-hour workday, 155, 162
elections: congressional, 108–9, 149; and
fraud, 26; in labor organizations, 40;
local and municipal, 100–101, 192;
presidential, 21, 146, 188; and violence, 64–65, 84–85
El Salvador Mining Company, 151–52, 155
Escalier, José María, 65, 84–85
Europe: Bolivians in, 146, 167; capital
from, 18; demand for metal in, 27,
65–66; and imperialism, 169; labor

movements in, 1; revolutions in, 5;
warfare in, 15, 47, 62
Extraordinary Miners' Congress, 195–97,
200
Eyzaguirre, Casto, 151–52

federalism, 21, 26
Federalist War, 21–25, 173
Federation of Secondary Students,
148–49
Federation of Students (Cochabamba),
189
Feminine Committee for the Defense of
the Working Woman, 184–85
Feminine Union of Various Occupa-
tions, 185
Fernández, Ernesto, 115, 123, 132–33,
138–39
Fernández, Nícanor, 118–120
Flores, Adolfo, 124–25
Flores, Santiago, 162–63
Francia Hotel, 124, 133, 137
football, 77, 110

Gallardo, Luis, 186–88, 191
Gamarra, Guillermo: after Uncía Mas-
sacre, 143; and appeal to union allies,
123; arrest of, 135; company pressure
on, 129–30, 134; imprisonment of,
139; and organization of Central La-
bor Federation of Uncía, 114–15
Gonzales, José, 96–97
González Flor, Raimundo, 184, 186–88
Goytia, Meltión, 135, 139
Great Depression, 4–6, 145–46, 185, 188,
190
Guillén, Major, 134, 141
Gutiérrez, Nícanor L., 53, 60
Gutiérrez Guerra, José, 65, 82, 85

hacienda system, 22, 86, 171, 174, 196. *See
also* agrarian reform

Hinojosa, Roberto, 188–89
Huallpa, Diego, 8–10
Huanchaca Mining Company, 21, 30, 105–06
Huanuni: company rivalries in, 36–37; mines and mills, 4; mine workers in, 100, 154–55; police in, 53–55, 181–82; political violence in, 65; schools in, 45; silver mining in, 32; strikes in, 82–83, 87–88, 91–92, 111–12, 151; tin production in, 146; unemployment in, 67; unions in, 172, 195

Inca School, 38, 44, 46–47
Inca Empire, 10, 167–68
Independence Day, Bolivian (August 6), 45–47, 61–62, 77, 142, 151
Indians: in census of 1900, 30; and the Chayanta rebellion, 174–75; clothing of, 183; and early colonial mining, 8–11; and education, 41–42; and the Federalist War, 22–25; and the First National Indian Congress, 195; and involuntary labor, 71; as *kajchas*, 14–15; and the labor movement, 166, 171–73, 179, 198; and the *mita*, 12–13; stereotypes of, 53, 59–60. *See also* Aymara; Quechua
Industrious Society of Artisans (Oruro), 39–40. *See also* Mutual Aid Society of Artisans (Oruro)
"International, The," 166, 170
Irahola, David, 84, 86
Iraizós, Francisco, 121–22, 128, 131
Iraola, Hermógenes, 112, 151
Itos mine, 31, 98, 172, 180
Iturralde, Abel, 103–04

Japo Mining Company, 66, 160–61
Jesús de Machaca, 86–87

kajcheo, 13–18, 32–37, 94–95

Klein, Herbert, 64, 147

Langer, Erick, 174
La justicia del Inca, 167–69
La Paz (city): as capital, 21; Central Labor Federation of Uncía workers in, 120–26; death of Gualberto Villarroel in, 195; during Federalist War, 22–23; individuals from, 63–64; labor organizations in, 91, 102, 133, 155, 169–70, 176–78; Nationalist Revolution in, 198–200; newspapers in, 143; population, 2; and railroads, 26; strikes in, 104, 107, 148, 150, 188
La Paz (department), 24, 28, 68, 86–87
La Salvadora Mining Company: and attempt to bribe union officials, 134; and Central Labor Federation of Uncía, 114–15, 120–21, 124–25, 129, 132; establishment of, 7–8; merger with Tin Company of Llallagua, 143; and the military, 126–27, 135–37; and paternalism, 75; production volume of, 27; and Uncía Massacre's aftermath, 139–42
Leclere, Nícanor, 40, 78
Ladies' Benefit Society, 70–71
League of Railroad Employees and Workers, 102–3. *See also* Railway Federation
Leftist Revolutionary Party, 195–96
Lemaitre, Melitón, 47, 59, 61, 65, 73, 77, 79
Liberal Party: and betrayal of Indian allies, 25; disappearance of, 194; and Federalist War, 21–22; and the labor movement, 76, 79–81, 87–88, 91–92, 149–50; political dominance of, 4, 25–26; and the Republican Party, 47, 63–65, 82–85; and the Socialist Party, 100–101; supporters of, 86; weakening of, 62

Llallagua: Chilean workers in, 75; government actions in, 57; growth of, 31; labor movement in, 113, 172, 196; mines and mills, 4; police in, 131; strikes in, 96–98; tin production in, 27, 146; unemployment in, 66; workers of, 90, 137. *See also,* Tin Company of Llallagua

Local Labor Federation of La Paz, 178. *See also* Workers' Labor Federation of La Paz

Lora Escóbar, Guillermo, 85, 195–96

Machacamarca, 4, 154, 172, 182
Machacamarca-Uncía Railway, 103–4, 143
Machacamarca-Uncía Railway Federation, 147–48
Maldonado, Melquiades, 120, 133, 139
Mallea Balboa, Enrique, 105–06
Marof, Tristan: 167–69, 172–75, 189, 195
Marx, Karl. *See* communism
Marxism. *See* communism
May 1 Workers' Philharmonic, 61, 77
May 25 Mutual Aid Society (Potosí), 48–49
May Day: and alcohol, 153; and appearance in Bolivia, 48, 107; becomes an official holiday, 158; events typical of, 38–39, 46, 50, 110, 113–14, 185, 187
mercury amalgamation, 10–11, 15, 20
Michel, David, 113–14, 118, 131
military, Bolivian: budget, 186; and the Chaco War, 193; conscription, 54–55, 58; and coups, 65, 82, 85, 177, 188–89; and elections, 84; and Indian rebellion, 86–87; and the Nationalist Revolution, 199–200; post-Chaco War, 5, 194–95; strengthening of, 39, 51; and strikes, 88, 90–91, 96; and the Uncía Massacre, 111–12, 123, 126–29, 132–37; and the Uncía Massacre's aftermath, 138, 141–42

Mining Company of Huanuni, 36–37
Mining Company of Oruro: government complaints about 33, 79–80; management of, 77, 87; and negotiations with workers, 92, 98, 108, 163, 186–87; subsidiaries of, 101, 161
Mining Federation of Pulacayo, 105–6
Miraflores mill, 88, 90
mita, 9–12, 15–16
Mitre, Antonio, 18, 31
Moisés, Gabriel, 186–88, 191
Montes, Ismael, 26, 58, 63–65
Morales, Constantino, 27, 36–37, 42–43, 45–46, 51, 53, 75
Morococala, 52–53, 60, 77, 97, 99–100, 159, 172
Murgia, N., 79–80
Moscow, 178, 189, 196
Mutual Aid Society of Artisans (Oruro), 38–40, 44–47, 49, 61–62, 77, 173. *See also* Industrious Society of Artisans (Oruro)

Nash, June, 5
National Department of Labor, 156–58, 161, 165
National Revolution of 1952, 1–2, 198–200
National Workers' Confederation. *See* Bolivian Labor Confederation
Nationalist Revolutionary Movement (MNR), 194–95, 199–200
Native Americans. *See* Indians
Navarro, Gustavo A. *See* Marof, Tristan
Nava, Máximo, 89–90
Negro Pabellón, 53, 66, 159, 172
North America, 18, 66, 72. *See also* United States of America
Noya, Germán, 114, 116, 121

Obligatory Workers' Savings Program, 156

Oruro (city): archives in, 75; in the colonial period, 9–10, 12; commerce in, 93, 99; elections in, 64–65, 84, 192; in the Federalist War, 23, 25; growth of tin mining in, 27, 32; Independence Day in, 61–62; individuals from, 108; labor meetings in, 106, 166, 169–70, 178; labor movement in, 8, 38, 46–47, 76–77, 155, 183; newspapers in, 63; police in, 53, 55, 78, 90; population, 2, 30–31; and railroads, 26, 51, 107; repatriates in, 70–71; schools in, 43–44, 48; Socialist Party in, 100; strikes in, 148, 186–87

Oruro (department): Chayanta rebellion in, 174; education in, 41–42; economic difficulties in, 49; emigration from, 69, 72–73; labor movement in 5, 172; labor meetings in, 195; mining in 4, 6; Nationalist Revolution in, 199; number of workers in, 28; political importance of, 85–86; state of siege in, 133; strikes in, 83, 92, 103–4, 161; unemployment in, 66, 68

Pacheco, Pablo: and Central Labor Federation of Uncía, 124–25, 129–33; as manager of Huanuni mine, 82–83; and the military, 126–28; and Uncía Massacre's aftermath, 139, 141–41

palliris, 179–80

Pando, José Manuel, 22, 25–26, 63.

Paraguay. *See* Chaco War

Paredes, Matías, 35–36

Paria, 67–68

Patiño, Simón I.: business properties of, 4, 27, 66, 87–88, 146–47, 161, 194; first claim of, 7–8; and paternalism, 45, 75, 130; purchase of Tin Company of Llallagua, 143; representatives of, 77, 82

Pazña, 79, 85–86

Penny and Duncan Mining Company, 36–37, 52–53, 60, 77, 99–100, 160

Perales, Ricardo, 92–93, 101, 104, 108–09

Peru, 11–12, 138–39, 163, 170

Plaza Alonso de Ibañez, 1, 135

pollera, 183–84

Ponce, Victoriano, 162–64

Poopó (city), 41, 101, 149–50, 153, 155, 172, 181

Poopó Province, 53, 180

Potosí (city): in the colonial period, 9–15; elections in, 84–85; labor activists from, 170, 186; labor meetings in, 16, 176–77; labor organizations in, 48; May Day in, 50; population of, 2; and railroads, 26

Potosí (department): Chayanta rebellion in, 174–75; emigration from, 72; employment practices in, 33; and the Federalist War, 23; growth of tin mining in, 27, 31–32; industrial importance of, 4, 6; labor meetings in, 195; labor movement in, 8, 172; nineteenth-century mining in, 16–17, 20–21; number of miners in, 28, 30; state of siege in, 133; unemployment in, 66, 68

priests, 15, 22, 24, 133, 149, 175

Pro-Indian League of Oruro, 173

Public Assistance (Oruro), 59–60, 94

Public Health (Oruro), Office of. *See* Public Assistance (Oruro)

Pulacayo, 21, 28–30, 105–6, 196–98, 200

Quechua, 19, 22, 42, 59, 189. *See also* Indians

Quespi, Agustín, 13–15

Quintela, Enrique, 148–49

Quinteros, José S., 57–59, 180

Quiroga, Melchor, 82–83

Radical Party, 101, 168

Railway Federation, 102–07, 126, 131–32,
144, 156, 161, 169. *See also* League of
Railroad Employees and Workers
Republican Party: consolidation of
power, 86; creation of, 26, 63–65;
defeat of the Liberal Party, 81–83,
85; disappearance of, 194–95; and
election violence, 84; ex-members
of, 167; internal disputes of, 103, 146,
188; and the labor movement, 62,
87, 91–92, 111–13; and legislative reform, 144–45, 154–58; repressive side
of, 96–97, 106–7, 109, 147–48; and
the Socialist Party, 100–102; and
working-class political clients,
149–53
Republican Workers' Party, 112, 151
Revolutionary Workers' Party, 195–96
Rivera, Gumercindo, 120–23, 128, 132–37,
139, 191
Rivera Cusicanqui, Silvia, 174
Rivero, Fermín, 84, 86
Russian Revolution, 5, 168

Saavedra, Bautista: and Central Labor
Federation of Uncía, 118, 120–22,
138; declares state of siege, 133–34;
elected president, 85; and establishment of Republican Party, 63–64;
and Indian communities, 86–87;
and the labor movement, 112; and
labor legislation, 147, 152–56, 161;
and the mining companies, 125, 137;
political allies, 103, 128; and political
moderation, 109; and political prisoners, 139; and political rivals,
145–46; as Republican Party leader,
167; and Republican Party victory,
84; worker faith in, 92, 101, 114, 135,
143, 150, 179
Salamanca, Daniel, 63–64, 84–85, 103,
146, 188, 192–93

Salinas Aldunate, Alberto, 75–76
San José mine, 23, 25, 31–33, 79–80, 92,
180
San José Workers' Society, 47–48, 78–79
Sánchez, Nicolás, 115, 132
Sanjinés, Víctor E., 42–45, 51, 53, 182
Santa Cruz (city), 2
Santa Cruz (department), 133
Santo Cristo Mining and Agricultural
Company, 92, 99, 172
Saravia, Silverio, 135, 139
Seleme, Antonio, 199
scrip, company, 33, 94
Siglo XX, 4, 172
Siles, Hernando: becomes president,
145–46; and labor legislation, 156–58;
and the labor movement, 170, 185; as
Oruro's prefect, 85; overthrow of,
177–78, 186, 188–91, 193; and political
repression, 172, 175
Socavón mine, 31, 78
soccer. *See* football
socialism. *See* communism
Socialist Party, 93, 100–102, 104–5, 107–9
Soruco Ipiña, Ricardo, 103–4, 128
soup kitchens, 49, 70–71, 190
Stalinism. *See* communism
state of siege, 63, 133–34, 146, 176
Sucre: artisans of, 18–19; as capital, 21;
labor activists from, 167, 170; labor
organizations in, 133, 176; population
of, 2; presidents from, 146; and railroads, 2
Syndicalist Federation of Bolivian
Mine Workers (FSTMB), 195–97,
199–200

Tejada Fariñez, Adalid, 99, 103–04, 107–08,
147–48
Tejada Sorzano, José Luis, 193–94
Téllez, Donato, 93, 101, 104, 109
Thesis of Pulacayo, 196–98, 200

Tin Company of Llallagua: and the Central Labor Federation of Uncía, 112–16, 121–23; and government officials, 119–20, 124; importance of, 27; and the military, 54, 127, 135; purchased by Simón I. Patiño, 143; strike at, 66, 96–98; and the Uncía Massacre's aftermath, 138–39, 142; worker complaints against, 75–76. *See also* Catavi; Llallagua

tinterillos, 173

Tórrez Ruiz, Gerardo, 112–13, 118, 131

Totoral mine, 85,181

Tragic Sunday, 188

Trotsky, Leon. *See* communism

Trotskyism. *See* communism

Tunari Cooperative, 61, 77

typhoid fever, 59–60

Uncía: growth of, 31–32; importance of, 27; labor activists from, 196; May Day in, 110; mines and mills, 4, 146; strikes in, 87–91, 96–97; unemployment in, 66. *See also* Central labor Federation of Uncía; Uncía Massacre

Uncía Massacre: aftermath, 138–42, 144–45; legacy of, 5–6, 143, 166; military buildup to, 126–28; narrative of, 1, 135–37; numbers killed, 111; precipitating events, 132–34. *See also* Central Labor Federation of Uncía; Uncía

Union of Llallagua's Workers, 116–18

United States of America, 66, 169. *Also see* North America

University of San Agustín, 42–43, 51

Uyuni, 51, 81, 102, 105, 131, 133

Vera P., J., 149–50

Vergara Rivas, Marcial, 87–68

Vicenti, Gregorio, 134, 139

Villarroel, Gualberto, 194–95

Villazón, 188–89

Villegas, José, 134–35, 138

Vinto Tin Company, 161–64

wayra, 10–11

Wiessing, Jorge, 87, 163–64

women: and abusive officials, 182–83; demographics of, 30; education of, 43; and elections, 65, 200; labor legislation about, 56, 58, 170; and labor organizations, 184–85; as merchants, 181; and protest, 135, 194; workers, 20, 179–80

Workers' Conference of Potosí (1929), 176–77

Workers' Congress: First, 106–7, 169–70; Fourth, 175, 177–79, 186, 189; Second, 92, 170; Third, 92, 166–67, 170–72, 174–77, 185

Workers' Democratic Institution, 80–81

Workers' Labor Federation of Cochabamba, 133, 177

Workers' Labor Federation of La Paz, 133, 175–78. *See also* Local Labor Federation of La Paz

Workers' Labor Federation of Oruro: complaints against mining companies, 78, 98; founding of, 62, 76–77; government persecution of, 150; and the Great Depression, 190–91; and Independence Day, 151; Liberal Party reaction to, 80; members of, 40, 55, 93, 170, 173, 185; and national federations, 171–72; and solidarity with other unions, 104, 126, 133. *See also* Bolivian Labor Confederation

Workers' Labor Federation of Potosí, 133, 175

Workers' Labor Federation of Sucre, 133, 176

Workers' National Union, 185

Workers' Party, 191–92

Workers' Socialist Party (Oruro). *See* Socialist Party

Workers' Union of Artisans (Oruro). *See* Inca School

Workers' Union of Bakers, 61, 77

World War I: and Chile, 62–63, 68–69, 73, 76; and economic difficulties, 47, 49, 55; and price of tin, 65–66

Zabalaga, Dámaso, 162–64

Zárate Willka, Pablo, 22–24